Janice VanCleave's

BIG BOOK

OF SCIENCE

EXPERIMENTS

Janice VanCleave

JOSSEY-BASS™
A Wiley Brand

Published by Jossey-Bass
A Wiley Brand
111 River Street, Hoboken NJ 07030
www.josseybass.com

Jossey-Bass books and products are available through most bookstores. To contact Jossey-Bass directly call our Customer Care Department within the U.S. at 800-956-7739, outside the U.S. at 317-572-3986, or fax 317-572-4002.

Wiley also publishes its books in a variety of electronic formats and by print-on-demand. Some material included with standard print versions of this book may not be included in e-books or in print-on-demand. For more information about Wiley products, visit www.wiley.com.

Library of Congress Cataloging-in-Publication Data is available for this title

Cover illustrations: © Tina Cash Walsh
Cover design: Paul McCarthy
Printed in the United States of America
FIRST EDITION

Contents

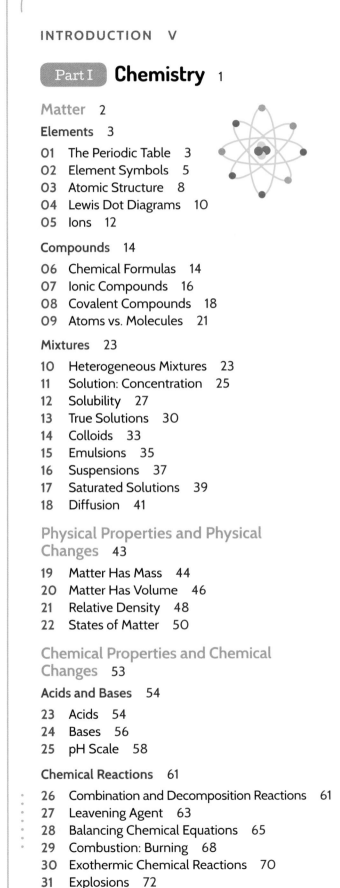

Introduction

Throughout the writing of this book, I imagined the reader delving into the exciting world of science exploration. It was and is my fervent hope that this science book will ignite a profound curiosity for scientific discovery in children of all ages! As this leads to a deeper understanding about the world around us, I believe that the future holds a rich promise for scientific challenges to be solved by these young scientists.

The order of presentation is designed to give you a platform to build on, starting with the basic foundation of all sciences, matter – the stuff the Universe is made up of. The activities in a specific topic do build in content, and you are encouraged to work through them in order. But although it is best to work your way through the book, *most* activities do stand on their own. (Some investigations require materials built in previous activities.) With the help of the glossary as well as introductions for the different topics, you can pick and choose any investigation and be rewarded with a successful experiment. Of course, your success depends on your attentiveness to following the procedure steps in order. Substituting equipment can affect the results for some activities, but for the most part just use your common sense about changes.

This book is designed to give the reader a taste of different sciences:

Chemistry   The study of the composition of matter and how it interacts, combines, and changes to form new substances.

Physics   The study of energy and forces and their interaction with matter.

Astronomy   The study of the Universe and Earth's position in it; the study of Earth's visible neighbors in space.

Earth Science   The study of the unique habitat that all known living creatures share – the Earth.

Biology   The study of the body systems of living organisms; the study of physical and biochemical changes.

The Activities

The activities follow a set step-by-step pattern, and generally start with a science problem to solve or purpose to investigate. The goal of this book is to guide you through the steps necessary in successfully completing a science experiment and to present methods of solving problems and discovering answers. It also provides a thought-provoking question about each experiment with steps for thinking through the information in order to arrive at a solution.

Introduction: Background information provides knowledge about the topic of the investigation.

See for Yourself: A list of necessary materials and step-by-step instructions on how to perform the experiment.

What Happened? A statement of what should happen; an explanation of why the results were achieved in terms that are understandable to readers who may not be familiar with the scientific terms introduced.

Challenge: A question related to the investigation, with step-by-step clues for thinking through the answer.

New terms appear in **bold** type and are defined in the Glossary.

General Instructions

1. **Read first.** Read each experiment completely before starting.

2. **Collect needed supplies.**   You will experience less frustration and more fun if all the necessary materials for the experiments are ready for instant use. You lose your train of thought when you have to stop and search for supplies.

3. **Experiment.**   Follow each step very carefully, never skip steps, and do not add your own. Safety is of the utmost importance, and by reading the experiment before starting, then following instructions exactly, you can feel confident that no unexpected results will occur.

4. **Observe.**   If your results are not the same as described in the experiment, carefully read the instructions and start over from the first step. Consider factors such as the temperature, humidity, lighting, and so on that might affect the results.

Measurements

Measuring quantities described in this book are given in the English imperial system followed by approximate metric equivalents in parentheses. Unless specifically noted, the quantities listed are not critical, and a variation of a very small amount more or less will not alter the results.

I hope you have fun as you learn about the beautiful world we live in!

–Janice VanCleave

Part I

CHEMISTRY

hemistry is the study of matter, its physical and chemical properties, and how it changes. This science involves all of one's senses: seeing, hearing, tasting, feeling, and smelling. It is listed first in this book because chemistry concepts are a springboard into the other sciences. You cannot understand the physics concept of electricity without understanding the chemistry of atoms, or the formation of crystals in caves in earth science, or biochemical reactions in the fruit ripening process in biology without understanding chemical reactions.

Chemistry is not restricted to scientists working in laboratories; instead, knowledge of chemistry is important in our everyday lives. Who knows? You might be on some reality show or confronted with an unexpected survival situation. You would be cut off from electrical devices. Chemistry knowledge would help you use available resources. Yes, your brain is your best survival tool in emergencies; but it is also the best problem-solving tool you have. Chemistry is all about problem solving, and the investigations in this book contain the foundation on which to build and sharpen your chemistry knowledge.

Matter

Matter is anything that occupies space and has mass (an amount of matter making up a material). Matter is the stuff that makes up the Universe. Figure 1 shows a flow chart for the different types of matter. The term pure substance refers to one kind of matter, such as an element or a compound; without the adjective "pure," the term substance is commonly used to refer to any material pure or not, and that is how it is used in this book. Mixture is a term that refers to the combination of different substances.

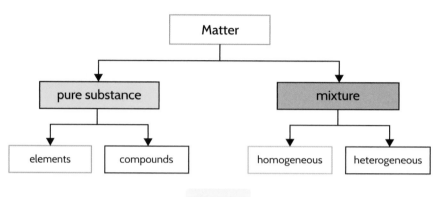

Figure 1

Elements

At this time, 118 different elements have been identified. The 94 elements that occur in nature are called natural elements, examples being carbon, oxygen, nitrogen, and sulfur. Synthetic elements are the 24 elements made by scientists in a laboratory. Synthetic elements include californium, plutonium, nobelium, and einsteinium.

The periodic table is a chart that lists all the known elements. The placement of elements on this table gives clues as to their physical structure, their physical characteristics, and how they might react with other elements. Understanding the periodic table is like having a special condensed code book.

Compounds

Compounds are substances made of two or more different elements combined in a certain ratio with the elements bonded (linked) together. There are two types of compounds, covalent and ionic. The difference between the two is in how they are bonded together. Covalent compounds have covalent bonds that form between two atoms that share electrons. Molecules are the smallest building blocks for covalent compounds that can exist independently. Ionic compounds have positive and negative ions as their building blocks.

Mixtures

Mixtures are the combination of two or more substances, where each substance retains its own chemical properties. There are two basic types of mixtures, homogeneous and heterogeneous. Homogeneous mixtures are the same throughout; they have the same uniform appearance as well as composition throughout. Heterogeneous mixtures are not the same throughout. This type of mixture has visibly different substances, such as a mixture of ice and soda or a mixture of fruit in a bowl.

01 The Periodic Table

The **periodic table of elements** contains 118 elements, of which 94 are natural and the remaining 24 are **synthetic**. Each element is given a specific number called the **atomic number**, used to place elements in a specific location on the table.

The rows on the periodic table are called **periods** and are numbered from 1 through 7; elements are arranged from left to right across each row by increasing atomic number. The columns on the table are called **groups** or **families** and are numbered from 1 through 18. The periodic table can be color-coded to identify the location of the major **types of elements**; each type falls in a region that overlaps different periods and groups. **Metals** are typically solids that are hard, but are easy to bend or stretch into a wire. **Nonmetals** typically are dull solids with characteristics opposite to those of metals.

See for Yourself
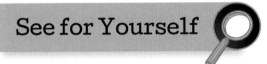

Materials

sheet of graph paper   pen
ruler   colored pens

What to Do

1. Use Figure 1 to create your own periodic table by drawing the boxes on graph paper, then number the periods and groups as shown. Keep and use your periodic table for other activities.

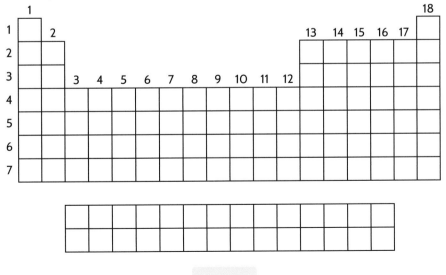

Figure 1

2. Use the numbers in Figure 2 as clues to help you number all 118 boxes on your periodic table. Remember, the numbers increase from left to right across each row.

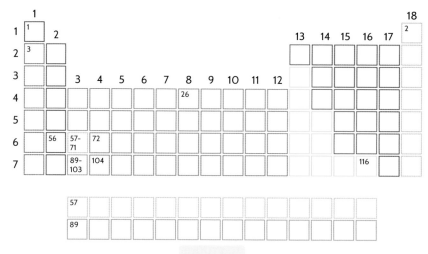

Figure 2

3. This time, use Figure 2 as a guide to color-code these nine different sections on your periodic table. The colors you choose aren't significant; one possible set may be:

purple (group 1): alkaline metals; very reactive metals.

blue (group 2): alkaline earth metals; more reactive than other metals, but less than alkaline metals.

lime green (groups 3–12): transition metals; have a different atomic structure from other metals.

yellow: basic metals.

red: metalloids; have metallic and nonmetallic characteristics.

dark green: basic nonmetals; group 17

comprises the halogen gases, which are the most reactive nonmetals.

pink (group 18): noble gases; react under special conditions.

light blue (period 6 elements 57–70): lanthanide series; separated from the table because of the difference in their physical atomic structure.

orange (period 7 elements 89–102): actinide series; separated from the table because of the difference in their physical atomic structure.

4. Add a legend to your periodic table that represents the color-coding used.

What Happened ❓

The different types of elements on the periodic table have been identified. There are more metals than any other type of element on the table. The nonmetals are listed on the right side of the periodic table. The red zig-zag line in Figure 2 contains metalloids, which have both metallic and nonmetallic properties. The metalloids basically separate the metals from the nonmetals.

Challenge ⭐

Can you use your periodic table to determine the element type of element #3, lithium (Li)?

Think!

- Element #3 is found in group 1 on the periodic table.
- Using the legend for your periodic table, identify the type of elements found in group 1.
- With the exception of element #1, hydrogen (H), which is a gas, all elements in group 1 of the periodic table are solid alkaline metals.
- Lithium (Li) is an alkaline metal.

02 Element Symbols

Elements, the building blocks of matter, are pure substances made up of **atoms**. A **chemical symbol** is much like a code that represents the name of an element. A chemical symbol has one or two letters. A capital letter is used for symbols with one letter – for example, H for hydrogen and C for carbon. Symbols with two letters start with a capital letter and the second letter is lowercase – for example, He for helium.

(Some older periodic tables have a few three-letter symbols, such as Uup for ununpentium. This means "115," which is the atomic number of this manmade element. As of 2016, all 118 elements have names and one- or two-letter symbols. Element 115 is called moscovium, Mc.)

The symbol and name do not always match, such as Na for sodium and Au for gold. (Na is from the Latin word *natrium* and Au is from the Latin word *aurium*.) Few people memorize all 118 known elements, but someone studying science should become familiar with the first 20 elements shown in the table. Element booklets can be used to become more familiar with individual elements and their symbols as well as their location on the periodic table.

Symbol	Name	Atomic Number
Al	aluminum	13
Ar	argon	18
B	boron	5
Be	berillium	4
C	carbon	6
Ca	calcium	20
Cl	chlorine	17
F	fluorine	9
H	hydrogen	1
He	helium	2
K	potassium	19
Li	lithium	3
Mg	magnesium	12
N	nitrogen	7
Na	sodium	11
Ne	neon	10
O	oxygen	8
P	phosphorus	15
S	sulfur	16
Si	silicon	14

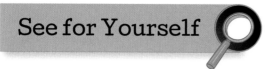

Materials

20 sheets of blank paper
black marker

your periodic table from experiment #1, "The Periodic Table"

What to Do

1. Make a booklet by folding one of the sheets of paper in half twice, first from top to bottom, and then from side to side (Figure 1).

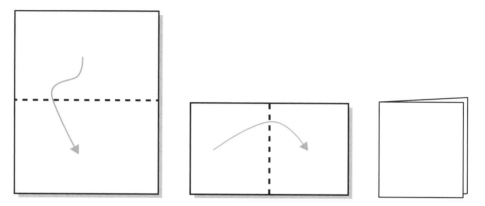

Figure 1

2. Prepare a booklet for aluminum, Al, the first element in the alphabetical list of elements by symbol in the table. Use the marker to print the symbol for aluminum and its atomic number on the front of the booklet and the name on the back as shown in Figure 2.

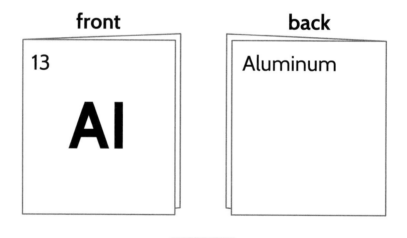

Figure 2

3. Repeat steps 1 and 2 making booklets for the remaining 19 elements in Table 1.

4. Stack the 20 booklets with symbols face up. One at a time, looking at the symbol of the first booklet in the stack, identify the name of the element.

5. Turn the top booklet over. If you correctly identified the name of the element lay it name side up on the table. If your answer was wrong, start a second stack of booklets with symbol side up.

6. Repeat step 5 until you have gone through all 20 booklets.

7. Start over using the new stack of booklets. Continue until you can correctly match the symbol and name of all 20 elements.

8. Now repeat step 5 giving the symbol for each name.

9. Keep the booklets and add information as you learn more about the elements.

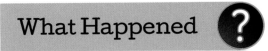

What Happened ?

Booklets for the first 20 elements on the periodic table were made and used to learn the symbols and names of these elements.

Challenge ★

Using your periodic table, can you organize the booklets in groups and periods?

Think!

- Periods are horizontal rows.
- Groups are vertical columns.
- Figure 3 shows the atomic numbers of the first 20 elements of the periodic table.

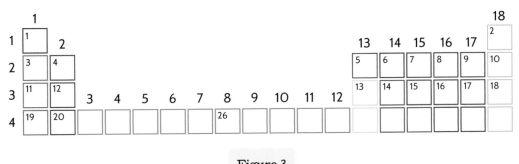

Figure 3

Using your booklets, add the first 20 symbols to your periodic table.

03 Atomic Structure

An atom is composed of two regions:

1. the center of the atom, called the **nucleus**, which contains protons (P^{1+}) and neutrons (n^0);

2. outside the nucleus, at fixed distances, are **energy levels** or orbitals with electrons (e^{1-}) having different amounts of energy.

The period number on the periodic table equals the number of energy levels for every element in that **period**. An element's **mass number** is the sum of the protons and neutrons in the nucleus of that element's atoms. An element's **atomic number** is equal to the number of protons in the nucleus and is equal to the number of electrons outside the nucleus in energy levels.

Figure 1 shows the atomic number, mass number and group A numbers for the first 20 elements. Add these to your own periodic table so that it can be used to draw atomic structures.

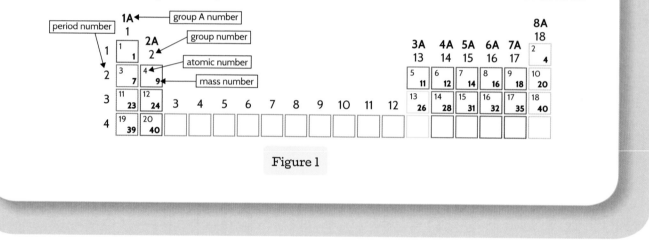

Figure 1

See for Yourself

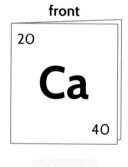

Figure 2

Materials

black marker
element booklets (from experiment #2)
periodic table (from experiment #1)

What to Do

1. For each element booklet, add the mass number to the symbol of each element. The symbol for calcium should look like this: $^{20}Ca_{40}$.

2. Use the atomic number of 20 and mass number of 40 to determine the number of neutrons in a calcium atom.

$$\#neutrons = mass\ number - atomic\ number$$

3. Inside the booklet for calcium, draw a circle and add the protons and neutrons found there.

4. Use the following to add the energy levels outside the nucleus:
   - Find the element in the periodic table:
     The period number of the element equals the number of energy levels.
   - Use curved lines to represent the energy levels, as shown in Figure 3.

5. Use the following to add electrons to each energy level:
   - The number of electrons in an atom is equal to the number of protons (atomic number).
   - For calcium there are 20 electrons: The first level has $2e^-$, second level has $8e^-$, third level has $8e^-$, and the fourth level has the remaining $2e^-$.

6. Repeat the previous procedure to draw atomic structures inside the remaining 19 element booklets.

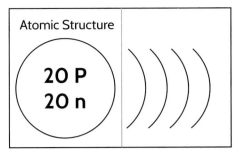

Atomic Structure

20 P
20 n

Figure 3

What Happened ❓

The atomic structures for elements #1 through #20 were drawn in element booklets. Although the atomic number of an element does not change, its mass number can. This is due to differences in the number of neutrons in the atoms of an element. Atoms of the same element with different numbers of neutrons are called isotopes. Magnesium has 18 isotopes, of which Mg-24 is the most common. Mg-24 represents a magnesium atom with a mass number of 24.

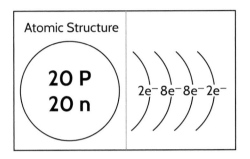

Atomic Structure

20 P
20 n

$2e^- \ 8e^- \ 8e^- \ 2e^-$

Figure 4

Challenge ⭐

Compare the hydrogen isotopes in Figure 5. How are the isotopes alike? How are the isotopes different?

Think!

- Each isotope of hydrogen has the same atomic number of one. This is because all atoms of hydrogen have the same number of protons, which is one.
- The isotopes all have the same number of energy levels and the same number of electrons. This is because the isotopes are all hydrogen atoms, which have the same number of electrons and protons.
- The isotopes all have a different mass number because, as isotopes, they all have a different number of neutrons.

Hydrogen Isotopes

hydrogen

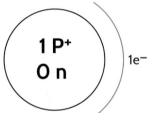

$1 \ P^+$
$0 \ n$

$1e^-$

deuterium

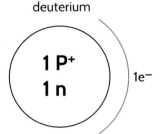

$1 \ P^+$
$1 \ n$

$1e^-$

tritium

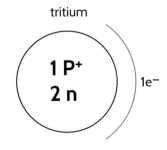

$1 \ P^+$
$2 \ n$

$1e^-$

Figure 5

04 Lewis Dot Diagrams

A **Lewis dot diagram** is a representation of an element's **valence electrons**, which are the electrons in an atom's outermost energy level. Lewis dot diagrams are composed of an element's symbol with dots representing electrons placed around the symbol. Lewis dot diagrams represent neutral atoms, which means the number of protons in the nucleus is equal to the total number of electrons outside the nucleus.

In reality, there is no set placement of electrons because they are in constant motion. If the position of an electron at any one time were marked, the pattern of electron movement would look much like the **electron cloud** illustration in Figure 1. Note the density of the cloud is greatest near the nucleus and least at its edges. This is because the attraction between the negatively charged electrons and the positively charged nucleus is greater the closer the electrons are to the nucleus.

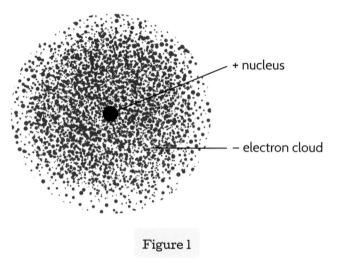

Figure 1

The Lewis dot diagram is used to show the number of valence electrons. The dot diagram for neon (Ne) in Figure 2 can be used as a guide for placing valence electrons. Make note that, for known elements, there are never more than eight valence electrons. Neon is in group 8A and has the maximum number of valence electrons. The number of valence electrons for group A elements is equal to the group A number. With the pattern for placing the electrons in Figure 2, dot diagrams for all group A elements are easy to draw.

$$\begin{array}{c} 6\ 3 \\ \cdot\ \cdot \\ 4\ \colon\ \mathbf{Ne}\ \colon\ 2 \\ 7\ \ \ \ \ \ \ \ 1 \\ \cdot\ \cdot \\ 5\ 8 \end{array}$$

Figure 2

See for Yourself

Materials

element booklets (from experiment #2)　　　periodic table (from experiment #1)
black marker

What to Do

1. Open the nitrogen element booklet and on the left side write the symbol for nitrogen below the atomic structure for nitrogen.

2. Use the following instructions to draw a dot diagram for nitrogen (N).
   - Locate nitrogen on the periodic table. The group A number of nitrogen is equal to its number of valence electrons.
   - Now, using the placement order of electrons shown in Figure 3 for nitrogen, make dots around the symbol, N.

Figure 3

3. Repeat the procedure drawing dot diagrams for each element inside their element booklet.

What Happened ?

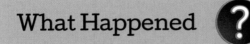

Nitrogen is in group 5A. Thus, all the elements in this vertical group have five valence electrons. Using Group A numbers, dot diagrams for each element #1 through #20 were drawn in their element booklets.

Ions are atoms that have either lost or gained electrons. Metals tend to lose their valence electrons, forming positive ions called cations; nonmetals tend to gain electrons, forming negative ions called anions.

Challenge ★

The Lewis dot diagrams can be used to show how cations and anions are formed. **Can you explain how the ions in Figure 4 are formed?**

Think!

- Nitrogen gains electrons and sodium loses electrons.
- Neutral atoms have the same amount of positive and negative charges; the same number of protons as electrons.
- Electrons have a negative charge; when electrons are gained by an atom it has more negative electrons than positive protons.
- Nitrogen gains three electrons, thus an anion with a 3– charge is formed.
- When an atom loses electrons, it becomes positively charged because it has more protons than electrons; sodium forms a cation with a 1+ charge.

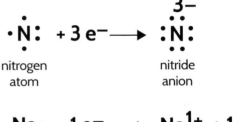

nitrogen atom

nitride anion

sodium atom

sodium ion

Figure 4

Did you notice that anions have a suffix of -ide, while cations maintain the name of the element? You will use this information in the next activity.

The electrons farthest from the nucleus are more likely to be involved in chemical reactions; these are the valence electrons.

05 Ions

Ions are atoms that have either gained or lost valence electrons, thus forming charged particles. For this activity, the formation of ions will be limited to elements #1 through #20 on the periodic table. Atoms that lose electrons form positive ions called cations. In Figure 1, the dot diagram for the element sodium is used to show the loss of its valence electron, thus forming a cation and one free electron. Note the atomic structure of sodium in Figure 1; when its valence electron is lost there are 10 remaining electrons and the nucleus still has 11 protons. The atom now has a positive charge because it has more protons than electrons.

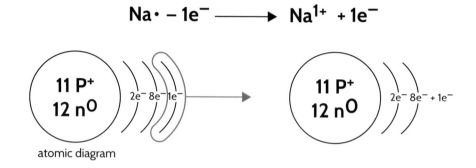

Figure 1

Electronegativity is a measure of how strongly electrons are attracted to the nucleus of an atom. The element with the lowest electronegativity is to the left in a period and at the bottom of a group.

Atoms that gain electrons form negative ions called anions. In Figure 2, the dot diagram for the element chlorine is used to show the formation of an anion. Chlorine atoms have an equal number of protons and electrons and seven valence electrons. The formation of a chloride ion occurs when a chlorine atom gains one electron to fill the outer energy level and forms an anion with a charge of negative 1. Note that the charge on an ion is written as a superscript above and to the right of the element's symbol. Charges on ions, whether positive or negative, are called valence charges.

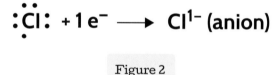

Figure 2

A general rule that can be used to determine whether an atom loses or gains electrons when reacting with another element is:

- Elements with 1, 2, or 3 valence electrons lose all valence electrons, forming cations.
- Elements with 5, 6, or 7 valence electrons gain electrons so that there are 8 valence electrons, forming anions.
- Elements with 4 valence electrons can gain electrons if they react with an element with a lower electronegativity, or lose 4 electrons if they react with an element with a higher electronegativity.
- The inert gases in group 8A do not generally form ions.

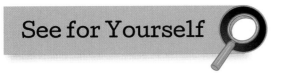
Materials

element booklets (from experiment #2)   black marker

What to Do

1. Start with the hydrogen booklet. Open the booklet and use the Lewis dot diagram to write an equation to show how hydrogen atoms form ions.

   - Use chlorine in Figure 2 as an example.
   - Write the symbol for hydrogen with its valence charge as a superscript.
   - Elements in groups 1A, 2A, and 3A tend to lose all their valence electrons, forming cations.
   - Elements in group 4A can lose or gain 4 electrons depending on what they react with. Write two equations for elements in this group.
   - Elements in groups 5A–7A gain up to 8 valance electrons, forming anions.
   - Elements in group 8A do not generally form ions. No equation is needed.

2. Repeat step 1, writing equations to show how each of the remaining 19 elements form ions, omitting group 8A.

3. Close the booklets and on the back of each booklet write the symbol and its valence charge in the upper left corner.

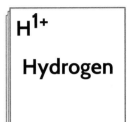

Figure 3

What Happened ?

The equation for ion formation of the first 20 elements on the periodic table was written in individual element booklets. The symbol and its valence charge were written on the back of each of the booklets.

Challenge

Can you identify the valence charge for the first 20 elements?

Think!

- One way to memorize the valence charges of elements is by using the element booklets.
- Stack the booklets with the symbol side up.
- Look at the symbol on the top booklet; identify the name of the symbol; and then identify the valence charge for the element.
- Turn the booklet over and check your answers.
- Repeat until you can identify the valence charge of all the first 20 elements. Note: Inert gases have no charge.

Chemical Formulas

A **compound** contains two or more different elements; for example, water is a compound containing two elements, hydrogen and oxygen. The chemical formula for water is H_2O. Every **chemical formula** is a combination of elemental symbols showing the elements as well as the number of atoms of each element.

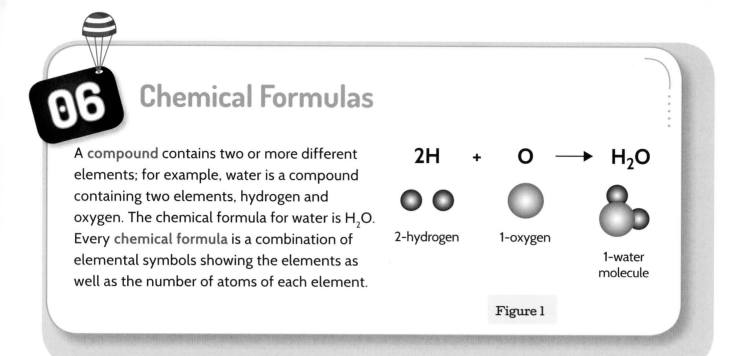

$$2H \quad + \quad O \longrightarrow H_2O$$

2-hydrogen   1-oxygen

1-water molecule

Figure 1

See for Yourself

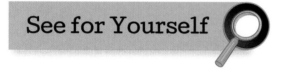

Materials

paper and pencil

What to Do

Identify the elements and number of atoms for the chemical formulas shown in the following table:

Chemical Formula	Elements	Symbols	Number of Atoms
NaCl			
$C_{12}H_{22}O_{11}$			

What Happened

Alphabet letters are used to write words, but elemental symbols are used to write chemical formulas for compounds. A word is composed of letters in a specific order; a chemical formula is composed of elemental symbols in a specific order. When writing words, such as "see," letters are repeated, but this is not true in chemical formulas.

Washing soda (Na_2CO_3) has three symbols: Na, C, and O. Subscripts for Na and O indicate the number of atoms of these elements. Thus, instead of writing the formula for baking soda as NaNaCOOO, subscripts follow a symbol to indicate the number of atoms. A symbol without a number indicates one atom, so no subscript is needed for C.

The kind and number of atoms in the chemical formula for table salt, NaCl, and for table sugar, $C_{12}H_{22}O_{11}$, are shown here:

NaCl

Atom Name	Atom Symbol	Number
Sodium	Na	1
Chlorine	Cl	1

$C_{12}H_{22}O_{11}$

Atom Name	Atom Symbol	Number
Carbon	C	12
Hydrogen	H	22
Oxygen	O	11

Challenge ⭐

Can you write the possible chemical formulas for the atomic structures in Figure 2?

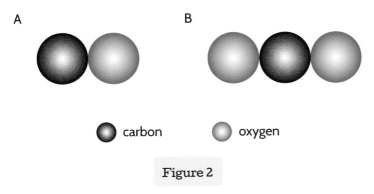

A   B

● carbon   ● oxygen

Figure 2

Think!

- What are the kind and number of atoms in each of the two atomic structures?
  (Structure A has 1 C and 1 O; structure B has 1 C and 2 O.)
- Carbon and oxygen are both in period 2 of the periodic table; oxygen is further to the right; thus, oxygen has the greater electronegativity (affinity for electrons) and will be the negative partner in the formula.
- When writing a formula, always write the positive element first and the negative element second.
- Structure A is carbon monoxide and its correct formula is CO; structure B is carbon dioxide and its formula is CO_2.
- It is important to write chemical formulas correctly. Slight differences matter. For example, the formulas CO and CO_2 contain the same elements (C carbon and O oxygen). But one formula is a poisonous gas and the other is a gas needed by plants to survive. The poisonous gas is CO, carbon monoxide; the gas that plants use to make food is CO_2, carbon dioxide.

Ionic Compounds

Compounds are formed when the atoms of two or more different elements bond together. Bonds between atoms are not physical structures; instead, they are electrostatic in nature, meaning there is an attraction between two differently charged particles. Ionic bonds form when there is an exchange of electrons between atoms, one giving up electrons thus forming a cation and the other accepting the electrons thus forming an anion. Ionic compounds are composed of cations and anions held together by ionic bonds (the electrostatic attraction between the cation and the anion). These charged particles combine in a ratio that gives the compound a net charge of zero.

A chemical formula for an ionic compound represents the lowest ratio between the cations and anions. For example, when calcium and chlorine react, the calcium loses its two valence electrons. Since chlorine atoms can only gain one electron, two atoms of chlorine are needed. Figure 1 shows the transfer of electrons and the chemical formula of the ionic compound formed. Note that a subscript of 2 indicates that two ions of chlorine are needed. Also, note that the symbol for the cation is written first in the formula.

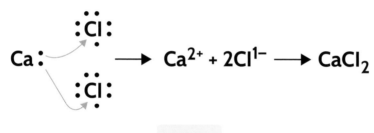

$$Ca + \ddot{Cl} \quad \ddot{Cl} \longrightarrow Ca^{2+} + 2Cl^{1-} \longrightarrow CaCl_2$$

Figure 1

Models can be used to demonstrate the formation of ionic compounds.

See for Yourself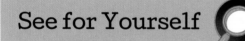

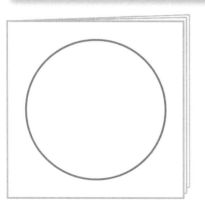

Materials

blank paper   ruler
pencil   scissors

What to Do

1. Fold the paper in half twice, first from top to bottom, and then from side to side.

2. Draw a circle as large as possible on the top layer, and then cut out this circle; cut through all four layers of paper.

3. Draw a circle in the center of each of the circle pieces.

Figure 2

4. On one of the cutouts, use the pencil and ruler to divide the outer circle into eight equal parts. Draw a dot to represent an electron in six of the sections.

5. Stack the remaining three cutout circles, and then draw one section of equal size to the sections in step 4. Cut out the center circle with this one section attached; add an electron to each as shown. Keep the cutout pieces and discard the remaining part of the circle.

6. Now that you have the "puzzle" pieces, put together an ionic compound by combining the pieces. Clue: Not all of the pieces are needed.

Group 6A

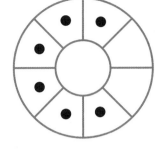

Figure 3

What Happened ❓

Ionic compounds are composed of cations and anions. Of the four pieces prepared, each of which represents an atom, one atom has six electrons and will gain two electrons when it reacts with another element. The remaining three atoms have one valence electron; these electrons will be lost. Atoms that lose electrons form cations. Atoms that gain electrons form anions. The cations have a 1+ charge and the anion has a 2− charge.

The ionic compound formed is made up of one anion and two cations. Make note that the ions are held together by the attractive force between the positive and negative ions. When ionic compounds dissolve in water, the ions separate.

Group 1A

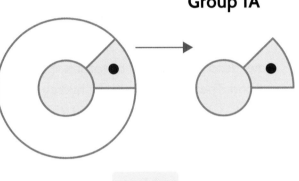

Figure 4

Challenge ⭐

The cation in the previous activity had a 1+ charge; this means it is a metal in group 1A. The anion has a valence charge of 2−; this means it is a nonmetal in group 6A. **Can you write a chemical formula that represents the model formed?**

Think!

- Pick one of the group 1A elements, such as potassium, K, and an element from group 6A, such as oxygen, O.
- Write the formula showing the valence charge on each ion: K^+O^{2-}.
- Since the magnitudes of the charges are not the same, use a subscript to change this. The correct formula is K_2O.
- Note: The name of the compound is potassium oxide. When naming ionic compounds with two elements, the cation's name is the name of the element. The anion's name is the root of the element's name plus the suffix "-ide."

08 Covalent Compounds

There are two basic kinds of compound, covalent compounds and ionic compounds. Ionic compounds are made up of cations and anions held together by ionic bonds. **Covalent compounds** are made up of **molecules**, which contain atoms of different elements held together by covalent bonds. A **covalent bond** forms when atoms share pairs of electrons. Covalent bonds generally form between nonmetals and between the atoms of diatomic molecules: H_2, N_2, O_2, F_2, Cl_2, Br_2, and I_2.

In Figure 1, a covalent bond is shown between hydrogen atoms. The ovals represent the outer energy level of each hydrogen atom. Much like a Venn diagram, where the energy levels overlap an electron pair is shown as being shared by the two atoms. Each hydrogen atom needs to gain one electron; thus, the two hydrogens share electrons, forming one covalent bond. The dash between the hydrogen symbols represents one covalent bond.

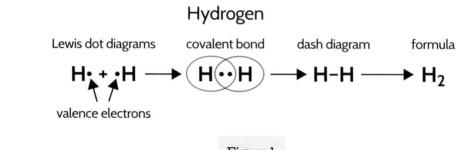

Figure 1

Ionic compounds are composed of cations and anions held together by ionic bonds. When ionic compounds dissolve in water, the ionic bonds break, and the cations and anions separate. Covalent compounds are composed of molecules held together by covalent bonds. When a covalent compound dissolves in water, the covalent bonds do not break; instead, single molecules of the compound separate from each other and spread out in the water. Models of covalent compounds can be made to demonstrate the strength of covalent bonding.

See for Yourself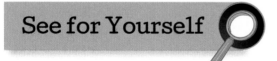

Materials

2 sheets of blank paper
pencil
scissors

paper punch
4 paper brads

What to Do

1. Fold one paper in half twice, first from top to bottom, and then from side to side.

2. Draw a circle as large as possible on the top layer, and then cut out this circle; cut through all four layers of paper. Keep three circles and discard the remaining paper.

3. Print the letter "C" in the center of one of the circles and the letter "O" in the center of two of the circles.

4. On the remaining paper, use the following to draw covalent bonds between these two nonmetals, carbon and oxygen:
   - Draw the Venn diagram as shown in Figure 2.
   - Mark "x"s for the oxygen electrons and dots for the carbon electrons.
   - In the overlapping areas between each atom, mark the electrons to be shared by each atom, as shown in Figure 3.

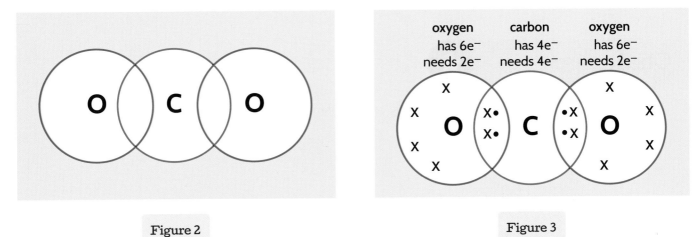

Figure 2

Figure 3

   - Add a dash diagram as shown in Figure 4. Remember that each covalent bond is made up of one pair of electrons.

5. Form a model of the molecule using the following:
   - Use the paper punch to cut two holes on opposite sides of the carbon (C) circle; punch two holes on one side of each oxygen (O) circle.
   - Connect the three circles with paper brads as shown in Figure 5, with carbon between the two oxygen atoms.

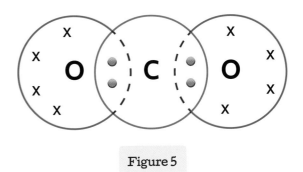

Figure 5

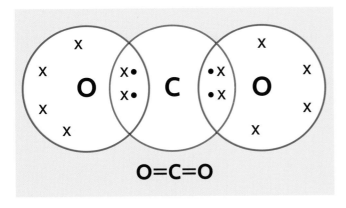

O=C=O

Figure 4

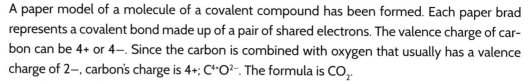

What Happened ?

A paper model of a molecule of a covalent compound has been formed. Each paper brad represents a covalent bond made up of a pair of shared electrons. The valence charge of carbon can be 4+ or 4−. Since the carbon is combined with oxygen that usually has a valence charge of 2−, carbon's charge is 4+; $C^{4+}O^{2-}$. The formula is CO_2.

Because there are only two kinds of elements in the molecule, it is called a **binary compound**. The names of binary compounds with covalent bonds include prefixes to identify the number of atoms of each element in the molecule; thus, the name of the formula is carbon dioxide. The prefix for "one" is mono, but it is not generally used when naming compounds. There are special cases such as carbon monoxide. The name of the positive element is written first and then the root of the negative element's name plus "ide" completes the name.

Challenge ★

Using the Greek prefixes, can you name these binary covalent compounds: N_2O_5; SO_3?

1. mono
2. di
3. tri
4. tetra
5. penta
6. hexa
7. hepta
8. octa
9. ennea
10. deca

Think!

- First identify the element names, which for N_2O_5 are nitrogen and oxygen, and for SO_3 sulfur and oxygen.
- Add prefixes for the number of atoms for each element in the formula: N_2O_5 is dinitrogen pentoxide, and SO_3 is sulfur trioxide.

FYI: The name is pentoxide instead of "pentaoxide" because there are two vowels together, a and o, so the a is dropped.

09 Atoms vs. Molecules

The atoms in molecules are connected by covalent bonds. A covalent bond is not tangible, meaning it is not a type of matter; instead, a covalent bond is an **electrostatic attraction** between atoms when the atoms share their electrons. Models, such as structural diagrams, use a straight line to represent a covalent bond. Three-dimensional models use materials such as toothpicks to represent the covalent bonds between atoms which are modeled in clay.

See for Yourself

Materials

sheet of blank paper
pen
ruler

2 lumps of clay: 1 red, 1 yellow
5 toothpicks
red and yellow crayons

What to Do

1. Divide the red clay into four equal parts. Shape each clay piece into a ball. Each ball represents an atom of hydrogen.

2. Divide the yellow clay into three equal parts. Shape each clay piece into a ball. Each ball represents an atom of oxygen.

3. Use the ruler, pen, and paper to prepare a "Matter Data" table, like this one:

Matter Data			
Atoms			
hydrogen 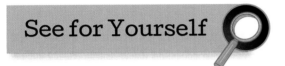		oxygen	
Molecules			
Name	Formula	Structure	Model
Hydrogen (diatomic)	H_2	H—H	
Oxygen (diatomic)	O_2	O=O	
Water	H_2O		

4. In the data table, make a colored drawing of each of the two kinds of atoms, as shown, hydrogen (red clay ball) and oxygen (yellow clay ball).

5. Form molecules using the clay balls for atoms and toothpicks for bonds. The structures listed in the "Matter Data" table indicate the number and location of the bonds between the atoms. For example, there are double bonds between the two oxygen atoms in the diatomic oxygen molecule (Figure 1).

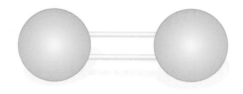

Diatomic
Oxygen Molecule

Figure 1

6. In the "Model" column of the table, make a colored drawing of each kind of molecule.

What Happened

You have made models of atoms and molecules and described the models on a data sheet. Clay models as well as colored diagrams of atoms and molecules were made. Two kinds of elements were represented, oxygen and hydrogen. The atoms of oxygen – a gas that is part of the air you breathe – form diatomic molecules. Hydrogen is generally found combined with other elements, but in its gas form hydrogen atoms combine with each other forming diatomic molecules. The structural diagrams of the oxygen, hydrogen, and water molecules indicate the number of covalent bonds as well as the direction of the bonds. In a water molecule, the hydrogen atoms combine with the oxygen at an angle of 105°.

Challenge

Can you make models of the molecules in the following table?

Simple Molecules to Make		
Name	Formula	Structure
Carbon dioxide	CO_2	O=C=O
Chlorine	Cl_2	Cl–Cl
Fluorine	F_2	F–F
Nitrogen	N_2	N≡N

Think!

There are five different types of elements represented: C, O, Cl, F, and N. You need five different colors of clay and nine toothpicks.

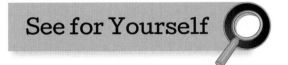

Heterogeneous Mixtures

Mixtures of different substances that are not the same throughout are called **heterogeneous mixtures**. A heterogeneous mixture can be formed by, for example, combining substances of different states of matter, such as ice and water, or things of different color.

See for Yourself

Materials

different-colored eraser caps (or similar colored objects, such as candy)

bowls, one for each eraser color

paper sack

What to Do

1. Separate the erasers by color, placing each color in a separate bowl.

Figure 1

2. Use your hand to pick out about half of the erasers from one of the bowls and place them in the paper sack.

3. Repeat step 2, taking samples of erasers from each of the remaining bowls.

4. Shake the sack to thoroughly mix the erasers.

5. Take a handful of erasers from the sack. This is your first sample. Lay these erasers on a table and separate them by color. Make note of the number of each color and record your results in a data table, such as this one:

Sample Number	Purple	Pink	Green	Yellow	ETC.
1					
2					
3					
4					
5					

6. Repeat step 5 four more times to give you five samples in total.

7. Compare the five samples of erasers taken from the sack. Were any of the samples the same?

What Happened

Each bowl had a homogeneous mixture of erasers, meaning all the erasers were alike. Combining the different colors of erasers in the sack produced a heterogeneous mixture. It is unlikely that any of the five samples taken from the sack were the same. This is because there were different colors and, generally, the odds are against any two samples taken from a heterogeneous mixture being the same. Thus, the sack had a heterogeneous mixture of erasers.

Challenge ⭐

Can you identify what kind of mixture the ocean is?

Think!

The ocean is made up of water with different substances, including salts, plants, and animals. This type of combination is an example of a heterogeneous mixture.

Figure 2

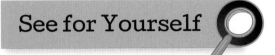

11 Solution: Concentration

A **solution** is a homogeneous mixture of two or more substances. A solution consists of a solute and a solvent. The **solute** is the substance that is dissolved (spread out) in the **solvent**. The **concentration** of a solution refers to the amount of solute added to the solvent. You can **dilute** a solution (reduce its concentration) by adding more solvent; the concentration of a solution can be increased by adding more solute or by decreasing the amount of solvent.

See for Yourself

Materials

black marker
4 transparent plastic cups or glasses
tap water
food coloring of your choice
  (red or blue work well)

4 stirring spoons
measuring cup, ¼ cup (63 mL)

What to Do

1. Use the marker to number the cups.

2. Fill each cup about one-half full with water.

3. Place one spoon in each cup.

4. Add 5 to 6 drops of food coloring to cup #1 (Figure 1) and stir.

5. Dip ¼ cup (63 mL) of colored water from cup #1, and then pour this water into cup #2 (Figure 2) and stir.

6. Transfer ¼ cup (63 mL) of colored water from cup #2 to cup #3 and stir.

7. Transfer ¼ cup (63 mL) of colored water from cup #3 to cup #4 and stir.

Figure 1

Figure 2

What Happened

Cup #1 has the most concentrated solution of food coloring in water. With each transfer of colored water, the ratio of food coloring to water decreased. Cup #4 is the most dilute solution. The more the color was diluted with water, the more transparent it became.

Challenge ⭐

Can you explain the statement, "The solution to pollution is not dilution"?

Figure 3

Think!

- What is pollution?

  Pollution is anything that harms our environment, such as exhaust gases from cars or pesticides running into a pond.
- Does pouring waste into a body of water completely get rid of it?

  No. Diluting the waste with water just spreads it out.

12 Solubility

Solubility is the measure of the ability of a solute to dissolve in a solvent when forming a solution. A solute must be attracted to a solvent for it to dissolve. Ionic compounds that are soluble in water break apart forming cations and anions. Water molecules are **bipolar** (they have charges on each end), thus the cations and anions are attracted to water molecules. Covalent compounds with molecules having even the slightest charge will also be attracted to water molecules. This happens at the atomic level, but you can observe the changes in a sugar (sucrose) cube as sugar molecules dissolve in water. Actually, the sugar molecules are pulled away from the cube by water molecules.

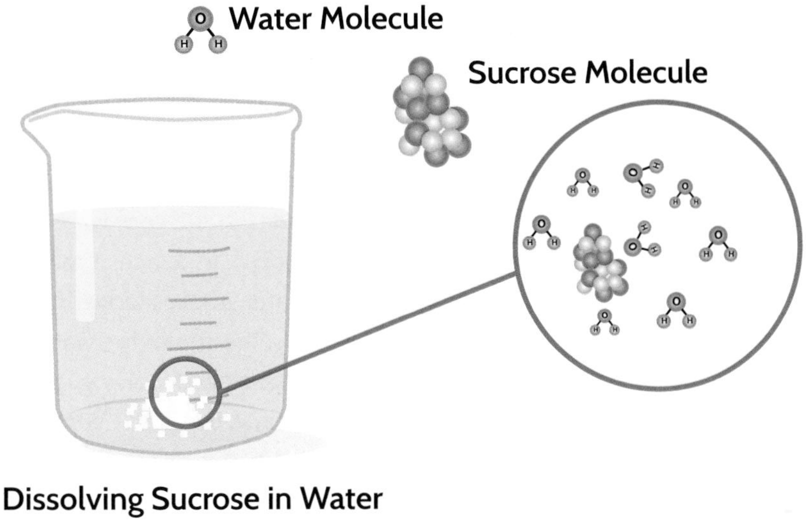

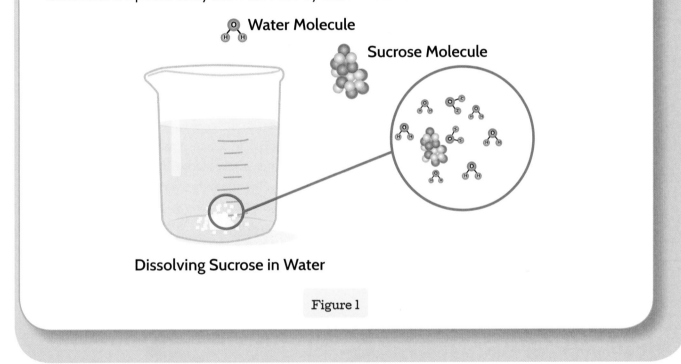

Figure 1

See for Yourself

Figure 2

Materials

transparent plastic cup
cool tap water
sugar cube

What to Do

1. Fill the cup with cool tap water.
2. Observe all the surfaces of the dry sugar cube.
3. Drop the sugar cube in the water.

4. Note changes in the surface of the sugar cube.

Figure 3

What Happened ?

The sugar cube began with relatively flat, square sides. When placed in water, bubbles rose from the cube. Bubbles are generally viewed as a sign that a chemical reaction is occurring, but this is not the case when a sugar cube dissolves in water. Instead, the bubbles are air that has been trapped between the grains of sugar in the cube and are released as the sugar molecules are removed. Water molecules in the cool water have less energy than at higher temperatures and thus move more slowly. In a race, it takes slow runners longer to finish. Likewise, when dissolving solutes in water, it takes longer for the solute to dissolve in cool water with slow-moving molecules. Thus, the cooler the water temperature the slower will be the rate of dissolving. In this activity, the slow dissolving rate allowed you to observe the changes in the sugar cube. The average time for all the sugar to dissolve and disperse throughout the water is about 10 minutes. Again, this depends on the water's temperature.

Figure 4

After studying Figure 5, can you describe three different methods of increasing the rate of dissolving?

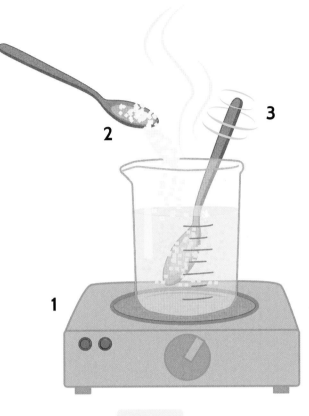

Figure 5

Think!

1. Cool water has slower-moving water molecules, thus increasing the temperature would result in faster-moving water molecules. The faster the molecules, the more often they will collide with the sugar cube. Raising the temperature of the solvent will increase the rate the solute (sugar) molecules are separated and dispersed.

2. Instead of a cube of sugar, granular sugar is used. The sugar cube has much less surface area than does the many separated grains of sugar. Thus, water molecules have access to more sugar molecules.

3. As well as dispersing the sugar, stirring moves the water and sugar around so that they have a better chance of being attracted to each other.

NOTE These methods also apply to increasing the dissolving rate of ionic compounds, such as salt, that break into ions.

True Solutions

A **true solution** has these characteristics:

- It's a homogeneous mixture of two or more substances.
- It has a uniform composition throughout.
- It doesn't separate upon standing.
- It's clear and transparent.
- It doesn't scatter light.
- Its components cannot be separated by filtration.

The components of a solution are a **solute** and a **solvent**, where the solute is dissolved and dispersed throughout the solvent.

See for Yourself

Materials

2 empty plastic water bottles with caps   flashlight
tap water   coffee filter
½ tsp (2.5 mL) of table salt (NaCl)   funnel

Figure 1

What to Do

1. Fill one bottle about three-fourths full with water.

2. Add the salt to the bottle of water and then close the bottle with its cap.

3. Shake the bottle vigorously to thoroughly mix its contents (Figure 1). If all the salt does not dissolve, add more water and repeat this step.

4. Observe the contents of the mixture in the bottle. Make note of the color and transparency of the mixture.

5. In a darkened room, hold the flashlight so that rays of light shine directly on one side of the bottle (Figure 2). Observe the mixture from one side. Make note of any visible path of light in the mixture as well as evidence that the light passes through it.

6. Allow the mixture to stand undisturbed for 5 minutes or more. Observe any change in the mixture, such as any separation of its components.

7. Place the coffee filter in the funnel, and then stand the funnel in the remaining water bottle.

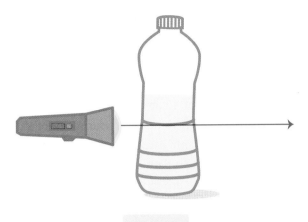

Figure 2

8. Again, shake the bottle of water and salt, and then pour the mixture into the filter-lined funnel (Figure 3). When all the liquid has passed through the funnel, observe the filter paper for any evidence of solid particles.

Figure 3

What Happened

The salt and water mixture produced a true solution. Like all true solutions, the mixture was homogeneous, meaning the particles of solute (salt) are thoroughly dispersed throughout the solvent (water); every sample of the mixture has the same solute to solvent ratio. The process of shining a light on mixtures to identify true solutions is called the **Tyndall effect**. True solutions are clear and transparent; no light path can be seen inside them. This is because the particles formed by the dissolved solute are too small to reflect light to your eyes. Instead, the light passes through the solution and illuminates objects on the other side of the bottle. The components did not separate upon standing, nor were they separated by filtration. These steps are used to identify a true solution from other mixtures.

Challenge

Can you identify the true solution in Figure 4?

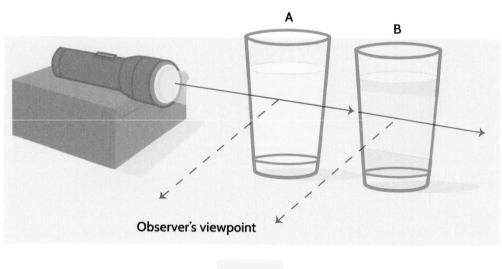

A   B

Observer's viewpoint

Figure 4

Think!

- Light rays pass through a true solution without being scattered. You only see light that reaches your eyes. If the light is not scattered toward your eyes, you do not see its path. Solution A is the true solution.
- A mixture in which the path of the light is visible is not a true solution. The light is visible in mixture B, thus it is not a true solution.

14 Colloids

A **colloid** is a mixture with suspended microscopic, undissolved particles dispersed throughout it. Colloids have a uniform composition throughout, and the colloidal particles do not settle, nor can they be separated by filtration. Thus, colloids have properties like true solutions. Colloidal particles are spherical with a diameter of about 0.001 to 0.000001 mm, which is larger than particles in solution. These particles are large enough to scatter light.

The Tyndall effect is a method used to distinguish a colloid from a true solution. This method is simple and requires only a beam of light, such as from a flashlight or laser. Light passes straight through a true solution, but a colloid scatters part of the light and the remaining portion passes through.

See for Yourself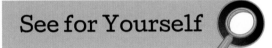

Materials

2 transparent drinking glasses
tap water
¼ tsp (1.25 mL) table salt
2 spoons

eyedropper
1 tsp (5 mL) milk
flashlight
helper

What to Do

1. Fill one of the glasses with tap water and then add the salt. Stir.
2. Fill the remaining glass with water and then add 2 to 3 drops of milk. Stir.
3. Line the two glasses up with the salt water solution in front of the milky solution.
4. Darken the room, and ask a helper to shine the flashlight on the side of the first glass with salt water.
5. Observe the glasses from the side and make note of the path of light. Can you see the light in both mixtures? Does the color of the mixture in each glass change because of the light?

What Happened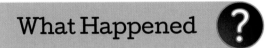

The milky water appears blue when the light shines on it. This is because milk contains microscopic fat particles suspended evenly throughout the liquid. The fat particles are the size of colloidal particles. Light from the flashlight is composed of different colors; the blend of these light colors produces what is called **white light.** The fat particles in the water scatter part of the light while the remaining light continues to pass through. The shorter wavelengths of light are more easily scattered; these are blue, indigo, and violet. Thus, the colloid mixture of water and milk takes on a bluish color. Scattering means the light moves out in all directions.

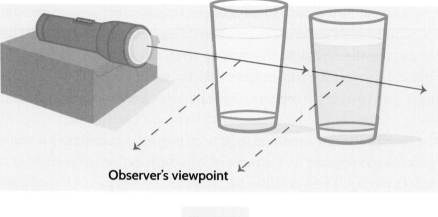

Observer's viewpoint

Figure 1

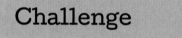
Challenge ⭐

The table lists the different types of colloids and gives a description of each. **Can you describe how each type of colloid is formed?**

Colloids

Fluid	Colloidal Particle	Colloidal Name	Example
Gas	Liquid	**Aerosol**	Fog
Gas	Solid	**Solid aerosol**	Smoke
Liquid	Gas	**Foam**	Whipped cream
Liquid	Liquid	**Emulsion**	Salad dressing
Liquid	Solid	**Sol**	Paint
Solid	Gas	**Solid foam**	Pumice
Solid	Liquid	**Gel**	Jelly
Solid	Solid	**Solid sol**	Colored glass

Think!

- Fog is an **aerosol**: water droplets are dispersed in air.
- Smoke is a **solid aerosol**: particles of carbon from a fire mix with air.
- Whipped cream is a **foam**: air is whipped into liquid cream.
- Salad dressing is an **emulsion**: oil droplets are dispersed throughout liquid vinegar.
- Paint is a **sol**: solid pigment particles are dispersed throughout water.
- Pumice is a **solid foam**: gases are mixed with lava and become trapped in a solid matrix as the lava cools and solidifies.
- Jelly is a **gel**: a solid has water trapped within a network formed by gelatin; it jiggles.
- Colored glass is a **solid sol**: solid colored particles are mixed with hot liquid glass; when cooled, the solid particles remain dispersed throughout glass.

15 Emulsions

Emulsions are a specific type of colloid containing two **immiscible** liquids, such as water and oil. The process of mixing two immiscible liquids is called **emulsification**, which means an **emulsifier** is added to the mixture. Figure 1 shows a simple diagram of an emulsifier used to form an oil and water emulsion. Note that one end of the emulsifier attracts water and the opposite end attracts oil. When an emulsifier is added, the oil and water no longer separate upon standing. *Voila!*, an emulsion is formed.

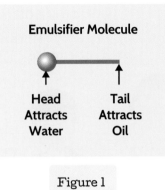

Emulsifier Molecule

Head
Attracts
Water

Tail
Attracts
Oil

Figure 1

Cream is an **oil-in-water emulsion** which has oil droplets dispersed (spread throughout) in water as shown in Figure 2. A protein in cream acts as an emulsifier, thus connecting the oil with surrounding water molecules.

Oil-in-Water Emulsion

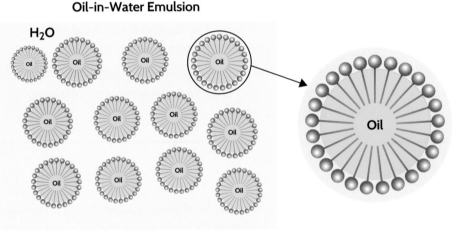

Figure 2

Churning is a process of agitating cream to form butter. Churning cream inverts this oil-in-water emulsion producing butter, which is a **water-in-oil emulsion**. Basically, butter is an inside-out version of cream with water droplets dispersed in oil instead of oil droplets dispersed in water (Figure 3).

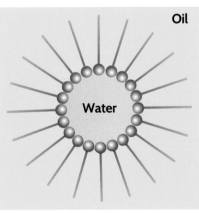

Water-in-Oil Emulsion

Oil

Water

Figure 3

See for Yourself

Materials

plastic jar with lid, 1 qt (1 L)
1 pint (500 mL) of heavy cream
  (whipping cream)
a marble

spoon
small bowl
tap water
measuring cups

Figure 4

What to Do

1. Wash the jar, lid, and marble with soapy water and then rinse with clear water.

2. Pour the cream into the jar. Add the clean marble, and then seal the jar with its lid.

3. Allow the jar to sit undisturbed at room temperature for about 2 hours.

4. Shake the jar until its contents is filled with bubbles and appears thick (Figure 4). Continue to shake the jar until there is a separation of the butter and the liquid.

5. Use a clean spoon to remove the clumps of butter from the jar and place them in the bowl. The liquid in the jar is called buttermilk, but it is mostly water and can be discarded.

6. Wash the butter by filling the bowl with cold tap water. Then, with clean hands, knead the butter to squeeze out any remaining buttermilk. Repeat this process using fresh water. You now have fresh churned butter.

What Happened

A simple explanation is that cream contains tiny fat globules surrounded by a membrane that keeps those globules separate from each other. Churning causes these fat globules to smash into each other causing the membrane to break and release the fat. The fat globules stick together and, as more globules break, the fat collection grows bigger and bigger. This collection of fat is butter, which is a water-in-oil emulsion – an inversion of oil-in-water. Cream and butter are examples of stable emulsions containing liquids that do not normally mix.

Challenge

Can you explain why laundry detergent helps to clean dirty, oily clothes?

Think!

* Water alone can only dissolve water-soluble dirt. Worn clothes are soiled by oil from your body as well as other materials that may not dissolve in water.
* In order to remove oils and other materials not soluble in water from dirty clothes, an emulsifier needs to be added to water.
* Detergent molecules act as an emulsifier with one end attracted to oil, and the other end attracted to water.

16 Suspensions

A **suspension** is a heterogeneous mixture containing particles larger than those in solutions or colloids; the large particles in a suspension settle on standing. Dirt or sand mixed with water is an example of a suspension.

See for Yourself

Materials

2 empty plastic water bottles, 1 cap
tap water
2 tablespoons (30 mL) of dirt or sand

flashlight
coffee filter
funnel

What to Do

1. Fill one bottle about half-full with water.
2. Add the dirt to the bottle of water. Close the bottle with the cap.
3. Shake the bottle vigorously to thoroughly mix its contents (Figure 1).
4. Observe the contents of the mixture in the bottle. Make note of the color and transparency of the mixture.
5. In a darkened room, hold the flashlight so that rays of light shine directly on one side of the bottle. Notice whether a path of light is visible in the mixture. Notice whether any of the light passes through the mixture.
6. Allow the mixture to stand undisturbed for at least 5 minutes. Observe any change in the mixture, such as any separation of its components.

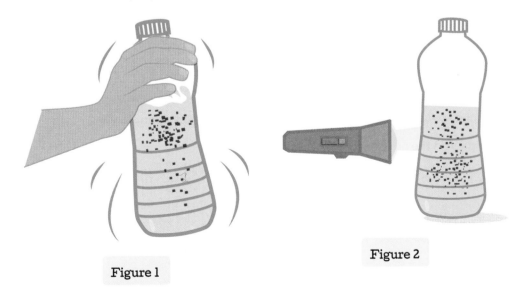

Figure 1

Figure 2

7. Place the coffee filter in the funnel, and then support the funnel in the remaining water bottle.

8. Again, shake the bottle of water and dirt, and then pour the mixture into the funnel (Figure 3). When all of the liquid has passed through the funnel, observe the filter paper for any evidence of solid particles.

What Happened

The dirt and water mixture produced a suspension, which is an example of a heterogeneous mixture. If the mixture is initially **opaque** (you cannot see through it; light doesn't pass through) then no light path can be seen inside the mixture and no light passes through to illuminate objects on the other side of the bottle. The undissolved particles precipitated upon standing and were separated from the mixture by filtration. These steps are used to identify suspensions.

Figure 3

Challenge

Can you identify the suspension in the table?

Sample	Mixture Type	Filtration	Standing
A	Heterogeneous	Components can be separated by filtration	Not stable; components separate upon standing
B	Homogeneous	Components cannot be separated by filtration	Stable; components do not separate upon standing

Think!

- A suspension is a heterogeneous mixture.
- The undissolved components of a suspension can be separated by filtration.
- The undissolved components of a suspension will separate upon standing.

So, sample A in the table describes a suspension.

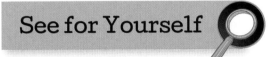

Saturated Solutions

A **saturated solution** contains the maximum amount of solute that can dissolve in a solvent at a specific temperature and pressure. Solvent temperature affects the solubility of table sugar. As the temperature increases the amount of sugar that will dissolve increases. This is why it is difficult to sweeten an icy drink with table sugar.

See for Yourself

Materials

three jars, 1 pint (500 mL) each
tap water
table sugar
measuring spoon 1 tsp (5 mL)
stirring spoon

3 or 4 ice cubes
coffee filter or paper towel
funnel
saucer

What to Do

1. Fill one jar half full with warn tap water, and then add 1 tsp (5 mL) of sugar. Stir until all the sugar has dissolved.

2. Continue adding sugar one spoon at a time until no more sugar will dissolve. Count the spoons of sugar that you used.

3. Fill the remaining jar half full with cold tap water, and then add the ice cubes. Stir for 3 to 4 s to lower the temperature of the water, and then remove and discard the ice.

4. Add 1 tsp (5 mL) of sugar to the cold water and then repeat step #2.

5. When no additional sugar will dissolve, add two more spoons of sugar. Stir vigorously, and then allow the jar to sit for about 5 minutes. Observe the contents of the jar periodically.

6. After sitting, decant (pour off) the clear liquid at the top of the jar into a funnel lined with a coffee filter. The filtrate (liquid passing through filter) is a saturated sugar solution. Any undissolved sugar on the filter paper is called the residue.

7. Allow the saturated sugar from step #6 to stand for 30 minutes or more to warm to room temperature, and then repeat step #2.

Figure 1

What Happened

More sugar should have dissolved in the warm water than in the colder water. After the saturated solution formed in the cold water warmed to room temperature, more sugar should have dissolved in it. Once the sugar starts to **precipitate** (settle to the bottom of the container), no matter how much you stir the solution, no more sugar will dissolve.

In Figure 2, can you identify which solution, A or B, will most likely be able to dissolve more sugar?

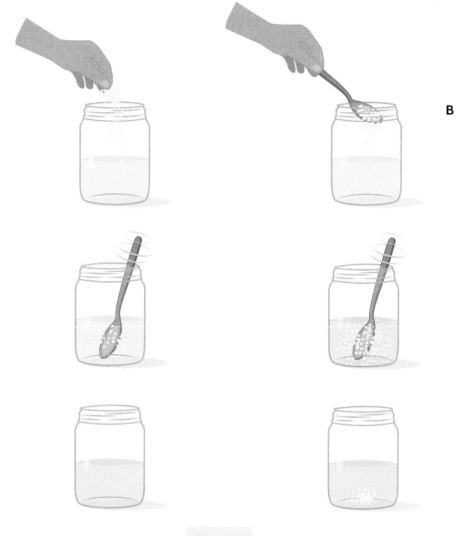

A   **B**

Figure 2

Think!

- Process "A" produces a solution of sugar and water. A small amount of sugar was added and the mixture was stirred.
- All the sugar dissolved in solution A. No sugar precipitated out of the solution. (A **precipitate** is undissolved solute that is pulled to the bottom of the glass by gravity.)
- Process "B" also produced a sugar solution. A large amount of sugar was added. After stirring, some of the sugar did not dissolve and was suspended in the solution. After sitting, the suspended sugar particles precipitated and settled on the bottom of the glass. This collection of undissolved sugar is called a sediment or a precipitate.

18 Diffusion

Diffusion is the spontaneous movement of particles in a **fluid** from an area of high particle concentration to an area of lower particle concentration. The **rate of diffusion** of a solute throughout a solvent is directly proportional to temperature. This means that as the temperature increases the solute moves faster through the solvent and the rate of diffusion increases.

See for Yourself

Materials

warm and cold tap water
2 ice cubes
2 glasses

yellow and blue food coloring
helper

What to Do

1. Fill one glass with cold tap water. Place the ice cubes in the water and stir for 4 to 5 seconds. Remove the ice from the glass.

2. Fill the remaining glass with warm tap water.

3. Ask a helper to assist in adding 3 drops of yellow and 3 drops of blue flood coloring simultaneously to the glass of cold water. Add the drops as far as possible from each other. Do not stir.

4. Immediately repeat this procedure adding the two colors to the glass of warm water (Figure 1).

COLD WATER   WARM WATER

Figure 1

5. Observe the movement of the coloring in the two glasses (Figure 2). Make note of how the water's temperature affects the rate the coloring diffuses throughout the water, as well as the final color of the solution.

What Happened ?

The yellow and blue food coloring spreads faster in the warm water than in the cold water. This is because diffusion depends on molecular movement. The molecules of the warm water have more energy and move faster than the water molecules in the cold water. The coloring is bounced around more in the warm water, thus it mixes faster than when added to cold water. As the yellow and blue coloring mix, the solution takes on a greenish color.

According to the **Particle Theory**, all matter is made of particles that are in constant motion; the speed of particle movement is directly proportional to the temperature. Figure 3 represents the motion of water molecules in warm and cold water; an increase in temperature increases particle movement.

Figure 2

Molecular Motion

Cold Water   Warm Water

Figure 3

Challenge ★

In Figure 4, can you explain why Character A smells the skunk but Character B doesn't?

A   B

Figure 4

Think!

- When something is baking, the smell drifts throughout the house, but it starts in the kitchen.
- We smell when vapor reaches our noses. Whatever is in the skunk spray, it first has to produce a vapor that diffuses out in all directions.
- It takes time for stinky skunk vapor to diffuse through the air, but Character B will soon be aware that a skunk has sprayed nearby.

FYI: Skunks spray a liquid chemical called *n*-butyl mercaptan. Like spraying liquid perfume, the liquid skunk spray clings to surfaces and some of these liquid molecules **evaporate** and mix with air. Even small amounts of the gas can be detected by some humans up to 3.5 miles (5.6 km) away.

Physical Properties and Physical Changes

Physical properties can be observed using the five senses of sight, hearing, touch, taste, and smell. The two basic groups of physical properties are:

Extensive properties: Extensive properties depend on the amount of matter, such as mass, weight, volume, length, area, and so on.

Intensive properties: Intensive properties are independent of quantities, thus the amount of matter doesn't affect measurements; examples include boiling point, melting point, density, and the state of matter.

Mass

Mass is the amount of matter in an object. Mass is a physical property that does not depend on gravity; instead, mass is a measurement of just how much stuff an object is made of. You will make a simple equal arm balance and use it to determine if air has mass.

Volume

Volume is how much space an object takes up. You can measure the volume of a box using a ruler; the volume of liquids can be determined with a measuring cup, but measuring the volume of irregular-shaped objects needs a special method. One such method is water displacement. You will discover how to use this easy technique and be able to use it to find the volume of irregular-shaped objects.

Relative Density

Density is a ratio, mass:volume. This ratio is usually expressed as a fraction, mass/volume. Substances have their own density which is not affected by how much you have. The density of water is 1 g/mL no matter whether you have a drop or a bucket full. Relative density is the comparison of densities; often an object's density is compared to the density of water. If an object floats in water, the object's density is less than that of water. Comparisons don't have to be with water. You will have fun comparing liquids and learn how to determine their relative densities.

States of Matter

States of matter are the physical forms matter can exist in. Four of the states of matter are solid, liquid, gas, and plasma. The state of a substance depends on the kinetic energy (KE) of its particles (atoms, ions, or molecules). Kinetic energy is the energy that an object has because it is in motion.

19 Matter Has Mass

Matter is anything that has mass and takes up space. **Volume** is the amount of space that something takes up. **Mass** measures the amount of stuff that something is made of. Gases are examples of matter; thus, gases have mass and take up space. Yes, even your exhaled breath has mass and volume.

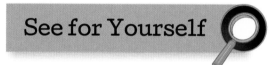
See for Yourself

Materials

two 9-inch (22-cm) round balloons
three 1-ft (30-cm) pieces of string
transparent tape

ruler (or a stick or even a clothes hanger)
pushpin

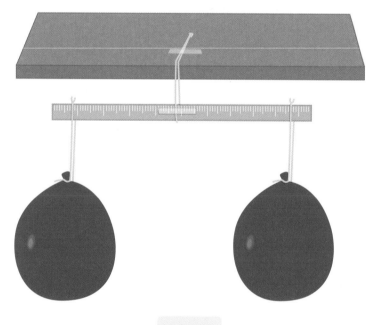

Figure 1

What to Do

1. Inflate the balloons so that they are as large as possible and of equal size. Make a note that, when filled with air, the sizes of the balloons increase. This is because air takes up space.

2. Tie a string to each balloon and then tape the free ends of the strings to the ruler, one on each end.

3. Use the remaining string to form a cradle around the center of the ruler, and then tape the free ends of the string to the edge of a table.

4. Adjust the position of the ruler in the string cradle until it is horizontal to the floor, and then secure the string to the ruler with tape.

5. Use the pushpin to make a hole in one of the balloons close to the knot. You do not want to pop the balloon.

6. Observe the two balloons, making note of any change in their position above the floor.

What Happened

Your exhaled **breath** is a mixture of gases, which are examples of matter. The expansion of the balloons gives proof that gases take up space.

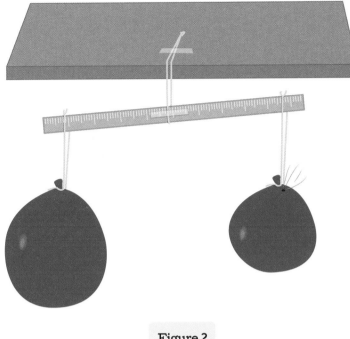

Figure 2

Assume the inflated balloons have equal mass when the ruler is balanced. When gas is released from one of the balloons, that balloon has less mass, resulting in a change in the position of the ruler; the ruler rotates around the supporting string with the less massive deflated balloon rising. While this experiment did not measure the magnitude of the mass or the volume of your exhaled breath, it did show that gases have mass and take up space.

Challenge ★

Can you use the previous information and explain why the balloon will not inflate inside the bottle in Figure 3?

Think!

- Air, like all matter, takes up space.
- There is air inside the bottle, which takes up space.
- The air inside the balloon takes up space, thus there is no room for the balloon to be inflated inside the bottle.
- Two things cannot occupy the same space at the same time.

See for Yourself

Put a balloon inside an empty bottle and pull the mouth of the balloon over the top of the bottle. Blow into the balloon.

Figure 3

Matter Has Volume

All types of matter take up space and all types of matter have volume. When an object is submerged in water, it pushes the water out of its way. In other words, the submerged object **displaces** the water. The amount of water displaced is equal to the volume of the object. The displaced water can be measured.

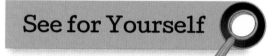

See for Yourself

Materials

jar, 1 qt (1 L)   marker

tap water   plum-size ball of clay (any color)

masking tape   fork

What to Do

1. Fill the jar about three-quarters full with water.

2. Place a piece of tape down the side of the jar and mark the water level on the tape (Figure 1).

3. Place the ball of clay in the jar and again mark the water level on the tape (Figure 2).

4. Insert the fork into the clay ball and remove it from the jar.

5. Dry the clay, then shape it like a snowman or person; make sure the clay is solid throughout, and then return it to the jar of water. Mark the new water level on the jar (Figure 3).

Figure 1

Figure 2

Figure 3

What Happened

The clay snowman displaced the same amount of water as the round ball of clay. No matter how you shape the clay, as long you make the clay solid throughout and do not remove or add any clay, each shape will displace the same amount of water. Thus, as long as a material is solid throughout, changing its shape does not change its volume.

Challenge

Can you determine the volume of the object shown in Figure 4?

Think!

- The initial water volume is 17.1 mL.
- With the submerged object, the water level rose to 19.8 mL.
- The absolute difference between the initial volume (V_i) without the object and the final volume (V_f) with the object is equal to the volume of the object (V_{object}).

$$V_{object} = V_f - V_i$$

$$V_{object} = 19.8\,\text{mL} - 17.1\,\text{mL} = 2.7\,\text{mL}$$

- The volume was determined by water displacement.

NOTE There is a curve in the surface of the water in the cylinder. This curve is called a **meniscus**, and the volume is read at the bottom of the meniscus.

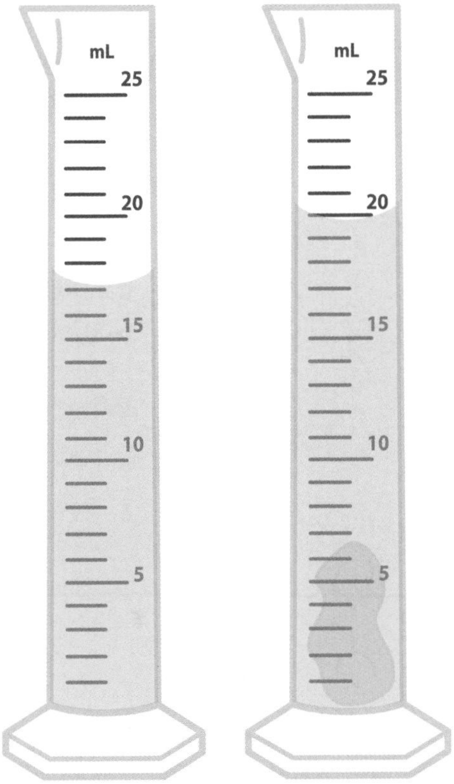

Figure 4

21 Relative Density

Density is the quantity of mass per unit volume. The formula for calculating density is $d = m/v$ (*d* for density; *m* for mass; and *v* for volume). Scientists measure density in g/mL or kg/L. **Relative density** is the comparison of the density of one material to another.

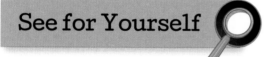

Materials

½ cup (125 mL) tap water
transparent drinking glass
blue food coloring

stirring spoon
½ cup (125 mL) dark corn syrup

What to Do

1. Pour the water into the glass, and then add drops of food coloring. Stir.

2. Slowly add the corn syrup to the glass without stirring.

Figure 1

Figure 2

What Happened

The corn syrup fell through the blue water and collected in a layer on the bottom of the glass. In comparison to water, the density of the corn syrup is greater.

The density of a material is often compared to the density of water; thus, it is important to know that water's density is 1 g/mL. While the density of corn syrup was not determined, from the experimental result you can state the density of corn syrup is greater than the density of water. The relative density of corn syrup is calculated by this equation:

$$D_R = > 1\,g/mL / 1\,g/mL$$

The units of g/mL would cancel out and the relative density for corn syrup would therefore be >1, which means corn syrup would sink through the water.

Challenge

Figure 3

If the relative density of cooking oil is less than 1, **can you predict what would happen if cooking oil was added to the glass with water and syrup from the previous activity?**

Think!

Since cooking oil has a relative density less than 1, its density would be less than 1 g/mL, and thus the oil would form a layer on top of the water as shown in Figure 3.

See for Yourself

Add cooking oil to the glass of syrup and water to confirm that oil floats on top of water.

22 States of Matter

The states of matter include solid, liquid, gas, and plasma. When pressure remains constant, state changes require either the addition of energy or the removal of energy from the substance. Changing from one state to another does not affect the chemical composition of the substance. A pure substance, such as water, can change from one state of matter to another but it is still water. Changing the state of matter doesn't change the amount of matter either.

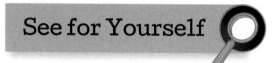

See for Yourself

Materials

clear bowl, 2 qt (2 L)   measuring cup, 1 cup (250 mL)
tap water   paper cup, 10 oz (300 mL)
marker   plate (to cover top of bowl)

What to Do

Figure 1

1. Fill the bowl about three-fourths full with water. Mark the water level on the bowl and write "#1."

2. Using the measuring cup, dip 1 cup of water from the bowl and pour it into the paper cup.

3. Mark the new water level "#2" on the bowl.

4. Cover the bowl with a plate to prevent the water from evaporating.

5. Place the cup of water in a freezer and allow the water to freeze.

6. Remove the ice from the cup and place it in the bowl of water. Mark the water level on the bowl as "#3."

7. Allow the block of ice to melt, and then mark "#4" at the water level on the bowl.

8. Compare the four water levels.

Figure 2   Figure 3   Figure 4

What Happened

Three of the water levels are the same, #1, #3, and #4. This is because one cup of water was removed from the bowl and one cup of water was returned; thus, freezing the liquid water did not affect the number of water molecules. Imagine that the ice could be lifted out of the water leaving a hole where it had been. After melting, the water from the ice would be just enough liquid to fill the hole.

NOTE When the cup was removed from the freezer, any water droplets on the outside of the cup were due to condensation of water vapor in the air.

Challenge ⭐

After observing Figure 5, can you explain how changing the state of water doesn't affect the identity of water?

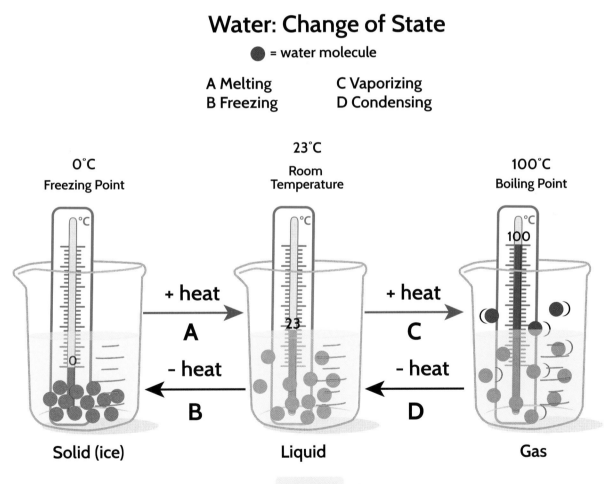

Water: Change of State

● = water molecule

A Melting   C Vaporizing
B Freezing   D Condensing

Figure 5

Think!

- Changes in the state of matter occur when there are changes in temperature. Temperature is a measure of how hot or cold something is. Temperature can be changed by adding or removing heat. As the temperature of water increases, its molecules move faster.

- Kinetic energy (KE) is a measure of the energy of moving objects; thus, the faster the water molecules move, the more kinetic energy they have. Ice molecules have the least kinetic energy. While not considered in the activity, molecules of water vapor in the air would have the greatest KE. No matter the amount of kinetic energy, the composition of a substance (such as water) stays the same. In other words, water molecules are chemically the same no matter how fast or slowly they move.

Chemical Properties and Chemical Changes

A **chemical property** describes the characteristics of a substance observed during a chemical reaction. A **chemical change** in a substance is when its atoms are rearranged into one or more new substances with a different composition. This can happen when a substance, such as hydrogen peroxide (H_2O_2), decomposes easily. Thus it is not a stable substance. When hydrogen peroxide decomposes, it forms water and oxygen.

Acids and Bases

Acids and bases are two different types of chemicals. Common acids are compounds with hydrogen as the positive ion, such as HCl (hydrochloric acid, found in the stomach). Common bases are compounds that have $(OH)^{1-}$ as the negative ion, such as $Mg(OH)_2$ (magnesium hydroxide, found in antacid medication).

pH Scale

The pH scale is a measure of how acidic or basic a substance is. The scale ranges from 0 to 14. A pH of 7 is neutral, meaning the substance is neither acidic nor basic. When a substance has a pH less than 7, it is acidic. The lower the pH the more acidic properties the substance has. A pH greater than 7 indicates the substance is basic. The higher the pH the more basic properties the substance has.

Chemical Reactions

A chemical reaction is the process that occurs when substances are chemically changed into one or more new substances. All chemical reactions result in chemical changes. The form in which chemical reactions are written is called a chemical equation:

$$Reactants \rightarrow Products$$

($\rightarrow$ This arrow is read as "yields": "reactants yield products.")

    Reactants are the starting substances. **Products** are the new substances formed from the rearrangement of the reactants' atoms.

    Chemical equations must be balanced. This means that there are an equal number of atoms of each kind of element on both sides of the equation. For example, diatomic hydrogen and oxygen combine forming water. The chemical equation for this reaction is:

$$2H_2 + O_2 \rightarrow 2H_2O$$

This equation needs a coefficient of 2 in front of the hydrogen and the water to balance the number of hydrogen and oxygen atoms in the reactants and product.

23 Acids

Acids are compounds that

- can donate a proton (hydrogen ion H^{1+}),
- change the color of blue litmus to red, and
- taste sour.

When you bite into a lemon, it tastes sour because it contains citric acid (Figure 1). A sour taste is one of the characteristics of all acids.

CAUTION While it is safe to eat sour foods, *the taste test is not a safe procedure* when investigating materials for the possible presence of an acid.

Instead, use a chemical indicator, which is a substance that makes a distinct observable change when in contact with certain substances. Blue litmus is an acid indicator that turns red when in contact with an acid.

Figure 1

See for Yourself

Materials

strip of blue litmus paper
strip of red litmus paper
white index card

eyedropper
white vinegar

What to Do

1. Lay the blue and red strips of litmus paper on the index card.
2. Using the eyedropper, place one drop of vinegar on the end of each litmus strip (Figures 2 and 3).
3. Repeat step 2 placing the drops of vinegar on the opposite, dry end of each litmus strip.

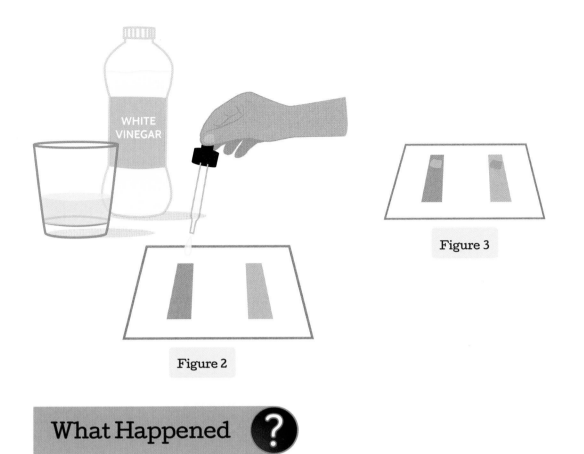

Figure 3

Figure 2

What Happened ?

Each procedure produces the same results, the blue litmus turns red and the red litmus gets wet, but has no color change (for more on red litmus, see the next experiment). You can conclude that vinegar is an acid.

The litmus test requires the acid be in a water solution. Thus, to test for the acidic properties of a solid or gas, they must first be dissolved in water. Vinegar is a solution of acetic acid in water. Aspirins are solid, thus to test with litmus paper, an aspirin has to be crushed and dissolved in water.

Challenge ⭐

After studying Figure 4, can you determine whether aspirin contains an acid?

Think!

- As in the previous procedure, litmus was used to test for the presence of an acid.
- The aspirin solution turned the blue litmus red and the red litmus just got wet.
- The conclusion from this litmus test was that aspirin does contain an acid.
- Researching the contents of aspirin revealed that the acid in aspirin is acetylsalicylic acid.

Figure 4

24 Bases

Bases might be thought to be chemical compounds with characteristics opposite to that of acids. Bases

- accept protons,
- have a pH higher than 7,
- taste bitter, and
- change red litmus blue.

But as with any investigation, *a taste test is not a safe test* and is not the best way to identify chemicals, acids, or bases. Indicators, such as litmus paper, can be used instead. Red litmus turns blue when in contact with a solution having a pH more than 7.

CAUTION Do not put any bases in your mouth. It is not safe to perform taste tests on these substances.

See for Yourself

Materials

strip of blue litmus paper
strip of red litmus paper
white index card

spray bottle of glass cleaner with ammonia
rubber gloves

What to Do

1. Lay the blue and red strips of litmus paper on the index card (Figure 1).

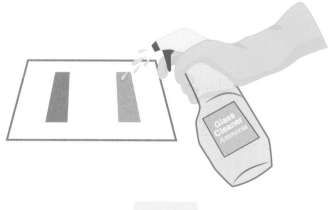

Figure 1

2. Spray the ends of the red and blue litmus strips with the glass cleaner (Figure 2).

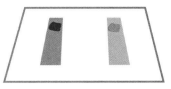

Figure 2

What Happened

Glass cleaner with ammonia is basic. A test for a base is red litmus, which turns blue when in contact with a basic solution. Bases have no effect on blue litmus. One way to remember the characteristics of a base is to remember: B is for base and B is for blue and B is for bitter. Bases turn litmus blue and have a bitter taste.

Oils stick to glass surfaces, such as windowpanes. Water alone is not effective in cleaning oily surfaces; this is because water and oil do not mix. Glass cleaners with ammonia are basic solutions. Bases are able to change oil molecules so that they are soluble in water.

Challenge ⭐

Lye is a strong base used in some drain cleaners. **Can you explain how lye might be able to unstop a clogged kitchen sink's drain, as in Figure 3?**

Figure 3

Think!

- Drains in kitchen sinks clog when cooking grease or oils stick to drainpipe walls. Add food particles, and the drain opening decreases until it finally closes off.
- The base sodium hydroxide is also known as lye or caustic soda. Note in Figure 3 that gloves are worn when pouring the lye drain cleaner. This is because, being **caustic**, lye can burn skin.
- Because lye is a strong base, it can react with more fatty materials so they are able to dissolve in water.

25 pH Scale

The special scale for measuring the acidic or basic nature of a substance is called the **pH scale**. The values on the pH scale range from 0 to 14, with the pH value of 7 being **neutral** (having no acidic or basic properties). Water has a pH value of 7. Acids have a pH less than 7, and bases have a pH greater than 7. The pH of a solution can be determined with an instrument called a pH meter or by using an **indicator** (a chemical that changes color in an acid and/or a base). For example, blue litmus turns red in a solution with a pH less than 7 and red litmus turns blue in a solution with a pH greater than 7.

pH Values of Common Products			
Name	pH	Name	pH
Stomach acid	1	Water	7
Lemon	2	Eggs	8
Grapes	3	Baking soda	9
Tomato	4	Soap	10
Banana	5	Cleaning ammonia	12
Milk	6	Lye	14

See for Yourself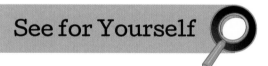

Materials

fine point black marker
piece of white poster board 14 by 24 inches
  (35 by 60 cm)
yardstick or meter stick

pen
scissors
crayons (optional)

What to Do

1. Use the marker and measuring stick to draw a line from top to bottom and 3 inches (7.5 cm) from one of the long sides on the poster board.

2. With the vertical line on the left, draw 15 horizontal lines starting at the vertical line and 1.5 inches (3.7 cm) apart.

3. Starting with the second horizontal line, number the lines 1 through 14, as shown in Figure 1.

4. Use the marker to add the title "pH Scale" at the top of the poster board.

5. Use the marker to add the labels "Neutral," "Acidic Concentration," and "Basic Concentration," and arrows as shown.
6. Add examples of common products to the pH model, as shown in Figure 1.

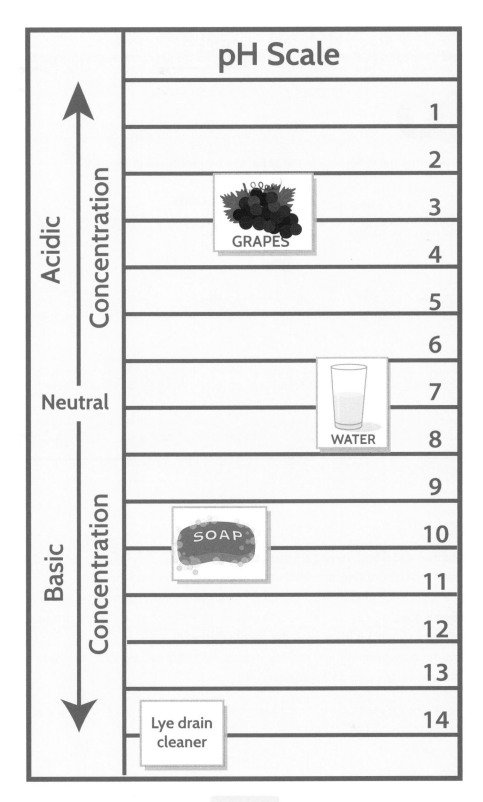

Figure 1

You have made a pH model showing some common substances and their pH values.

As the pH value of a substance decreases, its properties value increase. Thus, the lower the pH number, the stronger the acid. An increase in the pH value of a substance means an increase in the basic properties of the substance. Thus, the higher the pH number, the stronger the base.

Challenge ⭐

Can you describe the difference in the pH of the two solutions in Figure 2?

pH of Acid Solutions

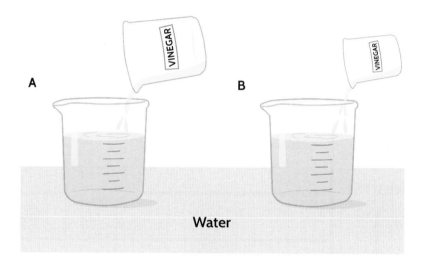

Figure 2

Think!

- Solutions A and B both have the same amount of water.
- Solution A has more vinegar added to the water than solution B does.
- The vinegar concentration in solution A is greater because it has more vinegar than solution B does.
- The pH of solution A is lower than the pH of solution B.
- I know this sounds wrong, and it always makes me take a second look, but the lower the pH, the greater the acid concentration.

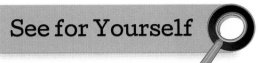

26 Combination and Decomposition Reactions

A chemical reaction occurs when the bonds between the atoms of a substance break and new bonds are formed. In other words, the new products are chemically different from the starting materials called reactants.

Combination Reaction

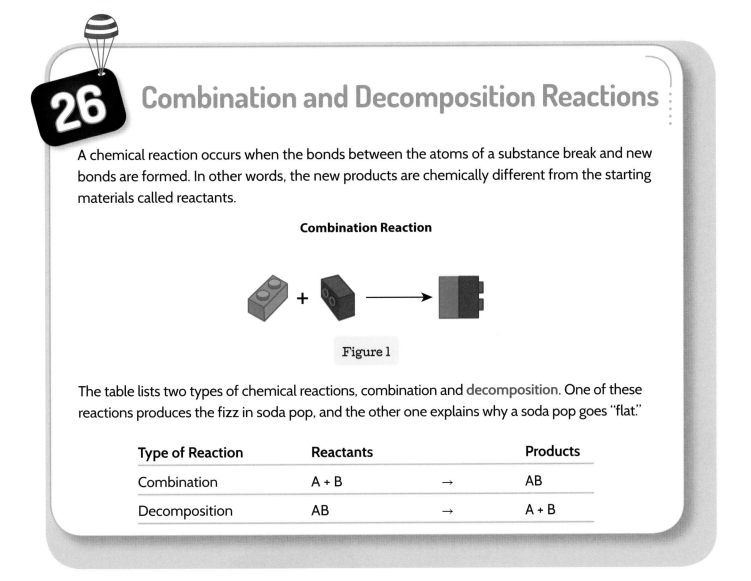

Figure 1

The table lists two types of chemical reactions, combination and **decomposition**. One of these reactions produces the fizz in soda pop, and the other one explains why a soda pop goes "flat."

Type of Reaction	Reactants		Products
Combination	A + B	→	AB
Decomposition	AB	→	A + B

See for Yourself

Materials

1 bottle of unopened cold soda pop   1 drinking glass

What to Do

1. Before opening the soda pop bottle, observe the content of the bottle. Make note of the presence of any bubbles.

2. Open and pour about half of the soda into the glass. Again, make note of the presence of any bubbles in the liquid.

What Happened ?

Soda pop contains carbonic acid, which is formed when carbon dioxide gas is forced into the liquid in the bottle at a low temperature and the bottle is quickly sealed. A closed bottle

Figure 2

of cold soda pop generally has no bubbles; this is because the carbon dioxide gas molecules are trapped inside the liquid. Some of the carbon dioxide molecules bond with water molecules forming carbonic acid. This is a combination reaction.

$$CO_2 + H_2O \rightarrow H_2CO_3$$

Carbon dioxide gas is not very soluble in water and, like all gases, more will dissolve at low temperatures. While the bottle of soda is closed, the high pressure on the carbon dioxide gas keeps the gas in solution. Opening the bottle releases this pressure and some of the gas escapes, taking with it some of the liquid soda mixture. Pouring the soda into a glass allows more gas to escape, and as it rises to the surface the gas bubbles form foam. But not all of the gas escapes; that is why the soda still has some fizz and tastes great. The remaining gas is actually being kept in the liquid because of the water's surface tension. **Surface tension** is a film-like formation across the surface of a liquid resulting from the strong attraction between surface molecules.

Water with carbon dioxide dissolved in it is said to be **carbonated**.

Carbonic acid is **unstable**, meaning it spontaneously decomposes forming carbon dioxide and water. In time, because of the decomposition of carbonic acid, all of the carbon dioxide gas leaves the liquid and the soda tastes "flat."

Challenge

Can you explain why drinking soda pop causes you to burp?

Figure 3

Think!

- There is a lot of carbon dioxide gas trapped in the liquid soda.
- When you drink the soda, you then have gas in your stomach.
- The buildup of gas causes the stomach to stretch, which triggers muscles at the lower end of the **esophagus** (the tube from your mouth to your stomach) to relax. Thus, the gas is allowed to escape. You burp!

27 Leavening Agent

A **leavening agent** is a substance used in doughs and batters that causes a foaming action that lightens and softens the mixtures. The foaming action is due to the formation of a gas, which expands the dough or batter, producing a porous structure.

This is why breads and cakes have a spongy texture. Baking soda, sodium hydrogen carbonate ($NaHCO_3$), is a leaving agent that produces a gas when it chemically reacts with an acid such as vinegar. This chemical reaction is a two-step process as shown by the two following equations. First, the baking soda reacts with vinegar producing sodium acetate and carbonic acid. Second, carbonic acid is unstable and decomposes forming water and carbon dioxide gas.

$$NaHCO + HC_2H_3O_2 \rightarrow NaC_2H_3O_2 + H_2CO_3$$

$$H_2CO_3 \rightarrow H_2O + CO_{2(gas)}$$

Chemists use this chemical property of baking soda to identify acids.

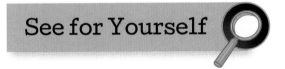

See for Yourself

Materials

safety goggles and protective gloves
plastic transparent cup

white vinegar
1 tbsp (15 mL) baking soda

What to Do

 CAUTION Put on your safety goggles before you start!

1. Add vinegar to the cup. Note: The vinegar should be at room temperature.

2. Now for the fun. Before adding the baking soda, make note that the purpose of this activity is to determine if vinegar is an acid. If it is, gas will be produced when vinegar and baking soda are mixed together. You want to make good observations of the results. Add the baking soda (Figure 1); is vinegar an acid or not?

Figure 1

Mounds of foam were produced (Figure 2); that's what happened. The results are much like blowing air through a straw into a soapy solution. Likewise, the release of the gas in the reaction of baking soda and vinegar indicates that vinegar is an acid. A chemical property of an acid is that when reacting with baking soda, gas is produced. Likewise, a chemical property of baking soda is that when combined with an acid, gas is produced.

Vinegar is a common acid found in many food products, such as pickles and salad dressing. It is not toxic, but it will hurt if it gets into a cut on your skin. The goggles protect your eyes from any splashes of vinegar.

Figure 2

Baking soda is one of the dry ingredients in baking powder, which is a dry leavening agent. Baking powder also contains cream of tartar (an acid) and cornstarch.

Figure 3

Challenge ⭐

Can you explain why the acid and baking soda mixture in a can of baking powder do not react?

Think!

The chemicals in baking powder are dry solids. When chemicals react, the particles of each chemical have to be able to move around, thus a liquid has to be added to baking powder for the chemicals to react.

28 Balancing Chemical Equations

A **chemical equation** uses elemental symbols and chemical formulas to represent a chemical reaction. A chemical reaction occurs when one or more substances are converted to different substances. For example, when mercury oxide, HgO, is heated, new substances are formed.

Note the structure of the chemical equation: There is an arrow separating the **reactants** (starting materials) from the **products** (results). The arrow represents "yields." It is important to remember that formulas of substances are first written correctly. For example, in Figure 1, oxygen is a diatomic molecule with a formula of O_2. The "2" subscript means there are two oxygen atoms combined, forming one molecule of oxygen represented by "2" joined red paper clips. Mercury is a single element. The equation is balanced by adding coefficients. Thus the the reactant and products have the same number of atoms of each elements. A "2" is placed in front of the reactant, 2HgO, and the product, 2Hg. The two green paper clips are not joined because mercury is not a diatomic molecule, so a coefficient of 2 is necessary to balance the equation.

Decomposition Reactions

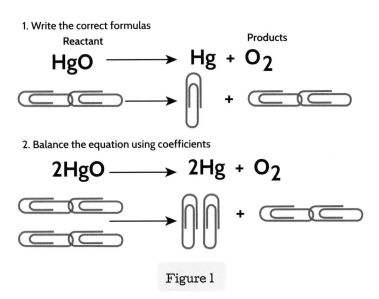

Figure 1

See for Yourself

Materials

4 different colors of plum-size balls of clay   10 toothpicks

What to Do

1. Shape the clay into different size balls as shown in Figure 2.

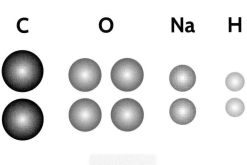

Figure 2

2. Connect the clay balls with toothpicks to form two separate models of NaHCO₃ as shown in Figure 3.

2 NaHCO₃

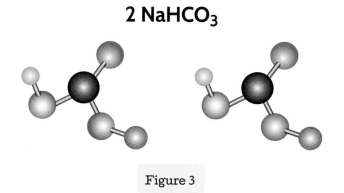

Figure 3

3. Use the following instructions to demonstrate the decomposition of NaHCO₃:

   • Form the product H₂O by removing one hydrogen and one oxygen from model A and combining them with one hydrogen from model B as shown in Figure 4.

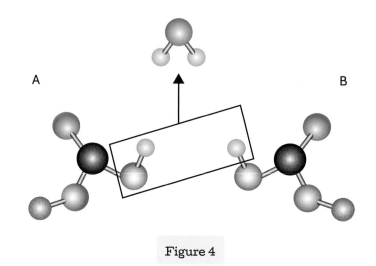

Figure 4

   • Remove the sodium (Na) atom from model A and attach it to model B as shown in Figure 5 to give Na₂CO₃. Add the water (H₂O) previously produced, and you have all the products for the decomposition of two molecules of NaHCO₃: Carbon dioxide, sodium carbonate, and water.

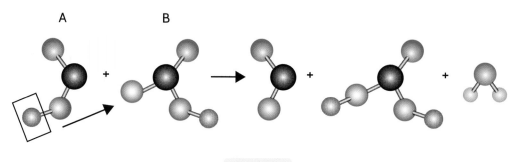

Figure 5

What Happened ?

The steps for the decomposition of $NaHCO_3$ are just to demonstrate that in a balanced chemical reaction *all* of the atoms in the reactants are used to form the products.

Law of Conservation of Mass: Matter is neither created nor destroyed during chemical reactions.

The toothpicks represent the electrostatic attraction, or bonds, between the atoms.

$$2NaHCO_3 \rightarrow CO_2 + Na_2CO_3 + H_2O$$

Challenge ★

Can you balance this chemical equation?

$$Fe + O_2 \rightarrow Fe_2O_3$$

Think!

- Compare the number of atoms for each element in the reactants and products.

$$Fe + O_2 \rightarrow Fe_2O_3$$

Reactants	Products
Fe-1	Fe-2
O-2	O-3

NOTE   When balancing a chemical reaction, you first make sure all the formulas are correctly written. *Never* change subscripts, and never use fractions as coefficients. When one of the reactants or products is a diatomic molecule, such as O_2, balance it first.

- Balance the diatomic oxygen molecule, O_2. There are two atoms of oxygen on the reactant side and three in the product.

  The common number for 2 and 3 is 6. This means you need 6 oxygen atoms in the reactant as well as in the product. A coefficient of 3 for the diatomic oxygen and a coefficient of 2 for the Fe_2O_3 balances the oxygen atoms.

$$Fe + 3O_2 \rightarrow 2Fe_2O_3$$

- Before taking a victory lap, check the other atoms in the equation. Oops! While oxygen is balanced, the iron (Fe) is not. But it is an easy fix. The product has 2 units of Fe_2O_3, as shown by the 2 coefficient. This means there are 4 atoms of Fe in the product. This is easily corrected by using a 4 coefficient for Fe as shown:

$$4Fe + 3O_2 \rightarrow 2Fe_2O_3$$

Yea!! Now we can celebrate, the equation is balanced.

29 Combustion: Burning

Combustion is commonly called burning, which requires a fuel, oxygen, and heat (ignition temperature). **Ignition temperature** is the amount of energy necessary for a fuel to release vapors and start to burn. The amount of heat necessary varies with the type of fuel. Combustion of a solid or liquid fuel takes place above the surface of the fuel where heat causes the fuel to vaporize. As long as there is fuel, oxygen, and heat, combustion continues. Limit any one of these and burning stops.

See for Yourself

Materials

2 tea candles
matches

wide-mouth glass jar, 1 qt (1 L)

What to Do

1. Set the candles on a flat surface.

2. Light the two candles.

3. When the candles are burning well, place the jar upside-down over one of the candles.

4. Observe the candles; compare and contrast how the candles burn.

Figure 1

CAUTION Take care when using matches. Ask an adult to help.

What Happened

First, energy from a burning match provided enough energy to ignite the candle's wick. Within seconds, pools of liquid wax collected around the wicks of both candles. Candle wicks absorb the liquid wax and the wax moves upward. The heat of the flame vaporizes the liquid wax, and it is the wax vapor that burns. Combustion reactions need energy to get started, but enough heat is produced to keep the reaction going.

The flames of the two candles are similar, but the burning time of the covered candle was shorter than that of the uncovered candle. The covered candle had fuel and heat but not enough oxygen, thus it stopped burning.

Can you explain a safe way for an adult to extinguish the grease fire in Figure 2?

Figure 2

Think!

- What does a fire need in order to continue to burn?
  Oxygen, fuel, and heat.
- How can a fire in a pan on a stove be extinguished?
  Remove necessary conditions for combustion: An adult must turn off the stove to remove the heat and cover the pan with a lid or cookie sheet to limit oxygen.

Figure 3

NOTE Never pour water on a grease fire because it causes the burning grease to splatter, thus spreading the fire.

30 Exothermic Chemical Reactions

An **exothermic reaction** is a chemical reaction that releases energy in the form of light and/or heat. The chemical equation would be like this:

reactants → products + energy

Combustion is an exothermic reaction. Rusting is an example of slow combustion; burning is an example of fast combustion.

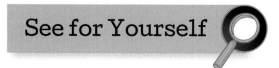

Materials

protective gloves
safety goggles
¼ cup (63 mL) of white vinegar
small bowl

2 steel wool pads without soap
 (available at hardware stores)
thermometer
jar, 1 qt (1 L)

What to Do

1. Wearing protective gloves and goggles, place one of the steel wool pads in the bowl, and then pour the vinegar over the steel wool.

2. Remove the steel wool pad and slightly squeeze to remove excess vinegar.

3. Make note of the temperature reading on the thermometer then wrap the moistened steel wool around the bulb end of the thermometer.

4. Stand the thermometer in the jar, wrapped end down (Figure 2).

Figure 1

Figure 2

5. Observe the temperature on the thermometer periodically for 3 or more minutes. Remove the thermometer

6. After 24 hours, compare the steel wool in the jar with remaining steel wool pad (Figure 3).

Figure 3

What Happened ?

The vinegar cleaned the protective coating from the steel wool to expose the iron. The iron chemically reacted with oxygen in the air producing iron oxide and energy. The rise in temperature indicated the released heat from the reaction. Rusting involves more than the simple combination of iron and oxygen atoms. Water is necessary for rusting to occur, but the conclusion for this reaction is that iron and oxygen combine producing iron oxide and heat energy.

Challenge ★

Can you explain how the experiment in Figure 4 demonstrates an exothermic reaction?

Think!

- What evidence is shown that indicates an exothermic reaction is taking place? The burning firework sparkler gives off energy in the form of light.
- Does the illustration indicate that heat is being released? While there are no temperature measurements shown, the sparkler is burning, which is a combustion reaction. All combustion reactions are exothermic, meaning heat is released.

FYI: When burning, sparklers can be as hot as 1800°F to 3000°F (1000°C to 1600°C). Note that water boils at 212°F (100°C). The sparkler can be around 15 times as hot as boiling water.

Figure 4

31 Explosions

An **explosion** is a sudden expansion and blowing apart of something with energy transmitted outward. An explosion can occur when gas is produced in a closed container, such as firecrackers. When ignited, the chemicals inside firecrackers produce gases. The tight paper wrapping around the chemicals limits the space for the expanding gases. Thus, the **pressure** (force/area) of these gases becomes so great that the paper container violently explodes releasing energy in the form of heat, light, and sound. The released gases expand at a speed faster than the speed of sound, which is 767 miles/h (1,235 km/h). The rapidly expanding waves of compressed gas create **sound waves**. Some explosions are safe; it just depends on the amount and kind of energy released.

See for Yourself!

Materials

safety goggles
tap water
sealable plastic bag

antacid tablet (Alka-Seltzer
   or generic version)
shallow pan

What to Do

CAUTION Put on your safety goggles before you begin!

1. Place a small amount of water inside the plastic bag.
2. Seal the bag closed except for a small opening.
3. Drop the antacid tablet through the opening in the bag and quickly seal the bag closed.
4. Lay the bag in the pan, and then observe the bag and its contents.

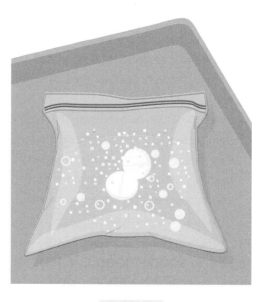

Figure 1

What Happened ?

Alka-Seltzer and similar antacid products react with water producing carbon dioxide gas. When two or more substances are mixed together and new substances are produced, the change is called a chemical reaction.

The production of carbon dioxide inside the sealed bag results in the bag being inflated. At some point the bag can no longer expand. The weakest part of the bag is where it is sealed. With enough pressure the seal opens and the compressed carbon dioxide gas inside the bag rapidly expands creating a sound. The escaping gas can cause the water and dissolved antacid to spray out, thus the need for the goggles.

I am sorry if you were expecting a sonic boom! While the sound is not as loud as a firecracker, it is loud enough that you know that it is not safe to close any container in which gas is being produced.

Challenge ★

Can you explain why a bag of potato chips inside a closed car on a hot summer day can explode with a loud BANG!?

Think!

- Is there a gas inside a bag of potato chips? Yep! Air is inside the bag.
- What happens to gas when it gets hot? Heat makes gas particles move faster and farther away from each other. Thus, gases expand when heated.
- What effect does the speed of gas particles have on the bag? The faster gas particles move the more often they hit the inside of the bag and with greater force. The heated gas causes the potato chip bag to expand.
- Why does the bag of potato chips explode with a loud BANG!? The compressed air inside the bag rapidly expands as it exits the open bag creating sound waves.

While I couldn't resist the cute car filled with potato chips, the bag of chips that exploded in my car didn't spray chips out. The sound was loud enough for me to stop the car and check to see what blew up.

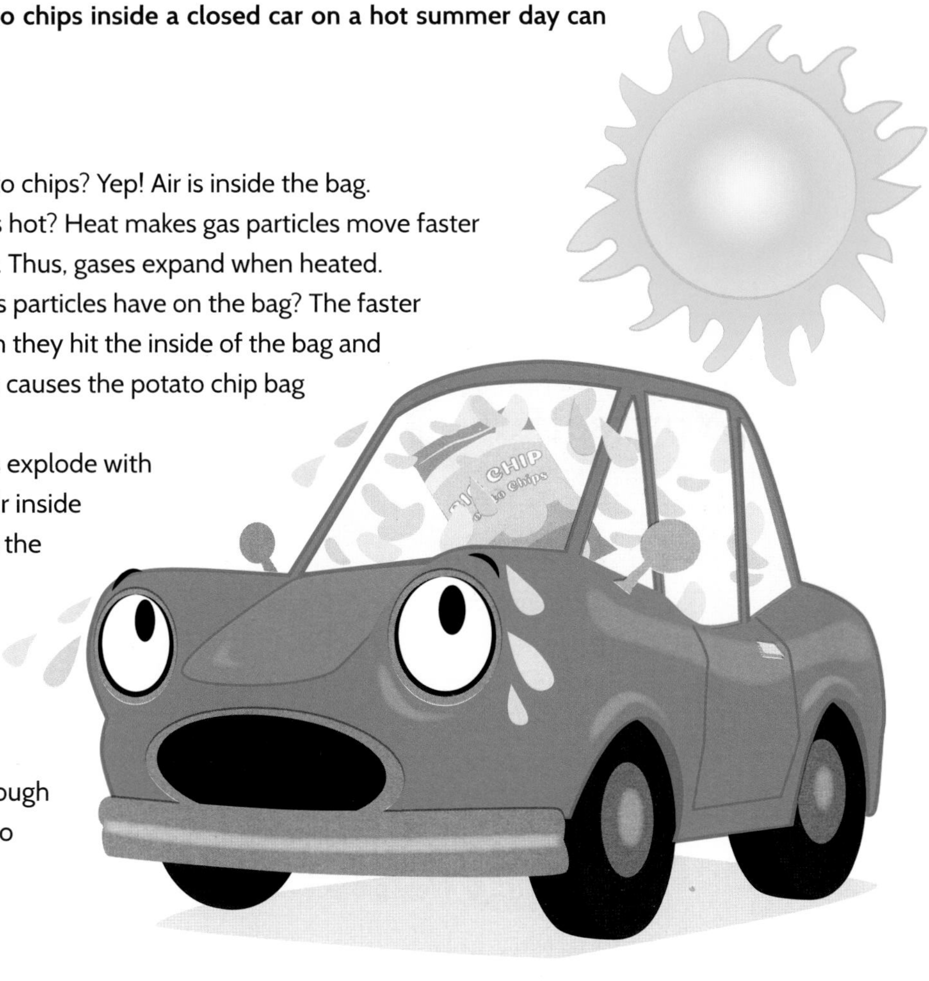

Figure 2

Slime is a **cross-linked polymer**, which has links between the polymer molecules. One way of visualizing the basic structure of cross-linked polymers is to think of a ladder (Figure 1), the two sides of the ladder being the polymer molecules and the steps of the ladder being the cross-links. The slime can be made by mixing glue with borax.

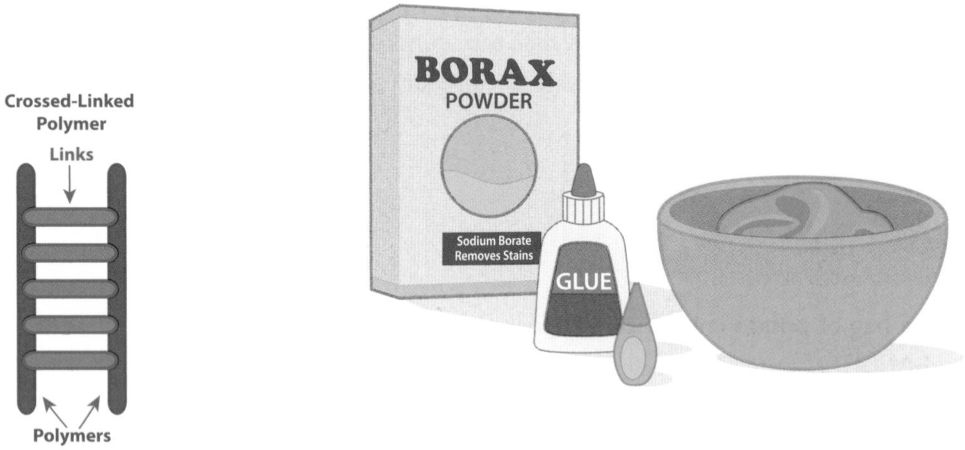

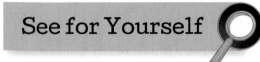

Crossed-Linked Polymer

Links

Polymers

BORAX POWDER

Sodium Borate Removes Stains

GLUE

Figure 1

See for Yourself

Materials

measuring cup, 1 cup (250 mL)

tap water

1 tsp (5 mL) borax, such as 20 Mule Team Borax

stirring spoon

bowl, 1 cup (250 mL) or larger

PVA glue, such as Elmer's white school glue

food coloring

waxed paper

paper towels

measuring spoon, 1 tbsp (15 mL)

CAUTION Wear protective gloves during this experiment.

What to Do

1. Fill the measuring cup with ½ cup (125 mL) of water.

2. Add the borax to the water in the cup. Stir until all the borax has dissolved.

3. In the bowl, put 1 tablespoon (15 mL) of water and 1 tablespoon (15 mL) of glue. Add 4 to 5 drops of food coloring. Stir until the solution is thoroughly mixed.

4. Pour the borax solution into the bowl containing the glue–water solution.

5. Stir the mixture slowly until a thick glob of slime is formed. This takes only a few seconds.

6. Lay out a sheet of waxed paper.

7. Dip the slime out of the bowl with your hands (Figure 2).

8. Form the slime into one lump then place it on the piece of waxed paper. Observe the slime and note any changes in its shape.

9. Dry your hands, then pick up the slime and roll it into a ball. Drop the slime ball to determine whether it will bounce (Figure 3).

10. Slowly pull on the slime and stretch it. Repeat this, but quickly pull on the two sides of the slime. Compare the results when slow and quick pressure is applied to the slime.

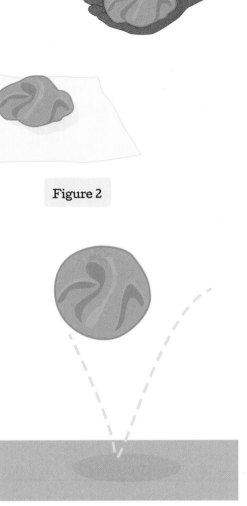

Figure 2

What Happened ?

Elmer's glue and other comparable school glues are **polyvinyl adhesives (PVA)**. PVA means the glue contains molecules of polyvinyl acetate. Mixing PVA glue with a solution of borax results in a chemical reaction; the product is slime.

PVA glue solution + borax solution → slime

Viscosity measures how easily fluids flow; the thicker the fluid, the greater its viscosity. The two reactants, PVA glue and borax, are not as viscous as the product, slime. The reason for this change in viscosity is that the borax forms links between the PVA molecules. These links restrict the motion of the PVA molecules. Slime is a **non-Newtonian fluid**, which is a fluid whose viscosity increases when under sudden stress. The slime broke when sudden pressure was applied, but stretched under slow continuous pressure.

Figure 3

Individual
Polymer Chains

Challenge ⭐

Can you explain why some cross-linked molecules (Figure 4) form one giant super-molecule large enough to hold in your hand?

Think!

- Cross-linking between polymer chains creates one molecule.
- Polymer chains can be very long; when one chain is linked to another and then another and then another and so on, this cross-linked molecule can be one gargantuan molecule large enough to hold in your hand.

Cross-linked
Polymer Chains

Figure 4

75

Part II

PHYSICS

Physics is the study of matter and energy and how they interact; physics is a study of how forces affect the motion of objects. Sir Isaac Newton (1642–1727) developed three laws that relate an object's motion to the forces acting on it.

A **force** is a push or pulling action on an object. Forces are measured in pounds (lb) or Newtons (N), where 1 lb = 4.5 N. This unit addresses three types of force: contact forces, noncontact forces, and turning forces.

A **contact force** is directly applied to an object, such as the upward **buoyant force** applied by water that keeps a cruise ship afloat. Friction is an opposing contact force, meaning if you push a box one way, the direction of friction between the box and the surface it is moved over is in the opposite direction.

Noncontact forces never come in contact with the object, such as gravity (a pulling type of force) or magnetism (which can push or pull). Gravity pulls things toward Earth's center. Of course, all bodies have gravity; the more massive a body is, the greater is its force of gravity. When someone jumps up on a trampoline, they do not keep going because Earth's gravity pulls them down. Just for a short time, they **freefall**, which occurs when gravity is the only force acting on them. Freefalling gives a feeling of **weightlessness**. Astronauts float around in spacecraft: Are they weightless? You'll find out as you investigate the force of gravity.

Forces do not always cause **linear motion**, which is motion in a straight line. **Torque** is a **turning force** that causes things to move in a circular path around some center point; torque causes things to rotate about their centers.

Energy is the ability to do **work**, which is described as the product of force times the distance an object moves. **Kinetic energy** (KE) is the energy a moving object has. This leads us back to Newton's Laws of Motion and how forces affect motion.

Heat and **light** are other types of energy that are addressed in this unit. You'll discover why some things glow in the dark; why things have different colors; and how lenses are able to bend light. Have you ever wondered why a tiled floor feels cold but a rug in the same room is warm? It's all about heat and light, and you'll find the answers as you investigate heat and light energy sources.

Electricity is another type of energy we use every day. We expect the lights to come on when we click a switch. But where does this energy come from and how does it get to your light switch? Why don't all the lights in your house go off when one light bulb burns out? Answers to these questions will be discovered as you investigate different types of electrical paths called **series circuits** and **parallel circuits**. You will safely explore, without the slightest tingle, how conductive the human body is with a science toy called an **energy ball**.

There are so many physics topics not represented, but hopefully the activities in this physics section will give you a desire to learn more about the forces and energy in the world around you.

Newton's Laws of Motion

In one of the more well-known stories about Sir Isaac Newton (1642–1727), he "discovered" gravity when an apple fell on his head. (An apple falling on Newton is possible, since there were apple trees on his mother's farm where he lived.)

Before introducing Newton's Laws of Motion, remember that a force is any pushing or pulling action on an object. Push and pull are not types of force; instead, they are the directions in which forces are applied. You pull something toward you; you push something away from you.

A net force is the vector sum of all forces acting on an object: the resulting force and direction when all the pushing and pulling on an object is considered. A net force is an unbalanced force, meaning no forces are acting against it.

Newton's laws are not something serious science students breeze through, because they are not restricted to physics studies. Instead, they apply to anything that is in motion, be it a satellite in space, a race car, or a baseball pitch.

Newton's First Law of Motion

This law describes inertia as a property of matter whereby matter resists changes in its velocity (speed and direction). In a nutshell, an object's velocity cannot be changed unless a net force acts on it. If the velocity is zero, the object is stationary; if the velocity is constant, the object is in motion at a constant velocity.

The amount of inertia that matter has is proportional to its mass; however, inertia and mass are not the same thing. The greater an object's inertia, the greater must be the force to change its motion.

Newton's Second Law of Motion

Newton's Second Law of Motion describes the amount of force needed to accelerate an object with a specific mass. This law can be expressed as an equation: $F = ma$. The equation is read as "force equals mass times acceleration." While it is not always labeled, the force is a net force. Thus, the direction of acceleration is determined by the direction of the net force. Acceleration measures the change of velocity in a time period.

Linear acceleration is in a straight line. An example of linear acceleration is when an object freefalls, meaning it falls with only gravity acting on it. Because gravity is a constant force, the falling object continues to *accelerate* toward Earth at a rate of 32 feet per second per second, or 32 ft/s². In metric this is 9.8 meters per second per second, which is written as 9.8 m/s².

Angular acceleration is rotational, meaning the motion is marking out a curved path about a center point. A merry-go-round accelerates when it is given a push, but then quickly experiences deceleration, which is negative acceleration: a decrease in velocity per unit of time.

Newton's Third Law of Motion

This is the action-reaction law, which states that for every action there is a reaction of equal force but in the opposite direction. It is important to know that this law describes two separate forces acting on two different objects. Earth pulls you down with a force equal to your weight; your body pulls up on Earth with an equal force. Because the mass of Earth is so much greater than your mass, the force you apply doesn't affect Earth. On the other hand, Earth's force on you keeps you pulled toward the ground. Another example of this action-reaction law of motion is when a ball is thrown against a wall (action force), and the wall pushes on the ball with an equal force (reaction force) but in the opposite direction. This action/reaction pair of forces causes the ball to hit and then bounce off the wall.

33 Newton's First Law of Motion: Inertia

Newton's First Law of Motion describes how an object's inertia affects its response to a force. **Inertia** is a property of matter that resists any change in its velocity. With zero velocity an object is at rest and will remain in this stationary state unless a net force acts on it. If an object is moving at a constant velocity and without any force acting against this motion, it will continue to move with no change in velocity unless a net force acts on it.

The more massive an object is the greater is its inertia. Mass and inertia are not equal; instead, they are directly related. For example, if the mass of an object is doubled, the object's inertia doubles. This would result in twice the force being needed to change its state of motion.

See for Yourself 🔍

Materials

empty 1 qt (1 L) plastic soda bottle with lid   tap water
piece of blank paper   paper towel

What to Do

1. Lay the paper on a table with part of the paper extending past the table's edge.

2. Stand the empty soda bottle on one end of the paper as shown.

3. Holding the edge of the paper, quickly pull the paper straight outward, as in Figure 1. The objective is to pull the paper out from under the bottle, leaving the bottle standing. Notice any movement of the bottle.

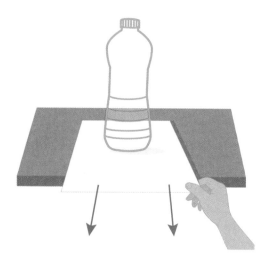

Figure 1

4. Fill the bottle with water, and seal the bottle with its lid.
5. Dry the outside of the bottle with the paper towel, and then stand the bottle on the paper as before.
6. Repeat step 3 (Figure 2).

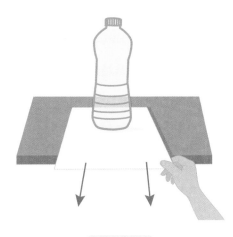

What Happened ❓

It was easier to pull the paper out from under the more massive bottle without knocking the bottle over because mass and inertia are directly related; an increase in mass increases inertia. When the paper was moved quickly, the more massive bottle remained in place because its inertia was great enough not to be affected by the paper's motion.

Figure 2

Challenge ⭐

Can you explain what will happen if the plastic embroidery hoop in Figure 3 is quickly removed?

Think!

- All matter has mass and takes up space. Thus, all matter has inertia.
- Newton's First Law of Motion describes inertia as the tendency of matter not to change its state of motion. This means that stationary objects, such as the marker, tend to remain in place.
- If the marker has enough inertia not to be affected by the motion of the hoop, it will fall into the bottle when the hoop is quickly moved.
- The marker falls straight down because of the force of gravity acting on it.

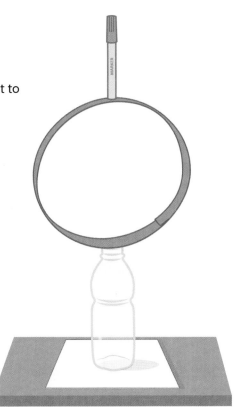

Figure 3

34 Newton's Second Law of Motion

Newton's Second Law of Motion states that a net force acting on an object causes it to accelerate. Acceleration is a change of velocity during a time period. It is important to understand that a net force is the result of the summation of all forces acting on an object; a net force is a **vector**, meaning it has magnitude and direction.

In Figure 1, there are different forces acting on the box, represented by the red arrows. When two forces act on the same object with equal forces in opposite directions, these forces cancel each other, thus the forces are balanced and the net force is zero. But, if one of the forces is greater than the other, the difference between the forces is called the **resultant force** or net force. The box accelerates in the direction of this resultant (net) force. The magnitude of the acceleration depends on the mass of the box.

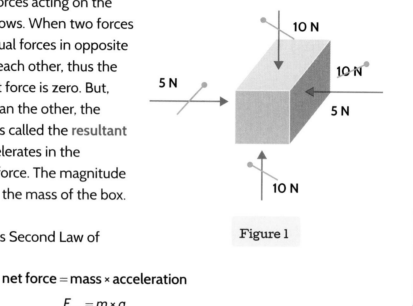

Net force

Figure 1

The equation that expresses this Second Law of Motion is:

$$\text{net force} = \text{mass} \times \text{acceleration}$$

$$F_{net} = m \times a$$

See for Yourself

Materials

scissors
two 5 oz (150 mL) paper cups
ruler
masking tape

yardstick (meterstick)
glass marble
towel

What to Do

1. Cut one of the paper cups down to a height of about 1 inch (2.5 cm).

2. Tape the short cup on to one end of the measuring stick.

3. Tape the taller cup to the stick about 4 inches (10 cm) away from the first cup.

4. Tape the other end of the measuring stick to a point just above the floor, as shown in Figure 2. The stick must be loose enough so its opposite end can be easily raised up and down.

5. Lay the towel on the floor under the stick.

6. Place the marble in the short cup.

7. Hold the stick with your fingers about 8 inches (20 cm) from the free end, just behind the tall cup.

8. Raise the end of the measuring stick about 20 inches (50 cm) from the floor.

9. Get ready to be amazed. At the moment you release the stick, give it a gentle push downward.

   Were you surprised that the marble moved from the short cup to the taller cup? If this did not happen (Oops!), try this:

   Trouble Shooting: If the marble doesn't fall into the large cup, then adjust how hard you push down on the stick.

1. Push a little harder if the marble falls short of the cup.

2. Decrease the downward push if the marble moves past the taller cup.

Figure 2

What Happened ❓

When Earth's gravity is the net force acting on an object, the object will accelerate at a rate of 32 feet per second per second (32 ft/s², 9.8 m/s²). The downward push on the stick increased its acceleration and it fell faster than did the marble. Actually, the stick fell out from under the marble, leaving the marble to freefall (Figure 3), so the faster-moving measuring stick fell from under the unsecured marble. Gravity pulled the marble in a vertical path toward the floor. The curved path of the falling stick placed the taller cup under the falling marble.

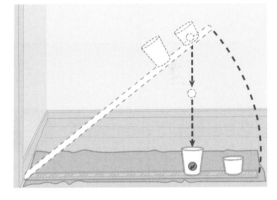

Figure 3

Challenge ⭐

Can you predict which of the wagons in Figure 4 will have a greater acceleration?

Think!

- Newton's Second Law of Motion is $F = m \times a$.
- Force A = Force B; mass A < mass B.
- Since the force on each wagon is the same, with more mass in wagon B, it will not be pulled as fast as wagon A.

Newton's Second Law of Motion
$F = ma$

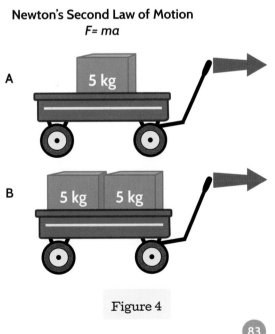

Figure 4

35 Newton's Third Law of Motion

Newton's Third Law of Motion says that for every action, there is an equal but opposite reaction. This means that if you push on an object, the object pushes back with an equal force, but in the opposite direction. This law describes a pair of forces, an action force and a reaction force. A balloon can be used to demonstrate how a rocket can accelerate in space (Figure 1).

Figure 1

See for Yourself

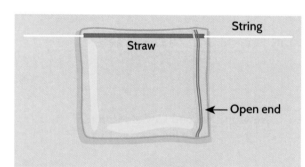

Figure 2

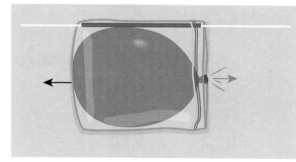

Figure 3

Materials

drinking straw	string
plastic bag, 1-gallon size (4 L)	round balloon, 9 inches (23 cm)
scissors	spring clothespin

What to Do

1. Place the straw inside the bag as shown in Figure 2.
2. Cut a small hole in the side of the bag, and then thread the string through the straw.
3. Secure the ends of the string so that it is stretched tight across the room, perhaps between two door handles.
4. Slide the bag to its starting position, which will be at one end of the string where the "rocket engine" will be inserted inside the bag.
5. Prepare the "rocket engine" by inflating the balloon. Twist the open end and clip it with a clothespin.
6. Put the balloon inside the bag and remove the clothespin.

What Happened ?

Like a rocket blasting off, the balloon moved forward opposite to the direction of the escaping air. The force of the air escaping is the action force; the forward motion of the balloon is the reaction force.

A very important thing to remember about action–reaction forces is that even though they are of equal forces in opposite directions, they are *not* examples of balanced forces. This is because the forces are acting on different objects. Yes, before the balloon was opened, the total force of the air inside pushing out on the balloon equaled the total force of the stretched balloon's force pushing in on the air. Since the air was pushing in all directions, there was no net force in any one direction. Figure 4A represents the forces of air pushing out on the surface of the closed balloon. Figure 4B represents the forces of air inside the balloon when the balloon's mouth is opened. When the air escapes through the opening, the net force of air inside the balloon changes. Now there is an unbalanced force of air pushing up on the balloon; thus, the balloon moves in the direction of this net force.

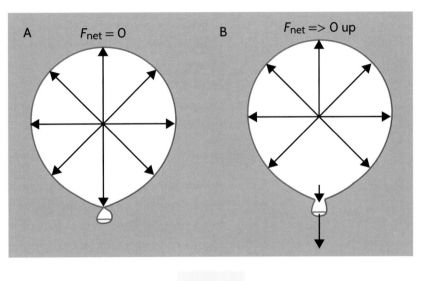

Figure 4

Challenge ⭐

Using the diagram in Figure 5, can you identify the two action–reaction forces?

Think!

- It doesn't matter which is identified as the action force, since the bat and ball are colliding with each other.
- Action–reaction forces can be expressed as:

   Action: Object A applies a force to object B in one direction.
   Reaction: Object B applies a force to object A in the opposite direction.

- **Action:** The bat applies a force to the ball in one direction.
   Reaction: The ball applies a force to the bat in the opposite direction.

Figure 5

NOTE   The ball and bat move in the direction of the force applied to them. These forces are equal, but the ball moves farther because its mass is so much smaller.

Forces

Noncontact forces, as the name implies, are forces that affect the motion of an object without being in direct contact. In this section, gravity is the noncontact force represented.

Earth's gravity is a noncontact force that pulls things toward the center of Earth. The weight of an object is the measure of the force of gravity acting on it. The force of gravity on an object is equal to the weight of the object. This force is equal to the product of the mass of the object times gravitational acceleration. On Earth, the acceleration as a result of the downward force of gravity is 32 ft/s² (9.8 m/s²). Momentum is the product of mass times velocity. The momentum activity in this study is directly related to acceleration due to gravity. Thus, the momentum of freefalling objects will be compared.

Contact forces are those forces applied directly to an object.

Friction is the force between any two surfaces in contact with each other. Static friction occurs between two surfaces that are not in motion. If the two surfaces are in contact long enough there is an exchange of surface molecules. They become bonded together and very difficult to separate. This is why it takes more force to get some objects to start moving. Kinetic friction is the resistance to the motion of one surface moving across another surface.

Drag is the contact force of fluids acting on objects moving through them, such as boats in water and aircraft in air.

Buoyant force is an upward-directed contact force of fluids acting on objects immersed in them. This can be objects in water or balloons in air. One of the activities guides you in calculating a buoyant force.

Torque causes rotation and is referred to as a turning force. Turning forces are contact forces that cause rotation about a center point. Examples are a wheel, a jar lid, or a seesaw. The magnitude of torque is the product of force applied times the distance the force is from the point of rotation. The point of rotation for a wheel or lid is its center; the point of rotation for a seesaw is the pivot, the point the board rotates around.

Balance has to do with torque applied to either side of the center of gravity of an object or system. The center of gravity is the point where the weight of an object or system is considered to be concentrated so that if supported at this point, the body or system would be balanced.

Stability is the resistance of an object to falling over. Again, the center of gravity is considered. It is actually all about balance and whether the torque acting on either side of the center of gravity is equal but in opposite directions. You can think of a seesaw and how the weight of each person produces a turning force on each end, one in a counterclockwise direction and the other clockwise. In this unit, a visual is used for showing how the center of gravity moves when an object is tilted and when the object becomes unstable and falls over.

36 Freefall

Freefall is when an object falls to Earth with gravity being the only downward force acting on it. Aristotle (384–322 BC), a Greek philosopher, taught his students that is was obvious that a leaf falls slower than a stone. Thus, he concluded that the acceleration of falling objects depended on their weight; therefore, lighter objects fall slower than do heavier objects.

For almost two thousand years, no one questioned Aristotle's common-sense logic. But in truth Aristotle's science was bad. Even so, Galileo Galilei (1564–1642), an astronomer, physicist, and engineer, was ridiculed for daring to argue against Aristotle. Galileo's experiments proved that mass does not affect the acceleration of falling objects. On Earth, all freefalling objects accelerate at the same rate of 32 ft/s^2 (9.8 m/s^2). If this is true, why do leaves fall slower than a stone?

Figure 1

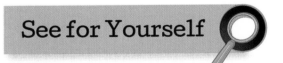

Materials

index card
book

What to Do

1. Hold the index card in one hand and the book in the other. Hold both of them parallel to the floor.

2. Raise the card and book chest high as in Figure 2 and drop them simultaneously.

3. Make note which of the two, the card or the book, hits the floor first.

Figure 2

Figure 3

What Happened ?

The index card fluttered about while the book fell straight down reaching the floor first. The card fluttered about because of **air resistance**, which is a force that occurs when gas molecules in air hit a moving object. This force is called **drag** and it acts in the opposite direction to the moving object through air, thus slowing the object down. The time taken for the card to fall was longer than for the book. Air resistance becomes insignificant with large objects.

Challenge ★

Can you predict what would happen if the activity were repeated with the card riding on top of the book as in Figure 3?

Think!

If mass has no affect on the acceleration of falling objects, then, without the effect of air resistance, the card should fall at the same rate as the book. The card and book would fall together.

See for Yourself

Place the card on the book. Make sure that no part of the card extends past the edge of the book. Hold the book as before and allow it to freefall to the floor.

37 Gravity

Gravity is the force that attracts objects toward the center of Earth or towards any other body with mass. The more massive a body is, the greater is its force of gravity. Yes, your body has mass and your body is pulling on planet Earth. Your force of gravity on Earth is insignificant compared to Earth's force of gravity on you. Earth's force of gravity is a **vector** quantity (which means it has magnitude and direction), which is directed toward the center of Earth, also referred to as vertical or **down**. A **plumb bob** is a weight freely hanging on a string; it is a tool to determine a vertical line.

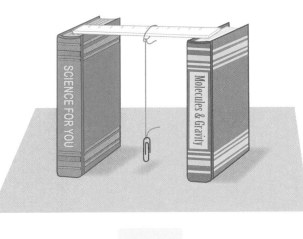

Figure 1

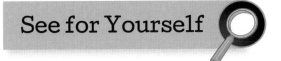

Materials

string about 12 inches (30 cm) long
metal paper clip

ruler
2 large books of equal height

What to Do

1. Tie one end of the string to the paper clip, and then tie the opposite end of the string around the center of the ruler.

2. Stand the two books about 10 inches (25 cm) apart on a flat surface.

3. Support the ends of the ruler on the tops of the books.

4. Observe the position of the string and paper clip.

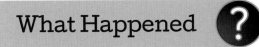

Earth's gravitational force of attraction pulls the free-hanging paper clip down, toward the center of Earth. The hanging paper clip is a simple plumb bob.

In Figure 2, can you explain why the string and paper clip are not affected by the position of the ruler?

Figure 2

Think!

The hanging paper clip is being pulled down by Earth's gravity. Movement of the ruler doesn't affect the free-hanging paper clip, because Earth's gravity continues to pull on it.

See for Yourself

Move the ends of the ruler up and down while observing the position of the hanging paper clip.

38 Momentum

Momentum is matter in motion. All matter has mass, so, if an object is moving, it has momentum. The amount of momentum that an object has depends on two variables: the mass of the object; and how fast the object is moving, that is, its velocity. The equation for calculating the magnitude of an object's momentum is

$$\text{momentum} = \text{mass} \times \text{velocity}$$

Momentum is a vector quantity, meaning it has direction as well as magnitude.

In Figure 1, a large rock and a small ball are dropped and freefall to the ground. Air resistance affects all falling objects, but the more massive the object is, the more air resistance becomes insignificant. Thus, disregarding air resistance, the acceleration of gravity on the rock and the ball is the same, being 32 ft/s^2 (9.8 m/s^2). The falling rock and the falling ball may reach the ground at the same time and with the same velocity, but their momentum is not the same. This is because momentum also depends on mass.

Figure 1

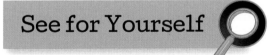

See for Yourself

Materials

shoebox or comparable size box
sand

3 rocks: 1 large, 1 medium, and 1 small
ruler

What to Do

1. Fill the shoebox with 2 inches (5 cm) or more of sand and stick the ruler upright in it as in Figure 2.

2. Hold the largest rock 12 inches (30 cm) above the surface of the sand, and then release it.

Figure 2

3. Remove the stone from the sand without disturbing the impression it made in the sand's surface.

4. Repeat steps 2 and 3 using the medium-size rock, dropping the rock so it lands in a new spot on the sand. Repeat again using the smallest rock.

5. Compare the impressions made in the sand by the three rocks.

What Happened ?

It is important to understand that all objects fall at the same acceleration. Thus, the rocks in this investigation all accelerated at the same rate and their time of falling was the same. Thus, they each had the same speed when they landed. The indentations in the sand were different; the more massive rocks made deeper indentations. The rock with the largest mass had the largest momentum; the greatest impact made the deepest impression.

Challenge ★

Imagine that an apple is dropped into a hole cut through the Earth from one side to the other passing through the center (Figure 3). **Can you identify where in its fall through the Earth the apple would have the most and least momentum?**

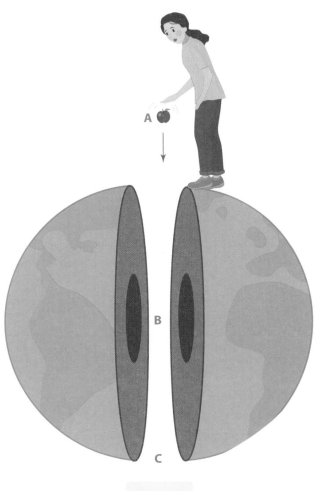

Figure 3

Think!

- Earth's gravity is a vector directed toward the center of Earth.
- In the imaginary hole through Earth, the apple would start at A with no velocity, thus no momentum.
- The apple would accelerate to its maximum velocity when it reaches point B, which is the center of Earth. At this point, the apple would have its greatest momentum.
- The apple would continue to fall, but would start slowing down because it is moving in the opposite direction to Earth's gravity. The velocity of the falling apple would be decreasing at a rate of 32 ft/s² (9.8 m/s²); this is negative acceleration or simply deceleration. At position C, the apple would have zero velocity and zero momentum as it did at the start of this imaginary journey.

39 Apparent Weightlessness

Weight is a measure of the downward force of Earth's gravity acting on an object. *Actual* **weightlessness** would be the total absence of gravity, which at this time is not possible. But, the *sensation* of being weightless occurs during any freefall, such as when riding on a roller coaster as it goes over the top of a hill. This sensation is called **apparent weightlessness**. All freefalling bodies experience this sensation of weightlessness.

Figure 1

See for Yourself

Materials

sharpened pencil
paper cup
tap water

smartphone
helper

What to Do

1. Perform this activity outdoors. Be aware that water might splatter and get you wet.

2. Use the pencil to punch a hole on the side of the cup near its bottom.

3. With your finger covering the hole, fill the cup with water.

4. Hold the cup as high as possible, with the covered hole pointing away from you.

5. Ask your helper to be ready to use the smartphone to video the cup when you release it.

6. Drop the cup.

7. Repeat this investigation several times so that you have several videos to observe.

8. Observe the videos of the falling cup. Stop the videos to observe the hole in the cup before the cup hits the ground.

Paper cup
Water
Pencil hole

Figure 3

Figure 2

What Happened

The water should not pour out of the hole during the time the cup is in freefall. This is because the cup and water were both falling at the same acceleration. The cup and water experienced apparent weightlessness because there was no force of support acting on them. As long as they were freefalling, the water would stay in the cup.

Did you know that astronauts in orbit are not weightless? It's true. Astronauts only experience apparent weightlessness.

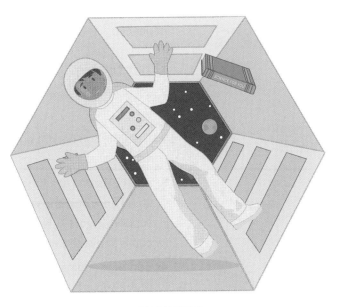

Figure 4

Challenge

Can you explain why astronauts in orbit are not weightless?

Think!

There are two ways to experience the sensation of weightlessness:
- One way is to actually not have any force of gravity acting on you. At this time, even in deep space, the force of gravity is present, but it is reduced.
- Apparent weightlessness is a feeling of being weightless during freefall.

While orbiting Earth, a spacecraft and everything in it is falling at the same rate, just like the water in the cup. Astronauts are not weightless. Instead, the spacecraft and the astronauts are freefalling around the Earth and experience apparent weightlessness. It is a continuous state of freefalling.

95

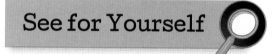
Buoyancy is the ability of an object to rise or sink in a fluid (gas or liquid). A **buoyant force** is an upward force by a fluid on an object immersed in it. The amount of buoyant force on an object is equal to the weight of the fluid displaced by the object. When the buoyant force is equal to the object's total weight, the object floats.

See for Yourself

Materials

large bowl   small coins

paper cup

What to Do

1. Fill the bowl about three-fourths full with water.

2. Hold the cup upright on the surface of the water.

3. Add coins one at a time until the cup will stand upright in the water without any support (Figure 1). Notice how much of the cup is above the water's surface.

4. Continue adding coins to the cup until most of the cup is below the surface of the water but the cup continues to stand upright (Figure 2).

Figure 1

What Happened ❓

At first, the cup floats upright with most of the cup above the water's surface (Figure 3). The part of the cup below the water's surface displaces water. The buoyant force (F_b) is equal to the weight of this displaced water. The cup floats because

Figure 2

the total weight of the cup (F_{wt}) and its contents is equal to the weight of the displaced water, which is the buoyant force. As more coins are added, more of the cup sinks below the water's surface. Thus, the cup displaces more of the water. As before, as long as the weight of the water displaced is equal to the weight of the cup, the cup will float. As the cup sank lower in the water, the surface level of the water rose an amount equal to the additional water displaced by the cup.

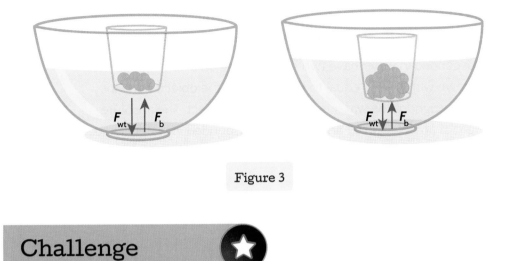

Figure 3

Challenge ⭐

Can you explain why a balloon inflated with helium gas floats in air?

Figure 4

Think!

- As the balloon is being inflated, it pushes the surrounding air aside. This is because two things cannot occupy the same space at the same time.
- The weight of the displaced air is equal to the buoyant force acting on the balloon.
- The balloon floats if its weight is equal to the buoyant force of air pushing up on it. The balloon will fly away if the buoyant force of air is greater than the weight of the balloon.

41 Buoyant Force

Weight measures the force of gravity acting on an object. Gravity on Earth is directed toward the Earth's center. Objects suspended in water have two forces acting on them in opposite directions: Gravity is pulling down with a force equal to the weight of the object; buoyancy is an upward force equal to the weight of the water displaced by the object. The absolute difference between the weight of an object in air and its weight suspended in water is equal to the **buoyant force**.

See for Yourself

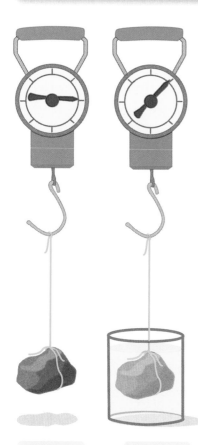

Figure 1   Figure 2

Materials

2 ft (60 cm) of string
fist-size rock
hand scale measuring
   in pounds or newtons

container filled with water
   (container must be large
   enough for the rock to fit inside)
tap water

What to Do

1. Tie one end of the string around the rock and the opposite end to the hand scale.
2. Hold the top of the scale, letting the rock hang freely. Make note of the weight measurement on the scale.
3. While holding the scale, lower the rock into the container of water.
4. Measure and record the weight of the rock while suspended in water.
5. Calculate the buoyant force using this equation:

$$\text{buoyant force } F_b = \text{weight of rock in air} - \text{weight of rock in water}$$

The weight of the rock in air is its true weight on Earth. The rock's weight in water was less, but the actual true weight of the rock had not changed. Instead, the upward buoyant force of water partially supported the rock, thus the rock's **apparent weight** was less.

Challenge ⭐

In Figure 3, the true weight is the same for both rocks. **Can you explain why the equal arm balance is tilted down on the right side?**

Think!

Both rocks have the same gravitational force pulling them down. The rock in the water has an upward buoyant force acting on it. Thus, the rock in the water has an overall resultant force down that is less than the weight of the rock in the air.

Figure 3

42 Friction

Friction is a type of contact force that opposes the motion of one surface moving over another. In Figure 1, force is being applied to the box. Because of inertia, getting an object to start moving is more difficult than keeping it in motion. **Static friction** is a "gripping" type of friction between stationary objects and the surface they are sitting on. **Kinetic friction** acts to stop an object from moving across a surface; it is also called sliding friction.

Figure 1

See for Yourself

Materials

rubber band (the wider the better)   jar with lid

What to Do

1. Ask an adult to tightly secure the lid on the jar.
2. Try to unscrew the lid from the jar with your bare hand. If the lid can be removed, make note of how difficult it was to turn the lid.
3. Replace the lid and ask the adult to again tightly secure the lid on the jar.
4. Place the rubber band around the lid as shown in Figure 2.
5. Now try to open the lid with the rubber band in place.

Figure 2

What Happened ?

When a jar lid is difficult to open, your hand tends to slip around the lid. This is because of the large static friction between the lid and the jar and the low static friction between your

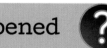

hand and the lid. Thus, your hand slides on the lid. The anti-slippery properties of the rubber band make the rubber band grip the lid as well as your hand, thus your hand doesn't tend to slip as before. The turning force (called **torque**) you apply with your hand may be enough to overcome the static friction between the lid and the jar. Once the static friction between the lid and the jar is overcome, less torque is needed to overcome the kinetic friction acting to prevent the turning of the lid. This demonstrates that static friction is generally greater than kinetic friction.

At the microscopic level, no surface is perfectly smooth. The rougher the surfaces the greater will be the static friction between two objects.

Challenge

In Figure 3, can you explain why there is static friction between the surface of the box and the surface of the table?

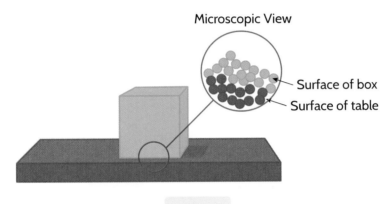

Microscopic View

Surface of box
Surface of table

Figure 3

Think!

- At the microscopic level, the particles of one surface move into open spaces in the other. It is in some ways similar to the surfaces being glued together, except glue is far more binding.
- The rougher the surfaces in contact, the more intermixing there will be of their molecules. Thus, the greater will be the static friction.

Torque is a force that starts something turning around a fixed point. A door rotates on its hinges; thus, you apply torque when you open a door. The top spins because torque has been applied.

Figure 1

Seesaws are a type of simple machine called a lever, which is a straight beam rotating around a fixed point called the fulcrum. Figure 2 shows the different parts of a lever that can be used to determine the torque needed to lift a load. The effort arm starts at the fulcrum and stops where the effort force (force applied to raise the load) is applied. The load arm starts at the fulcrum and stops at the load (object being moved). Torque is equal to the effort force times the effort arm distance. Other solid materials can act like a lever, such as a pencil.

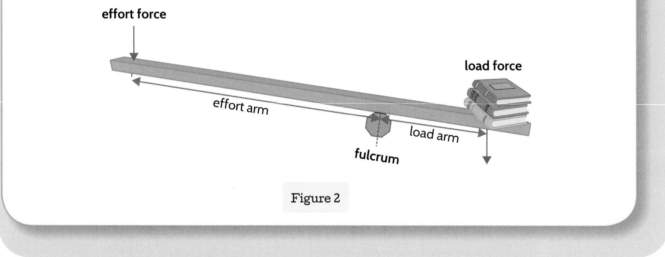

Figure 2

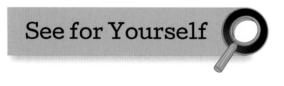
See for Yourself

Materials

stack of books   2 pencils

What to Do

1. Put the end of one of the pencils under the stack of books. This will be referred to as pencil #1.

2. Place the second pencil under the first pencil and close to the books. This will be referred to as pencil #2.

3. Push down on the end of pencil #1 and try to lift the books. Make a note of how much force was needed.

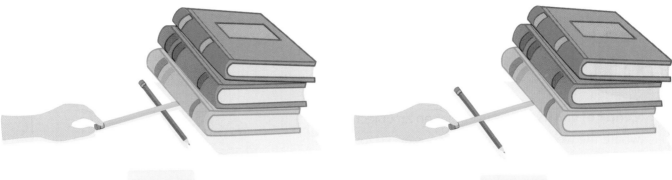

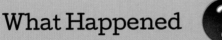
Figure 3

Figure 4

4. Change the position of pencil #2, moving it farther away from the stack of books.
5. Push down on the end of pencil #1 again and note how much force was needed to lift the books.

What Happened

In this activity, one pencil forms the lever beam and a second pencil forms the fulcrum.

When you pushed down on the end of pencil #1 it rotated around pencil #2, thus the books were raised. The position of the fulcrum changed the length of the effort arm. This investigation led you to discover that when using a lever, the longer the effort arm, the less effort force it takes to lift a load. This is because the torque applied is equal to the effort force times the length of the effort arm.

Challenge ⭐

Can you explain how the child in Figure 5 is able to lift the lady on the seesaw?

Think!

- The seesaw is a board with its center rotating around a fixed pivot point. Thus, the seesaw acts as a lever, with the fulcrum in the center.
- The weight of the child and the weight of the lady produce a torque (turning force) on each end of the lever.
- The magnitude of their torque is determined by multiplying their weight by their distance to the fulcrum. The lady weighs more but is closer to the fulcrum than the child. Thus, since the child's weight is lifting the lady, the torque the child applies is more than the torque applied by the lady.

Figure 5

44 Center of Gravity

Center of gravity (CG) is the point on an object where the weight of the body is considered to be concentrated; if the object is uniform, its CG is in the center; if supported at the CG, an object can be balanced as in Figure 1.

Many objects are not uniform, and their CG changes if the weight distribution changes or more weight is added or subtracted. But, like the cardboard square, to find the center of gravity experimentally one only needs to find the point where the object will balance if supported at that point.

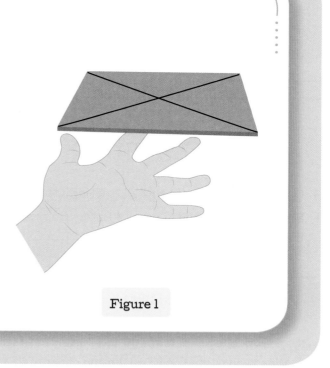

Figure 1

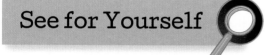
See for Yourself

Materials

18 inches (45 cm) of ¼-inch (0.63-cm) ribbon   dowel rod
transparent tape   lemon-size piece of modeling clay

What to Do

1. Use the ribbon to suspend the dowel rod as shown. The ribbon should form a cradle for the dowel rod to rest in. Secure the ends of the ribbon to the edge of a table.

2. Add about half of the clay to one end of the dowel rod.

3. Reposition the dowel rod so that it balances with the clay on one end.

4. Add a different amount of clay and repeat step 3.

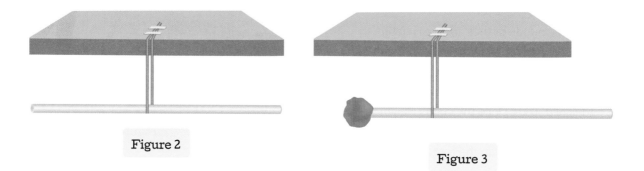

Figure 2

Figure 3

What Happened ❓

All matter behaves as though its weight is concentrated at one point called its center of gravity. The center of gravity of the rod is the point where, if supported, the rod will balance.

The rod can be compared to a seesaw that pivots around one point. When weight is added to one end, that end of the seesaw is pulled down and the opposite end moves up. Each end of a seesaw traces out a curved path. The turning force causing this rotation is called torque. The rod balances when the torque for side A equals the torque for side B.

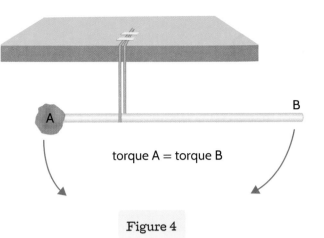

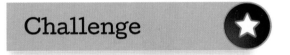
torque A = torque B

Figure 4

Challenge ⭐

Can you explain the outcome shown in Figure 5?

Think!

The can is balanced on the edge of a glass. The point where the can rests on the glass edge is the pivot point; thus, for the can to balance, its center of gravity must be in line with this point.

See for Yourself

Put a small amount of water in an empty soda can, and then balance the can on the edge of a glass as in Figure 5. It takes patience and possibly a bit of experimenting to determine the amount of water needed.

Figure 5

45 Stability

Being **stable** means an object is not likely to change, not likely to fall over.

The center of gravity of an object affects its stability. The lower an object's center of gravity is, the more stable the object. The higher the center of gravity the more likely the object will fall over.

An object will fall over if its center of gravity moves beyond the base of the object. A free-hanging weighted string can be used to identify just how far an object can be tilted and remain stable.

Figure 1

See for Yourself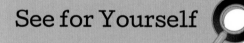

Materials

ruler
marker
empty box such as a cereal box
scissors

piece of string equal to the height of the box
metal washer
pushpin
large hardback book

What to Do

1. Use the ruler and marker to draw two diagonal lines across the face of the box to form a cross.

2. Tie a washer to one end of the string.

3. Insert the pushpin into the center of the X on the box.

4. Tie the free end of the string around the pushpin.

5. Lay the book on the edge of a table. Place the box on top so that the washer hangs freely over the edge of the table.

6. Slowly raise the end of the book, keeping the hanging string over the box.

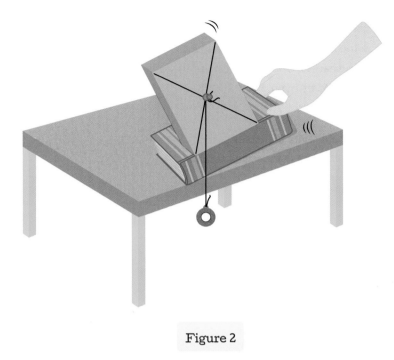

Figure 2

7. Continue raising the box until the string hangs past the bottom edge of the box.

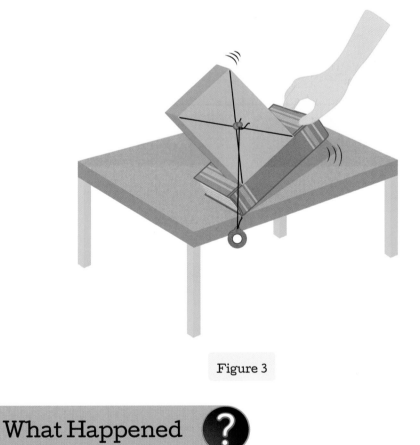

Figure 3

What Happened ?

The pushpin on the outside of the box points to the position of the box's center of gravity inside the box. The hanging string shows the direction in which the weight of the box is being pulled; the direction of gravity doesn't change; the force of gravity is always down, toward the center of Earth. As the box is being tilted, the string is not changing direction; instead, the box is tilting away from the string. The box continues to be stable with its base flat against the book until its center of gravity extends past the box's base. The hanging string allows you to visually observe the movement of the box's center of gravity. When the string passes the corner of the box, it indicates that the box's center of gravity is past the base of the box. When this happens, the box topples over.

Facts about stability:

- Lowering the center of gravity increases stability.
- Increasing the area of the base increases stability.

Challenge ⭐

Can you identify which of the football players in Figure 4, A or B, is more likely to fall over if hit by an opposing team's player?

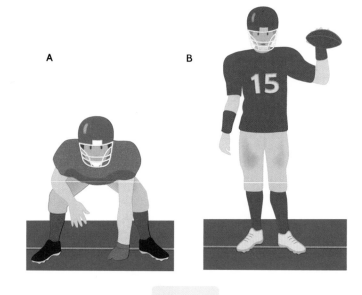

A   B

Figure 4

Think!

- The player with the widest base and lowest center of gravity will be the most stable.
- Player A has his feet separated giving him a wide base. This player also is crouched down giving him a low center of gravity.
- Player A is more stable than player B and harder to topple over when hit.

Heat

Heat is a form of energy that is transferred from a hot object to a cooler object. Heat is transferred in three different ways: conduction, convection, and radiation. Conduction and convection are the two processes that will be addressed in this section.

Conduction

Heat conduction occurs when two materials at different temperatures are in contact with each other. Heat always flows from an object at a higher temperature to the cooler object. This transfer of heat continues until both objects in contact are at the same temperature. Conduction occurs by collision of particles. Solid particles don't move from one place to another; instead, they vibrate in place. The hotter the object, the faster the vibration; even though they stay in place, solid particles can vibrate enough to collide with neighboring particles. With each collision, energy is transferred from the hotter molecule to the cooler one. The transfer of heat begins at the contact surfaces and spreads throughout the cooler material.

Convection

Convection of heat is a continuous circular pattern of rising warm fluid and sinking cooler fluid. This up-and-down movement due to differences in the temperature between regions is called a thermal convection current. This cycle of fluid movement continues as long as there is a difference in temperature between regions. Heat energy is transferred in Earth's atmosphere by the circulation of the air; just remember that hot air rises and cool air sinks, taking its place. This is true of liquids as well. Because convection is the movement of particles from one place to another, solids do not transfer heat by convection.

Conductors vs. Insulators

Conductors are materials in which heat is easily transferred from one particle to the next. Metals are among the best heat conductors. Fluids can conduct heat but not very well, thus fluids are poor heat conductors. Poor heat conductors are called insulators. Double-paned windows have air between the layers of glass, which retards the conduction of heat in or out of a building.

Heat Capacity

Heat capacity is a measure of the amount of heat needed for a substance to change its temperature. Water has the highest heat capacity of any liquid. Because of this, water is a good coolant. Coolants are liquids or gases used to take the heat away from something. Since heat moves from something hot to something colder, water can remove a lot of heat before it warms up.

46 Conduction of Heat

Heat conduction is the process of heat being transferred between two objects at different temperatures; the objects have to be in contact with each other. Conduction is best in solids because the solid particles are close together, which helps to transfer energy between them by vibration. Liquids do not conduct as well as solids, and gases are very poor conductors of heat. Energized solid atoms vibrate in place, but their vibrations are enough for them to bump into nearby neighboring atoms, transferring some of their energy. The conduction of heat in a solid is not visible because the solid molecules remain in place.

A device called Newton's cradle (Figure 1) can be used to model conduction of energy. The energy source comes from raising and then releasing one of the end spheres; this swinging sphere strikes the first sphere in the line. Since the device models energy conduction, what do you predict is going to happen to the line of spheres? Would the same happen with a row of marbles?

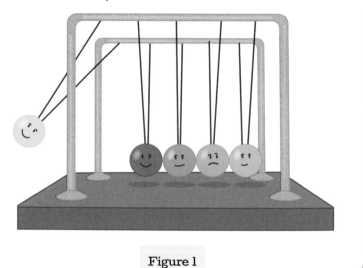

Figure 1

See for Yourself

Materials

book
6 marbles

What to Do

1. Open the book and line the marbles in the center crease as shown in Figure 2. Make sure the marbles are touching each other.

2. Move one end marble away from the others.

Figure 2

3. With your finger, flick this displaced marble so that it moves forward, striking the first marble in the line.

4. Repeat this experiment several times to confirm the results.

If you predicted that all the marbles would remain in place except the marble on the opposite end, then your prediction was supported. Asking a question, stating a **hypothesis** (an informed prediction of the answer to the question being investigated), and then experimentally testing your hypothesis is what science is all about. There will be times when your hypothesis is not supported by experimental results. This may or may not mean your hypothesis is wrong; instead, maybe an outside variable affected the results, such as changes in humidity or an ineffective way of applying force. Never change your hypothesis to fit the results. It is not about being right or wrong. Instead, it is all about learning more about the world around you. This experiment was designed to show that energy is conducted through solids without displacing the atoms making up the solids. The movement of the marble on the opposite end of the line confirmed that there had been a transfer of energy between the marbles in contact with each other. Heat can be conducted between objects of any state of matter, as long as they are in contact with each other; but solids are the best heat conductors. With the information from this investigation, make a prediction, also called a hypothesis, about the following problem.

Challenge

In Figure 3, what effect does the metal strip have on the temperature of the two cups of water?

Think!

- Most metals are solids at room temperature and are good heat conductors.
- Heat energy moves from a region of high temperature to a cooler region.
- Most metals are solids at room temperature and are good heat conductors.
- Without the metal strip there would be no transfer of heat between the cups.
- With the metal strip, heat from the warmer water is transferred to the cup with cooler water. This transfer continues until the water is the same temperature in both cups.

Figure 3

47 Convection

Convection is a heat transfer process: Energy is transferred from an area of higher energy to an area of lower energy. When fluids, such as air and water, are heated, their particles move farther apart; their density decreases, and they are more buoyant than surrounding fluid particles, thus they rise. The reverse is true when fluids are cooled: their density increases and they are less buoyant, thus they sink through surrounding fluids. The movement of fluids is called a current. When fluid motion is due to convection of heat, it is called a thermal convection current, which is always in a cyclical path as shown in Figure 1.

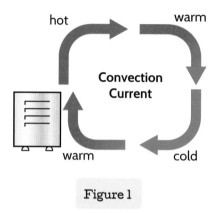

Figure 1

See for Yourself

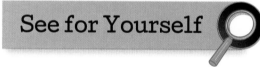

Materials

3 oz (90 mL) paper cup
tap water
blue food coloring

stirring spoon
1 qt (1 L) wide-mouth jar

What to Do

1. Fill the paper cup one-half full with water. Add food coloring and stir to make the water dark blue.

2. Place the cup of blue water in a freezer until the water is frozen solid.

3. When the ice is ready, fill the jar with warm tap water.

4. Remove the ice from the paper cup and place it in the jar of warm water.

5. Observe the contents of the jar for several minutes and then periodically during the day.

Figure 2

What Happened

The blue ice cube floats in the warm water and immediately begins to melt creating a cold, dense, blue water current that sinks below the ice. This cold water spreads along the bottom of the jar. Heat from the warm water in the jar as well as from the jar is transferred to the cold water. As the cold blue water warms, its molecules spread out, thus it rises because it is less dense and more buoyant. The ice continues to melt as heat is transferred to it from the warm water. There is an up-and-down cycle of water currents that continues until all of the ice melts and heat energy is evenly dispersed throughout the water.

Challenge

Can you explain the movement of the colored water in Figure 3?

Think!

- Why does one fluid rise and another sink? Fluids that rise are warmer and less dense than fluids that sink.
- A warm fluid rises because its density is less than a colder fluid.
- The blue liquid sinks because it is colder than the red fluid that is rising.

Figure 3

48 Conductors vs. Insulators

Materials in which heat quickly flows through are called conductors. Insulators are materials that minimize or retard heat transfer. The metal pot in Figure 1 is being heated. Metals are good heat conductors; thus, in a short time, heat will be transferred by conduction from one molecule to the next until the entire pot is heated, including the metal handle. The cloth mitten covering the hand is a poor conductor of heat, thus it insulates or protects the hand from being burned. Conductors feel colder than insulators do, even when they are both at the same temperature.

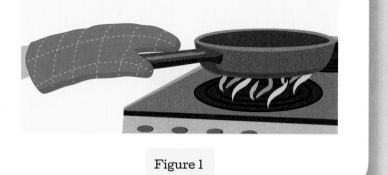

Figure 1

See for Yourself

Materials

metal spoon
towel

What to Do

1. Lay the towel on a table, or another flat surface.

2. Place the metal spoon on top of the towel.

3. Allow the towel and spoon to remain undisturbed for 20–30 minutes. This gives both items time to reach room temperature.

4. Touch the spoon with your fingers then touch the towel. Do they feel the same or does one feel colder than the other?

Metal Spoon

Cloth Towel

Figure 2

What Happened

The metal spoon and cloth towel are both at room temperature; your body temperature is higher than room temperature. Since both the towel and the spoon are cooler than your body, we might predict that heat would flow from your fingers to each one of them. If there had been an equal loss of heat from your body, the spoon and towel would have both felt cold; this didn't happen.

Instead, the spoon felt colder than the cloth. This is because the cloth towel is an insulator, which retards heat flow. On the other hand, metals are very good conductors, which allow heat to be freely transferred through them. When you touched the metal spoon, heat moved away from your skin to the metal, lowering the temperature of your skin. The nerves in your fingers sensed this heat loss, "reported" it to your brain, and, *voila*, the spoon felt cold. This explains why a tiled floor feels colder than a rug when they are actually both at room temperature.

Challenge

Using what you have learned in this activity, can you explain why the aluminum ice-cream scoop in Figure 3 removes ice cream more easily from the carton?

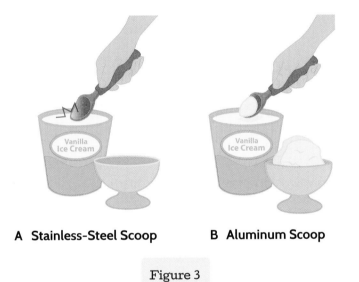

A Stainless-Steel Scoop   B Aluminum Scoop

Figure 3

Think!

- The shape of the scoops is the same, but this activity is about conductors and insulators.
- The scoops are made of different metals and all metals are good conductors. One of the metals must be a better conductor than the other. Now how does the ability to conduct heat affect being a better ice-cream scoop?
- The colder the ice cream, the harder it is to scoop out. So, warming the ice cream would make it easier to scoop. If aluminum is a better conductor of heat, then heat from the scoop is transferred to the ice cream raising its temperature and making the ice cream where the scoop touches softer and easier to scoop out.

FACT   Aluminum ice-cream scoops have a heat conductivity that is about 6.9 times that of stainless steel. This means heat moves 6.9 times as fast through the aluminum scoop than the stainless-steel one. Heating either of the metal scoops in warm water would make it easier to scoop out the ice cream.

Heat Capacity

Heat capacity is a measure of the amount of heat needed to change the temperature of a substance. Water has such a high heat capacity that it can be used as a **coolant**, which is a substance used to remove the heat from another material. One doesn't normally heat water inside a balloon, but it can be done because water keeps the balloon cool.

See for Yourself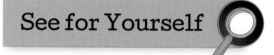

Materials

two 8-inch (20-cm) round latex balloons
paper towel
matches

tea candle
safety goggles

What to Do

CAUTION   Put on your safety goggles before you start!

1. Stretch the mouth of one balloon over the end of a water faucet and hold it in place while you slowly fill the balloon to apple size with water.

2. Remove the balloon from the faucet and while holding the balloon over the sink blow into the balloon until it is about the size of a cantaloupe. Tie a knot in the balloon to seal it, and then dry the outside of the balloon with a paper towel.

3. Blow into the second balloon, inflating it with air to about the same size as the water/air-filled balloon. Tie a knot to seal it.

4. Light the candle. Have an adult help you with this part.

5. Wearing your safety goggles, hold the air-filled balloon at arm's length about 2 ft (60 cm) above the candle flame. Slowly lower the air-filled balloon toward the candle. Make note of what happens.

6. Repeat step #5 using the water-filled balloon. Make sure the water in the balloon is held over the flame as shown in Figure 2.

Figure 1

CAUTION   Remove the balloon from the heat as soon as you have made your observation.

What Happened ❓

The air-filled balloon pops before the flame touches it. Inflating the balloon stretches the latex, thus the thin layer of latex quickly heats to its melting point of 248°F (120°C) and bursts with a BANG!!

The water-filled balloon doesn't burst when heated, not even when it touches the flame. Latex is an insulator, meaning it doesn't easily transfer heat. But the balloon's latex walls are too thin to restrict heat flow. Thus, the latex molecules transfer their heat to water molecules by conduction, and then thermal convection currents keep cool water molecules moving across the latex above the flame. Thus, the water inside the balloon keeps the latex from reaching its melting point. If heated long enough, the water inside the balloon will boil. This is because liquid water boils at 212°F (100°C) and in its liquid state water doesn't get any hotter; so, the water never gets hot enough for the latex to melt. The water acts as a coolant, which absorbs heat from the latex keeping the latex cool.

Figure 2

CAUTION Even though the water inside the balloon can boil, it is not safe to do this. You could be burned if the balloon burst.

Challenge ⭐

Can you explain how the girl in Figure 3 is being cooled by pouring water on her face?

Think!

- Water is a coolant and as such it can absorb a lot of heat before its temperature increases. The water absorbs heat from the girl's skin, thus reducing the temperature of her skin.
- As some of the water absorbs heat from the girl's skin, it evaporates. Remember that evaporation is the vaporization of water below the boiling point of water. Thus, water is cooling the skin by conduction of heat from the skin to the water and the heated water molecules are removed via evaporation.

Figure 3

Light

Light is a term generally used when referring to visible light; but visible light is only a small part of light energy known as **electromagnetic radiation (EMR or ER)**. All light is wave energy, but it also has particle characteristics and these particles are called **photons**. Light doesn't need matter to travel from place to place. The **electromagnetic spectrum** is the range of light radiation in order of wavelengths.

White light is perceived when the light is a combination of all visible light, from red with the longest wavelength and lowest energy, to violet with the shortest wavelength and highest energy. When white light is separated one sees a rainbow of colors; ROYGBIV is an acronym for the sequence of colors in the visible light spectrum from longest to shortest wavelength:

Red   Orange   Yellow   Green   Blue   Indigo   Violet

Light can be absorbed, reflected, or transmitted by materials. When white light strikes a material, the color of the material depends on the part of the light that is reflected to your eye; if no light is reflected all would be absorbed and the material would appear to be black; if all the light is reflected, the material would appear to be white; if only one color, such as red, is reflected, all the other colors would be absorbed and the material would appear to be red.

Incandescence refers to the production of light by heating. The Sun, campfires, and candles all produce incandescent light. **Luminescence** (cold light) is the production of light by a substance that has not been heated. Instead of heat, a high-energy form of light such as ultraviolet light can activate electrons in some chemicals, resulting in the electrons moving farther from an atom's nucleus. The electrons are said to be in an **excited state**. These electrons lose this energy and return to their **ground state** or natural position. The energy lost by the electrons is in the form of photons, that is, light energy. **Phosphors** are chemicals that emit photons in the form of visible light. Phosphors are found in **fluorescent** and **phosphorescent** materials. These materials will be investigated using a black light as the source of high-energy ultraviolet light, UV.

Transparent is generally defined as something you can see through; it describes the characteristics of a material in which visible light can pass through with no change in its direction. **Opaque** refers to things visible light cannot pass through, and **translucent** means some of the visible light is blocked and the light passing through is scattered.

Scattering of light is the process of light being absorbed by a material and emitting it in many different directions.

Dispersion of light is the splitting of white light into its separate colors. This happens because light **refracts** or bends when it changes speed as it moves from a medium with a different density from the medium it is entering. Each light color refracts at a different angle. An example is when light moves from air into a prism, and then out into air again.

Incident light is light that strikes the surface of a material.

Lenses are curved transparent surfaces of glass or plastic. When incident light strikes the surface of a lens at an angle, it is refracted but not dispersed. The light enters the lens at an angle, is refracted, and exits at the same angle it entered the lens. The surface of **convex lenses** curves outward, while the surface of **concave lenses** curves inward. Convex lenses **converge** light, or bring it to a point, while concave lenses **diverge**, or spread out, the light.

50 Electromagnetic Spectrum

Electromagnetic radiation (EMR or ER) (Figure 1), also known as light energy, doesn't require matter to move from place to place. EMR is wave energy that travels through space at the speed of light, which is about 186,000 miles per second (300,000 km/s). This speed decreases when light travels through mediums of different density.

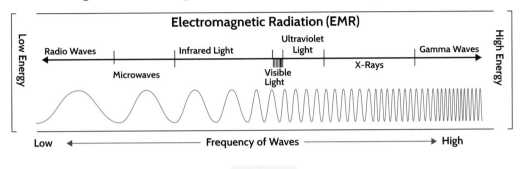

Figure 1

Light waves are **transverse waves**, which means they have a shape like water waves. **Wavelength** is the distance between each wave (Figure 2) and **wave frequency** is the number of waves that pass a point in a time period. Since all EMR waves travel at the same speed, those with short waves have a higher frequency and more energy, and vice versa. Water waves can demonstrate the difference between short and long waves, as well as frequency.

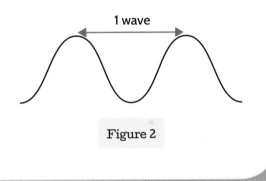

Figure 2

See for Yourself

Materials

glass rectangular baking dish
(the longer the better)
four food cans of equal height
(or any substitute that will raise the dish)

pencil
overhead light
tap water

What to Do

1. Use the food cans to raise the glass dish above a flat surface by supporting each end with two cans of food. An overhead light is needed in order to cast shadows below the dish. Note: Substitute anything for the cans that can elevate and securely support the dish.

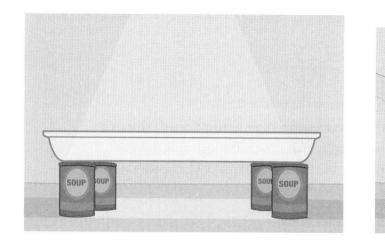

Figure 3   Figure 4

2. Fill the glass dish about half-full with water.

3. When the water is calm, create a wave in the water by inserting the pencil in the water at one end of the dish and then quickly removing the pencil.

4. Observe the shadow of the wave on the surface below the dish.

5. Repeat steps 3 and 4, but insert the pencil in the water five or more times as you slowly count, one and two and three and so on. Make note of the distance between the water waves.

6. Repeat the wave-making process, but speed up the frequency by inserting and raising the pencil faster. As before, make note of the distance between the waves.

What Happened ?

A water wave is created each time you touch the water. The faster you touch the water, the greater the number of waves and the closer the waves are to each other. Water waves can be used to show what EMR waves are like. The speed of EMR waves is the product of frequency × wavelength. **Frequency** is the number of waves formed in one second. **Wavelength** is the distance between each wave. No matter the type of EMR, be it gamma, visible light, or radio waves, the product of each wave's frequency times its wavelength is 1.86×10^5 miles/s (3×10^5 km/s).

Challenge ⭐

Using Figure 1, can you describe the relationship between the wavelength, frequency, and energy of EMR?

Think!

- Gamma waves have the greatest energy, the highest frequency, and the shortest wavelengths.
- Radio waves have the least energy, the lowest frequency, and the longest wavelengths.
- As the wavelength of EMR radiation increases, the energy and frequency of waves decrease.

51 Photons

Light has wave characteristics, but it also has characteristics like particles. But unlike the properties of matter, the particles of light have no mass and do not take up space. Yikes! Sounds a bit like "ghost" particles. But there have been experiments that support this, and the particles of light have been given the name of **photons**.

Photons are not all alike in that they each contain a specific amount of light energy. The photon energy of light is inversely proportional to the wavelength of light. Thus, in the visible light spectrum, photons of red light with its long wavelength have less energy than photons of blue light with its shorter wavelength.

Sunlight is called "**white light**," which contains the entire visible light spectrum; from least to greatest energy it contains red, orange, yellow, green, blue, indigo, and violet light. The difference in the photon energy of different colors affects the **fading** of dye colors when exposed to sunlight.

See for Yourself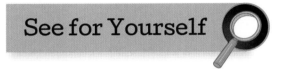

Materials

2 sheets of construction paper,
   1 red and 1 blue
scissors

transparent tape
1 manila folder

What to Do

1. Fold the red sheet of paper in half lengthwise. Unfold the paper and cut along the fold line (Figure 1).
2. Tape one half of the red paper to the inside of a window receiving direct sunlight. Place the other half of the red paper in the folder.
3. Repeat steps #1 and #2 using the blue paper (Figure 2).
4. After a week or longer, remove the papers from the window and observe both sides. Compare the papers from the window to those stored in the manila folder. Compare the fading of the two different colors of paper.

What Happened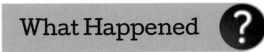

The sides of the papers facing the outside receive direct sunlight. The sides of the papers facing the room receive some sunlight reflected from objects in the room as well as light from

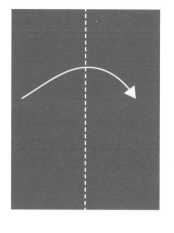

Figure 1

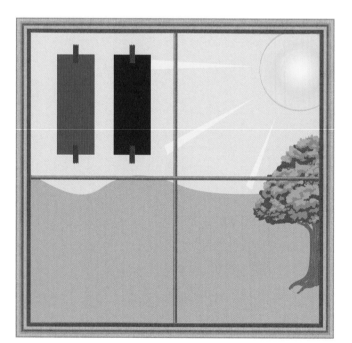

Figure 2

Direct sunlight   Indirect sunlight   Folder
(outward facing)   (inward facing)

Figure 3

other sources in the room. The papers in the folder are not exposed to light. Both the red and blue papers receiving direct sunlight faded the most (the red papers are shown in Figure 3).

Photodegradation is the fading of dye colors due to exposure to light, generally sunlight. Dyes have molecules with light-absorbing regions. These parts of a molecule are called **chromophores**. The chromophores in the red paper absorb all the photons of the different light colors except red, which is reflected. This means the least energetic red photons are reflected and the remaining high-energy photons are absorbed. These photons can break bonds in the chromophores, destroying their ability to absorb light and reflect light. With fewer chromophores reflecting red light, the intensity of the red color decreases. In other words, the color fades. The reverse is true for the blue paper, which reflects high-energy blue photons and absorbs the less energetic photons. While the blue paper fades, generally blue dyes do not fade as fast as red dyes.

Challenge ⭐

Can you explain why sunlight passes through glass in windows?

Figure 4

Think!

- Red paper looks red because it absorbs all visible light photons except red photons, which are reflected.
- Black materials absorb all visible light photons, and white materials reflect all visible light photons.
- If a material doesn't absorb or reflect visible light photons, then there is nothing in the material to stop the photons and they pass through it. Glass is said to be transparent to visible light photons.

FYI: Glass is not transparent to infrared light.

52 Phosphors

A **phosphor** is a chemical substance in which when the electrons in its atoms are energized, they jump to a higher energy level. This simply means the electrons can move farther away from their normal position, called the ground state. Energized electrons are said to be **excited**, but this state is temporary. Excited electrons lose their excess energy by emitting photons of visible light, and then return to ground state. Photons are particles representing a quantity of light. Some phosphors can be energized with visible light, but all phosphors can be energized with ultraviolet light (UV). Phosphors may or may not contain the element phosphorus (P).

Fluorescent highlighters contain ink with phosphors that emit photons of energy equal to that of the color of the ink. In other words, a yellow fluorescent highlighter contains phosphors that emit both yellow photons from the yellow dye in the ink plus yellow photons emitted by excited electrons activated by UV light.

See for Yourself

Materials

yellow fluorescent highlighter
yellow highlighter (not fluorescent)

white index card
pencil

What to Do

1. Using the two highlighters, draw and color in two squares on the index card.

2. Use the pencil to label the fluorescent marker patch "YES," and the regular non-fluorescent marker patch "NO."

3. Allow the ink on the card to dry. This should take 1 minute or less.

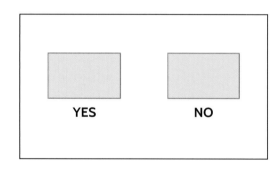

Figure 1

4. Stand outdoors so you are facing away from the Sun. Hold the card with its ink side in front of you; the card should be in the shadow of your body.

5. Observe any difference in the brightness of the two ink marks on the card.

CAUTION Never look directly at the Sun. It could permanently damage your eyes.

What Happened ?

Both colored squares receive the same amount of sunlight; both colored squares reflect yellow visible light. But the yellow square made with the fluorescent highlighter is much brighter. This is because the phosphors in the fluorescent highlighter ink convert some of the invisible UV light from the Sun into visible yellow light. This yellow light is no different from the reflected visible yellow light from the Sun. The fluorescent highlighter is brighter because it emits more photons of yellow light, which makes its yellow ink appear super bright. The ink in the regular marker only reflects the visible yellow light from the Sun and, in comparison, appears dull.

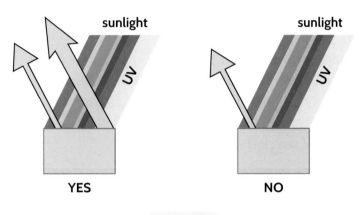

YES   NO

Figure 2

Challenge ★

After studying Figure 3, can you list the steps of fluorescence of a phosphor?

Think!

1. An electron of a phosphor atom is excited by absorbing high-energy photons of light, such as from UV light.

2. The excited electron jumps to a higher energy level, a level farther away from the atom's nucleus.

3. The excited electron loses photons of visible light.

4. The electron then falls back to its original position, which is called its ground state.

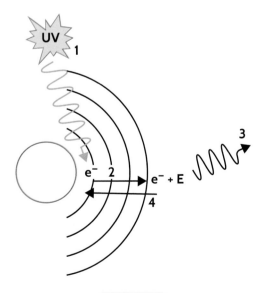

Figure 3

53 Fluorescence

Fluorescence is a type of **luminescence**, meaning heat is not used in the production of visible light. Instead of heat, high-energy ultraviolet light will cause some materials to emit different colors of visible light. Materials that fluoresce contain phosphors, which are chemicals that absorb UV photons causing electrons in the chemical's atoms to move to higher energy levels (Figure 1). These excited, energized electrons release the absorbed energy in the form of photons of visible light.

All phosphors emit visible light, but some only emit light during the time they are being energized. These phosphors are said to be **fluorescent**. The color of the glow depends on the type of photon emitted. Parts of some living organisms are fluorescent, such as teeth, urine, and the exoskeleton of some scorpions (Figure 2). Parts of some plants are fluorescent, such as the **quinine** that comes from the bark of the cinchona tree.

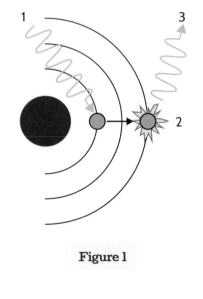

Figure 1

Figure 2

See for Yourself

Materials

bottle of tonic water with quinine   black light

CAUTION Do not stare directly into the black light, as it can damage your eyes.

What to Do

1. Observe the tonic water and make a note of whether the light glows under the light in your room.

2. Take the tonic water outdoors and determine whether sunlight makes the liquid glow.

3. In a darkened room, shine the black light on the tonic water. Observe the liquid with the black light on, and then again when you turn the light off.

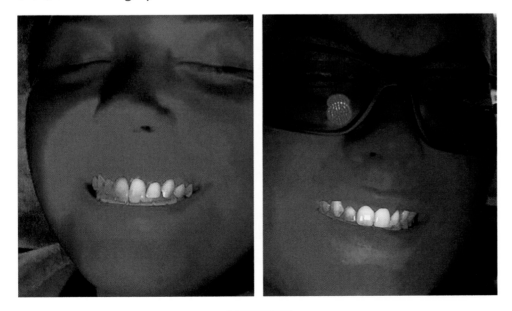

What Happened ❓

Black lights give off ultraviolet-A light, which is a type of high-energy light invisible to people. UV light photons have higher energy than visible light photons. UV from sunlight might make the tonic water glow, but it would be difficult to see because of the brightness of sunlight. The material in tonic water that makes the liquid glow is quinine, which contains phosphors. Phosphors in the quinine absorb UV photons and emit blue visible light photons.

Challenge ⭐

Can you discover other common things that fluoresce under a black light?

Think!

- Shine the black light on other things, such as olive oil, laundry detergent with brighteners, and don't forget your teeth.

Figure 4

- Take your black light to the grocery store and discover other things that fluoresce under this source of UV light.

Figure 3

54 Phosphorescence

Phosphorescence, like fluorescence, is visible light emitted as excited electrons return to their ground state. The difference is that the release of energy is slower for phosphorescence; the electrons lose some of the activation energy and fall to a lower energy level, and finally back to ground state, as shown in Figure 1.

While materials that fluoresce stop emitting light as soon as the activation energy is removed, phosphorescent materials continue to glow for seconds to hours after the activation energy is removed. Thus, these materials will glow in the dark.

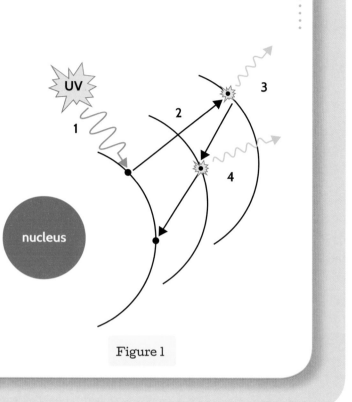

Figure 1

See for Yourself

Materials

glow-in-the-dark tape
masking tape
sheet of black paper

petroleum jelly (such as Vaseline)
black light

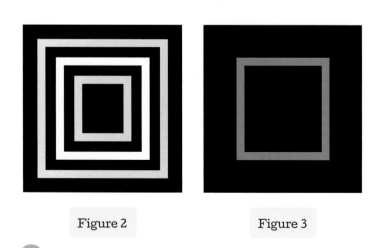

Figure 2   Figure 3

What to Do

1. Use the tape to form a design, such as the concentric squares shown here, on the paper. Alternate the tape so that the first square is masking tape, the second square is glow tape, and the outside square is again masking tape (see Figure 2).

2. Use your finger to cover the masking tape forming the inside square with petroleum jelly.

3. Darken the room and shine the black light on the black paper with the tape squares for about 30 seconds. You can measure the time by counting slowly to 30.

4. Turn the black light off and make note if any of the squares glow in the dark and, if so, note their color (see Figure 3).

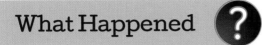

What Happened ?

The tape coated with petroleum jelly as well as the glow tape both glow while the black light shines on them. But only the glow tape continues to glow after the activating energy source, the black light, is removed. The petroleum jelly has a bluish-white glow color, and the glow tape is a specific color identified on the package.

The petroleum jelly is a fluorescent material but the glow tape is coated with a phosphorescent chemical that loses the energy absorbed a little at a time as the electrons fall back to lower energy levels until they reach their ground state.

Challenge ⭐

In Figure 4, can you select the setup, A or B, that most represents the loss of energy by phosphorescent materials?

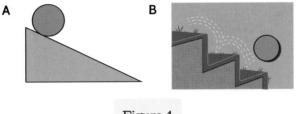

Figure 4

Think!

- The ball in A is rolling down a ramp. This ball moves from the top to the bottom without stopping. It is more like fluorescent materials that lose their energy quickly.
- The ball in B is rolling down steps. This ball is more like phosphorescent materials that jump down the energy levels losing photons of energy with each jump. All the excess energy will be lost by the time the ball reaches the bottom. This is like the energy lost by electrons in phosphorescence, and it is why these materials continue to glow even after the activating energy source is removed.

55 Colors You See

When light shines on the surface of a material, the molecules making up the material will reflect, absorb, and/or transmit the light. White light, such as sunlight, is made up of all the visible light waves. White light can also be produced by adding the proper intensity of red, green, and blue light. These three colors are the most the most common primary colors. When sunlight hits the surface of a green leaf (Figure 1), the molecules in the leaf's surface absorb all the visible light colors except green, which is reflected to your eyes. Some materials absorb some parts of the visible light and reflect and transmit other parts.

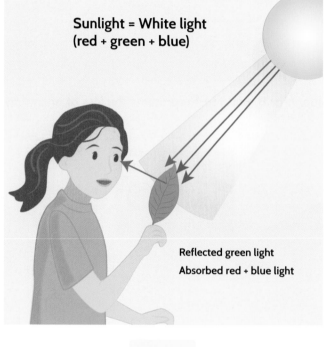

Sunlight = White light (red + green + blue)

Reflected green light
Absorbed red + blue light

Figure 1

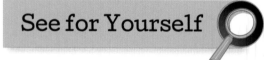

See for Yourself

Materials

white penlight

2 gummy bears, 1 red and 1 green

sheet of plain white paper

What to Do

1. Lay the paper on a flat surface.

2. Place the two gummy bears on the paper.

3. Darken the room, and then one at a time, shine the light on each candy piece.

4. While the light is shining on each candy piece, make note of any change in the candy's color as well as of any light that might pass through.

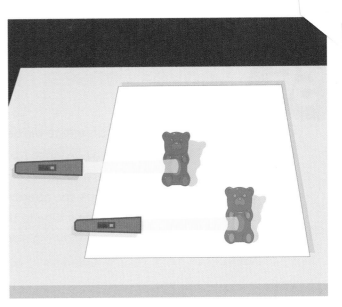

Figure 2

What Happened

White light has all the visible light colors. When white light shines on the red gummy bear, the candy looks red and a red shadow appears behind it. This is because red light is the only part of the white light that is *not* absorbed; instead, the red light is both reflected and transmitted. The red reflected light is why the gummy bear appears to be red; the red transmitted light forms the red shadow behind the bear. The green gummy bear responds in a like manner, except it is the green light that is not absorbed. Instead, the green light is reflected and transmitted.

Challenge

Can you describe what would happen if instead of white light red light was used in the previous activity?

Figure 3

Think!

- Shining a red light on the red gummy bear would have the same effect; the red light would be reflected and transmitted. This is because it is the only light color that the red candy doesn't absorb.
- Shining a red light on the green gummy bear is a different story. The green gummy bear absorbs all light colors except green; thus, the red light would be absorbed. Since no light is reflected, the candy would look darker. Also, no light is transmitted; therefore, there is no colored shadow behind the candy.

56 Convex Lenses: Focal Length

The **focal point** of a convex lens is where incident parallel light rays meet after being refracted by the lens. The **focal length** is the distance from the center of the lens to the focal point. Light from distant objects passes through a convex lens and forms an inverted image at or very near the lens' focal point. Thus, the approximate focal length of a lens can be determined by measuring the distance from the image to the lens.

See for Yourself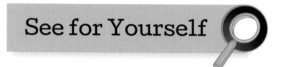

Materials

magnifying lens (convex lens)
piece of modeling clay about the size of
   a golf ball

sheet of white paper
ruler
helper

What to Do

1. On a sunny day, in a darkened room, use the clay to stand the magnifying lens so that it faces a window.

2. Hold a sheet of white paper on the side of the magnifier opposite the window.

3. Move the paper toward and away from the magnifying lens until the objects outside the window form a clear image on the paper.

Figure 1

4. Ask a helper to measure the distance from the center of the magnifying lens to the image on the paper. This will be the approximate focal length of the lens.

Figure 2

What Happened ?

A convex lens forms an inverted image at or near its focal point when the reflected light passing through the lens comes from a distant object, that is, an object at a distance of more than twice the focal length of the lens. The image is inverted, reduced in size, and real. A **real image** is one that can be projected on to a screen, which is the white paper in this activity. The focal length measured in this activity is slightly too large, because the image is always projected a bit past the focal point. The measurement is accurate enough for most uses.

Challenge ★

Can you explain why the paper in the previous activity was in no danger of getting hot while the paper is smoking in Figure 3?

Think!

- In the activity, indirect sunlight, which is sunlight reflected from objects, entered the lens. This light does not have enough energy to heat the paper.
- In Figure 3, direct sunlight entered the lens, which is held at a distance so the refracted light exiting the lens is focused on the paper.
- The heat from the focused sunlight is enough to ignite the paper.

CAUTION Adult supervision is needed any time a fire is made by focusing sunlight on flammable materials.

Figure 3

Convex Lenses: Rules of Refraction

A convex lens bulges out at its center and is thinner at its edges. The center of the lens is called the **optical center** and a straight line through its center is called the **principal axis**. There are rules for the directions of light passing through a convex lens that determine where real images will be located.

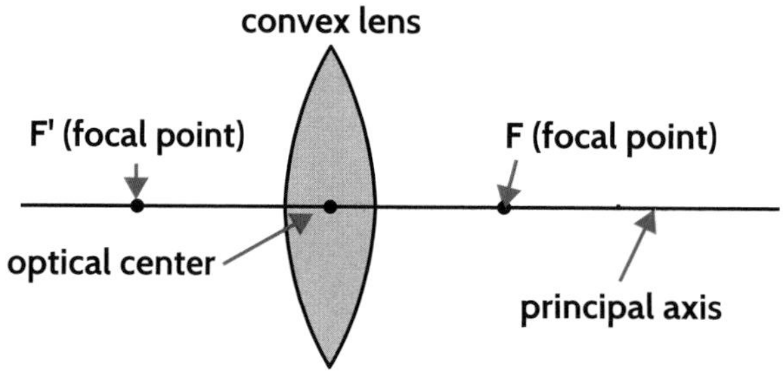

convex lens

F' (focal point)   F (focal point)

optical center

principal axis

Figure 1

See for Yourself

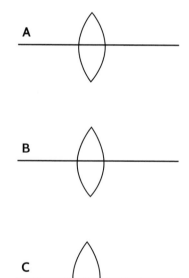

Materials

sheet of blank paper   ruler
pencil

What to Do

1. Draw three convex lenses on the paper with a line passing through the center of all three. Label the lenses A, B, and C as shown in Figure 2.

2. The following are three rules for the refraction of light rays by a convex lens. Use each rule to draw a single light ray through a convex lens as described.

   A. All incident light rays that are parallel to the principal axis of a convex lens are refracted so that they pass through the focal point.

   B. All incident light rays that pass through the center of a convex lens are not refracted; instead, the light ray continues in a straight line.

   C. All incident light rays that pass through F' before entering the lens are refracted so that they leave the lens parallel to the principal axis.

Figure 2

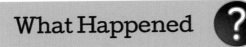
Three rules for the direction of refracted light rays from a convex lens were used to draw an example demonstrating each rule. A real image is formed where the three types of refracted light ray meet. While three different types of incident rays are shown, only two rays are needed to determine the location of an image.

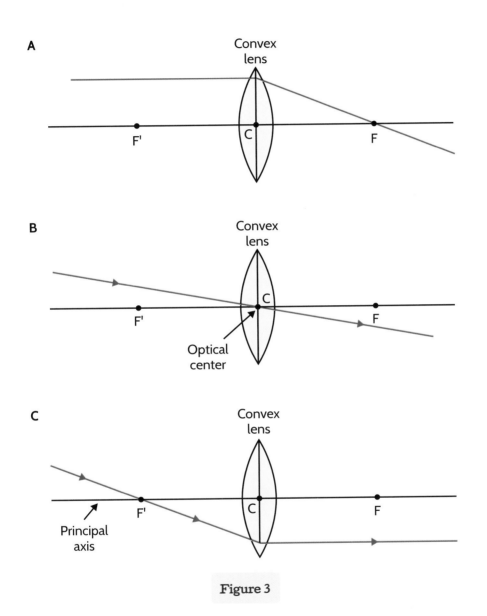

Figure 3

Can you use your diagrams of refracted rays in the previous investigation to determine the location of the image in Figure 4?

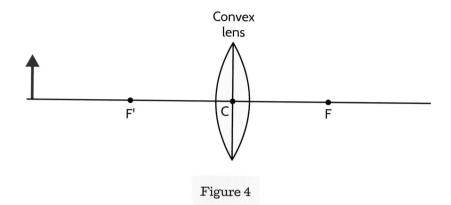

Figure 4

Think!

- Light rays parallel to the principal axis are refracted through the focal point.
- Light rays passing through the center of the lens continue in a straight line.
- Light rays passing through F' are refracted by the lens and leave as lines parallel to the principal axis. Figure 5 shows the location of the inverted images.

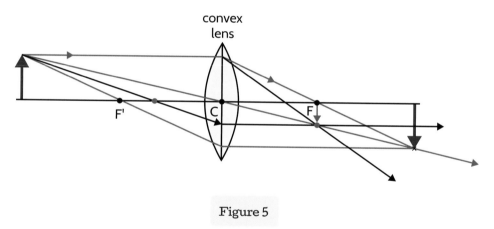

Figure 5

FYI: Figure 5 is the kind of image that the lens of your eye forms on the retina at the back of your eye. Everything you see is right-side-up because your brain flips the image messages it receives from your eyes.

Convex vs. Concave Lenses

A **convex lens** is thicker in the center than at its edges. This lens curves outward. Light rays from an object that are parallel to the lens' principal axis are refracted so that they **converge**, or meet at the lens' focal point. Convex lenses are called converging lenses.

While a convex lens converges light toward the principal axis, a **concave lens diverges** or spreads light away from the principal axis. As shown in Figure 1, diverging light rays are at an angle; if extrapolated they meet at F', which is the focal point on the same side as the source of the light.

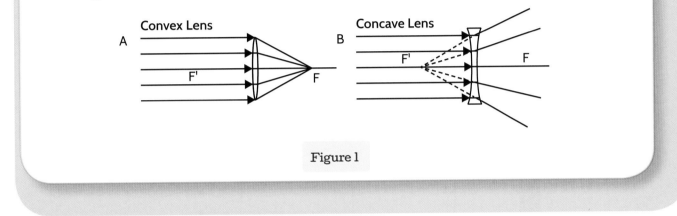

Figure 1

See for Yourself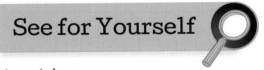

Material

lined paper   ruler
convex and concave lenses   marker
laser pen light   helper

What to Do

1. Use the marker to trace one line on the paper. This will be the lens' principal axis.

2. Place the convex lens on the paper so that the principal axis line passes through the lens' center as shown in Figure 2.

3. Hold the laser pen so that its light is parallel and to the right of the principal axis.

4. Ask your helper to mark the path of the refracted light exiting the lens.

5. Repeat steps 3 and 4 placing the laser pen to the left of the principal axis.

6. Repeat steps 1 through 5 using the concave lens (Figure 3).

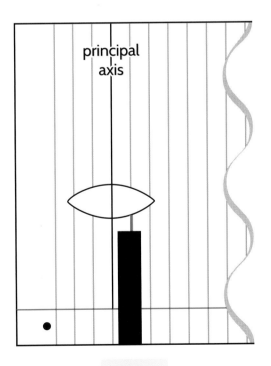

Figure 2

The convex lens refracted the light toward the centerline passing through the lens, called the principal axis. The two lines converged at one point on the principal axis, which is the focal point of the lens used.

The concave lens diverged the light passing through the lens so that neither of the two light rays passed through the principal axis.

While the concave lens diverges rays, it still produces an image that is virtual, meaning it cannot be projected on to a screen. Virtual images are formed on the same side of the lens as the object. Figure 4 shows dashed lines from the diverging rays that lead to F' (the focal point on the object's side of the lens). The rules for the formation of the virtual image formed by the concave lens are the same as those for the convex lens.

Figure 4 shows parallel light rays from an object passing through a concave lens. The small arrow is where the upright, diminished virtual image would be formed.

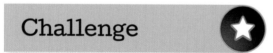

Figure 3

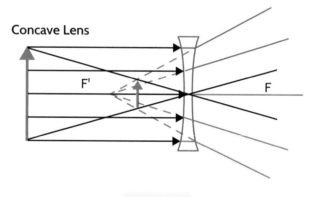

Figure 4

Challenge ★

After studying Figure 4, can you write the rules for locating the formation of a virtual image by a concave lens?

Think!

- Parallel light rays passing through a concave lens are diverged away from the primary axis.
- Diverging rays from a concave lens all lead back to F' (the focal point on the object's side of the lens). Dashed lines are used to show this extension of the diverging rays.
- Straight lines, one from the top and one from the bottom of the object, pass through the center of the lens. These lines cross the dashed lines and it is at these junctions where the top and bottom of the virtual image are formed.

Electricity

Electricity is a form of energy associated with the presence and movement of electrical charges. The buildup of stationary charges is called **static electricity** and moving charges are called **current electricity**.

Good heat conductors are also good electrical conductors; electrical insulators do not allow the transfer of electricity. Thermal currents move due to temperature differences; **electric currents** move due to a charge imbalance. There are two known types of charge, positive and negative. Protons in the nucleus of atoms have a positive charge of 1+. Electrons spinning around the outside of the nucleus have a negative charge of 1−.

A **battery** is a device that changes chemical energy into electrical energy. The ends of a battery are called **terminals** (points at which connections are made to an electrical device); one terminal is positive and the other is negative. The electrical energy in the battery cannot be used until a conductor, such as a metal wire or conducting tape, connects its two terminals.

The path through which electric charges move is called an **electric circuit**. A **series circuit** is one single circular path. If the path is complete from the positive to the negative terminals of the battery, the circuit is said to be a **closed circuit**. If any part of a series circuit is broken, the circuit is said to be an **open circuit**.

A **parallel circuit** is a combination of different circular paths connected to one battery source. Both series and parallel circuits will be investigated.

Series Circuit

When there is only one path for an electric **current** to follow, the electric **circuit** is called a **series circuit**. The arrows in the diagram represent the flow of electricity in a series circuit, which starts at the negative terminal of the battery, goes through the bulb, and ends at the positive terminal of the battery.

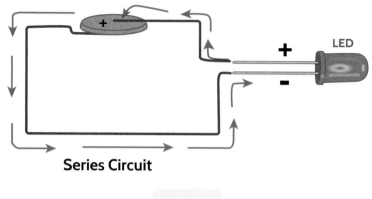

Series Circuit

Figure 1

If any part of a series circuit is broken, meaning there is a break in the path formed by the conductors, no current can flow; this is called an **open circuit** and the bulb will not glow. If there are no breaks in the path, it is a **closed circuit**.

See for Yourself

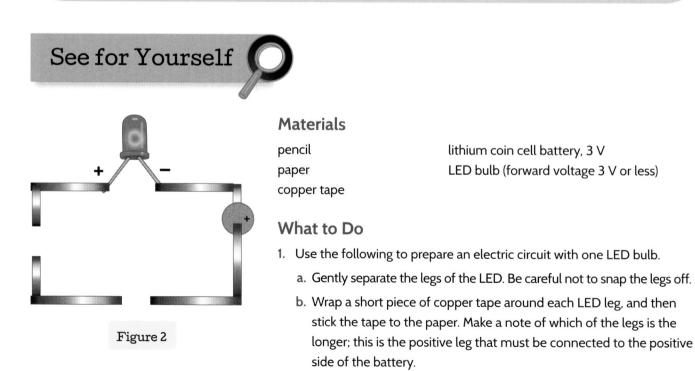

Figure 2

Materials

pencil   lithium coin cell battery, 3 V
paper   LED bulb (forward voltage 3 V or less)
copper tape

What to Do

1. Use the following to prepare an electric circuit with one LED bulb.

   a. Gently separate the legs of the LED. Be careful not to snap the legs off.

   b. Wrap a short piece of copper tape around each LED leg, and then stick the tape to the paper. Make a note of which of the legs is the longer; this is the positive leg that must be connected to the positive side of the battery.

   c. Connect the round battery with two strips of copper tape. Stick the copper tape to the paper as shown in Figure 2.

2. The diagram has a break in the copper wire, which represents a switch.

3. Close the gap in the tape with a short piece of copper tape.

What Happened

The **LED** light will glow if the circuit is closed. If the electrons from the battery flow in one circular path, then a series circuit is produced.

Challenge

If the LED does not glow, can you locate and solve the problem?

Think!

- The battery may not be getting a good connection. Is the tape tightly pressed against the sides of the battery? FYI: You could use a wooden spring clothespin to firmly press the tape to the battery.
- The LED may be connected wrongly. Does the tape on the long, positive leg of the LED lead to the positive battery terminal?
- The LED legs must each have a connection to the circuit, but should not be connected together. Figure 3 shows the correct way and an incorrect way of attaching the LED.
- The connections on the LED legs may not be tight enough.
- Tightly press all areas of overlapping copper tape to make sure they are making a good connection.

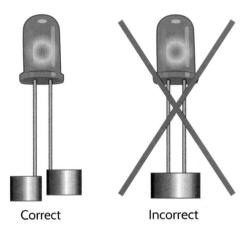

Correct   Incorrect

Figure 3

60 Parallel Circuit

A **parallel circuit** is made of two or more connected circles of conducting materials. In a series circuit, electricity moves in one complete circle passing from one light bulb to the next. Thus, each bulb becomes part of the circuit and if one is removed, the circuit is broken. But in a parallel circuit (Figure 1), there are separate but connected circuits. If a light bulb in one circuit burns out or is removed, the bulbs in the remaining circuits will still glow.

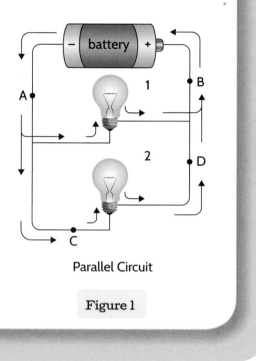

Parallel Circuit

Figure 1

See for Yourself

Materials

pencil
paper
copper tape

lithium coin cell battery, 3 V
2 or more LED bulbs (forward voltage 3 V, or less)

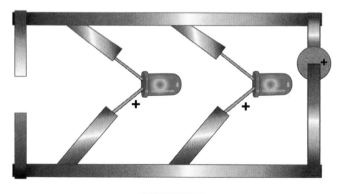

Figure 2

What to Do

1. Carry out the following steps to prepare an electric circuit with two or more LED bulbs:

   a. Gently separate the legs of the LEDs. Be careful not to snap the legs off.

   b. Wrap a short piece of copper tape around the legs of each LED and stick the tape to the paper. Mark the positive leg and make sure this leg is connected to the positive battery terminal.

   c. Connect the round battery with two strips of copper tape. Stick the copper tape to the paper as shown.

2. The diagram has a break in the copper wire, which represents a switch.

3. Close the gap in the tape with a short piece of copper tape.

What Happened

The **LED** lights glow and with the same brightness. Parallel circuits are used in buildings; this is why all the lights do not go off when one light bulb burns out. If the LED bulbs do not glow, use the trouble-shooting hints in experiment #59 "Series Circuit."

Challenge ⭐

Using Figure 3, can you determine which of the LEDs will glow if the circuit is broken at points A or B? What if the circuit is broken at points C or D?

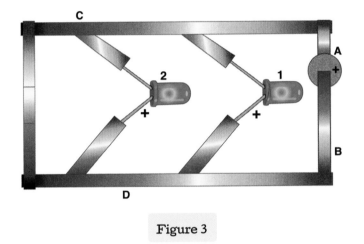

Figure 3

Think!

- If the circuit is broken at either A or B, the battery will be disconnected from the circuit and no current can flow.
- If the circuit is broken at points C or D, no current would flow through LED 2, but current would flow through LED 1.

See for Youself

Break the tape at A or B to see what happens.

Energy Ball

An **energy ball** is a device designed with an open circuit (Figure 1). When the circuit is closed the ball lights up and buzzes. An electric circuit is a path through which an electric current flows. Batteries are devices in which chemical energy is converted into electric energy. Conductors are materials through which electrical energy in the form of moving charges can pass.

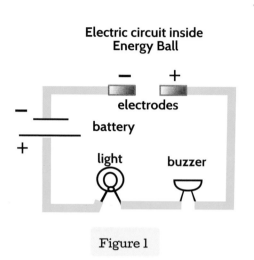

Electric circuit inside Energy Ball

Figure 1

A closed circuit is an unbroken circuit; an unbroken path of conductors. An open circuit has a break in the circuit; the path of conductors is broken. Now, with all the background information covered, energy balls are fun and a great way to learn more about current electricity.

See for Yourself

Materials

hand cream   energy ball

What to Do

1. Rub a very small amount of hand cream onto your hands.

2. On the outside of the energy ball are two metal strips. Hold the ball with your thumb on one metal strip and your index finger on the other strip.

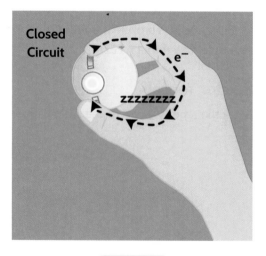

Figure 2

What Happened

The ball flashes a red light and buzzes. This happens because there is a battery, light, and buzzer inside the ball. When you touch the two metal strips, your hand acts as a conductor, which closes the circuit.

Yes, without even the slightest electric tingle, your body bridges the gap between the two metal strips, thus closing the circuit so there can be a flow of electric energy.

YES!! The energy ball is safe. There is so little current produced that even dry skin can block the flow of electrons. That is why hand cream is first applied to the skin. The human body is a conductor of electricity, but it also adds resistance to the flow of electric energy.

Challenge ⭐

Can you explain why the energy ball in Figure 3 lights up and buzzes?

Figure 3

Think!

- The four children are standing in a circle and hold hands, except two.
- Two of the children in the circle are not touching hands; instead these two are touching the metal strips on the energy ball; this makes the energy ball a link in the circle.
- The energy ball works when a conductor bridges the gap between the two metal strips; the bodies of the children form a conductor; electric current passes from the energy ball through the children and back into the ball.

NOTE Although they're not visible, there is a battery, an LED, and a buzzer connected in series inside the ball.

See for Yourself

I wonder... What effect does the number of people in the circle have on the light and sound of the energy ball? Discover this for yourself!

Part III

ASTRONOMY

Astronomy is the study of **celestial bodies**, which are natural bodies in space. In other words, astronomy is the study of the physical Universe as a whole. **Universe** is the name for all things in space, including Earth. At one time, the Universe was considered to be composed of only what could be seen in the sky with the unaided eye; everything in the sky seemed to rise above the horizon, move across the sky, and set below the opposite horizon. This put Earth at the center of the Universe with all other celestial bodies circling it. This **geocentric** model that made Earth the center of the Universe did not fit all observations. Thus, in time the **heliocentric** model of the Universe was suggested, with the Sun being the center of the Universe. Both views limited the Universe to only things visible to the unaided eye, which is amazing when you think of how many planets were identified. Early sky observers were only designing models of our **Solar System**, which is composed of the Sun with celestial bodies moving around it at different distances.

Today, it is known that our Solar System is not the entire Universe; instead, it is a very tiny part of a **galaxy** (a group of millions of stars, gas, dust, and other celestial bodies) called the Milky Way. This galaxy is just one of many galaxies in the Universe. It is also known that our Sun is not in the center of the Universe, being only in the center of our Solar System, which consists of eight major planets revolving around the Sun.

The Universe is much vaster than was believed by early astronomers, and as such we need special ways to measure distances as well as identify the position of visible celestial bodies. You will discover a few of the measuring units used by astronomers as well as how to measure sky distances with your hands.

The Sun and other stars are luminous, meaning they produce their own light; planets and moons, however, are nonluminous, but even so they appear to give off light. You will investigate the reflective power of a celestial body, which is called its albedo.

Earth's gravity pulls on the Moon; the Moon's gravity pulls on Earth. It's like a tug-of-war between these two bodies, which results in the two moving as a unit as if physically connected. The Moon rotates on its axis and at the same time revolves around Earth; but there is more: as part of the Earth–Moon system, the Moon and Earth revolve around the Sun. There is so much movement going on and some of it will be explored in this astronomy unit.

Last, but certainly not least, are stars. Ancient stories were made up about groups of stars, called constellations, which are shapes created by imaginary lines between the stars. Some shapes are easy to see, while others take a real stretch of the imagination.

Space Measurements

In this unit, we study different space measurements, including linear measurements for straight line distances and angular measurements for curved paths. Linear distance measurements from Earth to or between other celestial bodies include astronomical units (AU) and light-years.

- One AU is equal to the distance between Earth and the Sun, which is about 93 million miles (150 million km).
- One light-year is the distance that light can travel in the time of one Earth year.

One of the angular distance measurement units is degrees (°). This is different from temperature measurements in degrees, but has the same symbol. An angular degree simply measures angles based on the distance around a circle being 360°. Thus, one degree is 1/360 of a circle. Angular measurements of celestial bodies, such as the position of the Moon or stars above the horizon, can be made using your hands. Holding your fist at arm's length, the width of your fist is about 10°. Other hand measurements for measuring angular distances will be used to investigate angular distances between stars.

Apparent measurements are only the comparison of the size or distance of celestial bodies. For example, the Moon and the Sun both appear to be about the same size in the sky, when actually the Sun is 400 times larger than the Moon. Even so, at times the Moon eclipses the Sun. Eclipse means to move in front of and block one's view of the other body. How this can happen when the actual sizes of the bodies may not be the same will be investigated.

Albedo is a measurement without units: It is a comparison of the amount of light received by a surface to the amount of light that is reflected. Neither the Earth nor the Moon is luminescent (meaning to produce light). Even so, light from the Moon (moonlight) falls on the Earth, and light from the Earth (earthshine) falls on the Moon. This apparent contradiction will be explained in this unit.

CAUTION Never look at the Sun. It can permanently damage your eyes.

62 Models of the Universe

Aristotle (384–322 BC) was possibly the most important scientist for over 2000 years. What Aristotle thought was viewed as the absolute truth. Aristotle taught that the Universe was everything visible in the sky and that it all revolved around the Earth.

Later scientists, such as the Greek astronomer Ptolemy (AD 100–170), proposed a model for Aristotle's **geocentric** (Earth-centered) ideas for the Universe. Ptolemy's model had a motionless Earth with other celestial bodies revolving around it. You have to admit that this makes sense; when you observe the sky, the Sun, the Moon, and stars do appear to move across the sky together. So, let's start with the geocentric universe model and discover how it compares with the **heliocentric** (Sun-centered) model that was proposed by the Polish astronomer Nicolaus Copernicus (1473–1543) in a book published after his death in 1543.

See for Yourself

Materials

yardstick (meterstick)

piece of poster board 22 by 28 inches (55 by 70 cm)

pencil

piece of string 26 inches (65 cm) long

black marker

What to Do

1. Lay the yardstick (meterstick) across the middle of the poster board, parallel with the longest side.

2. Using the pencil, make nine small dots on the poster board next to the yardstick, one every 3 inches (7.5 cm) from the end. The last dot will be 1 inch (2.5 cm) from the edge of the poster board.

3. Tie a loop in one end of the string.

4. Insert the pencil point through the loop and stand the point on the second dot from the left side of the paper. Pull the string outward to stretch it over the first dot. Hold the string on the first dot with your thumb as you move the pencil across the poster board to draw as much of a circle as possible.

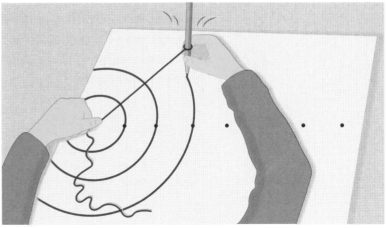

Figure 1

5. Repeat step 4 for each of the remaining dots; for each dot start with the pencil point on the dot, and then stretch the string to the first dot where the string will be held.

6. Using the marker, draw circles at each dot and add the names of the celestial bodies in this order from Earth: Moon, Mercury, Venus, Sun, Mars, Jupiter, and Saturn, with stars beyond Saturn.

What Happened

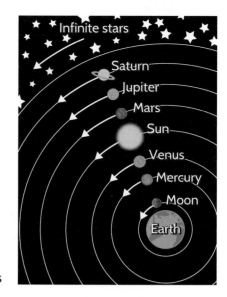

Figure 2

You have made a geocentric model of the Universe as Ptolemy and other scientists believed it to be.

No one seriously questioned Ptolemy's model until 1543, when Nicolaus Copernicus's book was published suggesting that the Sun was the center of the Universe. This is called the heliocentric (Sun-centered) model. Copernicus was not the first to view the Universe as sun-centered. The astronomer Aristarchus (310–230 BC) introduced this idea more than a thousand years previously, but few accepted it.

Challenge

Compare Figure 2 with Figure 3. Can you describe how these two models differ?

Think!

- "Geocentric" means Earth-centered while "helio-centric" means Sun-centered.
- Note that when one switches the position of Earth and the Sun, the order of the planets remains the same.
- The Moon, Sun, and planets all orbit Earth in the geocentric model. In the heliocentric model, the Moon orbits the Earth and as a pair they orbit the Sun, as do other planets.

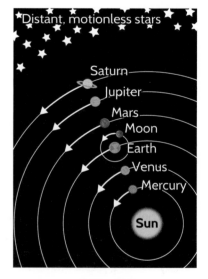

Figure 3

Space Measurements

The **astronomical unit (AU)** is mostly used to measure distances within our Solar System. One AU is the distance between the Sun and the Earth, which is 93 million miles (150 million km). To model the distances between celestial bodies, a scale must be used. This type of scale is not for weight measurements; instead, it is a ratio of a linear distance on the model used to represent the actual distance in space. For example, a scale of 1 AU/10 cm means that, since the actual distance from Earth to the Sun is 1 AU, on the model this distance is represented by 10 cm (Figure 1). Using a scale of 1 AU/10 cm, a reasonably small model comparing distances between celestial bodies within our Solar System can be made.

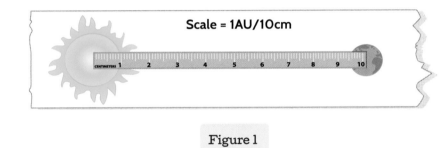

Scale = 1AU/10cm

Figure 1

See for Yourself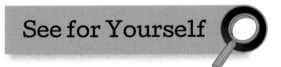

Materials

roll of adding machine tape 2¼ inches (5.6 cm) wide

scissors

transparent tape

meterstick or metric measuring tape

black markers

colored markers (optional)

What to Do

1. Measure and cut 132 inches (330 cm) of paper from the roll of tape.

2. Lay the long paper strip on a table or the floor. Secure the left end with tape.

3. Draw the Sun as shown in Figure 2 on the left end of the strip. Make a dot in the center of the Sun.

4. Add the celestial bodies listed in the following table. For each celestial body, measure their distance from the center dot of the Sun. Make a dot to represent the center of the celestial body.

Celestial Body	Distance (in AU)	Distance (in cm)
Sun	0	0
Mercury	0.4	4
Venus	0.7	7

Celestial Body	Distance (in AU)	Distance (in cm)
Earth	1.0	10
Mars	1.5	15
Asteroid belt	2.8	28
Jupiter	5.2	52
Saturn	9.6	96
Uranus	19.2	192
Neptune	30.0	300

5. Add information, such as names of the celestial bodies (Figure 2).

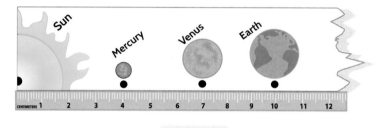

Figure 2

What Happened ?

A scale model of the distances from the Sun to each planet and the asteroid belt in our Solar System was made. Using the scale

1 AU = 10 cm, the distance from the Sun to Neptune, the outermost planet, is 300 cm.

The AU unit is too small to measure distances outside our Solar System, such as to stars. Astronomers created another unit called a **light-year**: the distance that light moving at a speed of 186,000 miles (300,000 kilometers) every second will travel during one Earth year.

Challenge ★

Using Figure 3, can you calculate the distance of one light-year in kilometers?

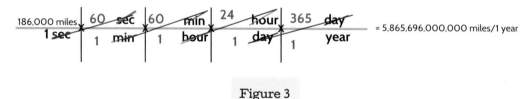

Figure 3

Think!

- Light travels 300,000 kilometers in 1 second; the problem is finding out how many kilometers it travels in 1 year. Figure 3 shows the dimensional analysis for changing the time unit of second to the time unit of year.
- All that needs to be done is to replace 186,000 miles with 300,000 km, and then do the calculations. Now it is your turn.
- If your calculations are correct, the answer will be 9,460,800,000,000 kilometers per year. WOW!

64 Apparent Sizes of Celestial Objects

The **apparent size** of objects is how large they appear to a viewer. At a distance, objects appear to be smaller than they really are. This is especially true for celestial bodies. The Sun is about 400 times larger than the Moon; yet in the sky, the two appear to be circular disks with about the same diameter. When Earth, the Moon, and the Sun are in line with each other (in that order), viewing from Earth, the Moon blocks light from the Sun. This is called a **solar eclipse** and occurs because the Moon is closer to Earth than the Sun is, giving it a larger apparent size. All objects close to you look bigger than they would at a distance.

Figure 1

See for Yourself

Materials

pencil
white blank paper
scissors

masking tape
your thumb!

What to Do

1. Draw a large circle on the paper.

2. Cut the circle out and tape it to a wall at eye level.

3. Stand in front of the paper and as far away as possible.

4. Close your left eye, and hold your right thumb at arm's length from your open right eye.

5. Sight the white circle and determine how much of the object your thumb covers up.

6. Slowly move your thumb toward your open eye until it is close to but not touching your eye. As you move your thumb, make note of how much of the white circle is covered by your thumb.

Figure 2

As the distance between your eye and your thumb decreased, your thumb blocked more of your view of the white circle. The closer your thumb was to your eye, the larger was its apparent size in comparison to the white circle. The same thing happens with the Moon and the Sun. Although the Sun is about 400 times as large as the Moon, the Sun is about 400 times farther from the Earth than is the Moon. So, to an observer on Earth, the apparent sizes of the Moon and the Sun are the same. Thus, from Earth, the Moon and the Sun appear to be equal-sized disks in the sky.

Challenge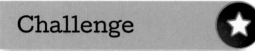

Can you explain why the telephone poles in Figure 3 get smaller and smaller?

Figure 3

Think!

- The diagram represents the apparent size of telephone poles at different distances from a viewer.
- The telephone poles, like your thumb in the previous activity, are larger when closer to the viewing point.
- You can conclude that the apparent size of the telephone poles decreases with distance from the viewer.

65 Angular Distances

In order to compare and describe the position of celestial bodies viewed in the sky, a method of measuring the distance between them is needed. As an observer on Earth, the sky appears to be a dome with its circular edge resting on the horizon. Celestial bodies appear to rise from one horizon, move across the sky, and set below the horizon on the opposite side. This is an angular movement, thus is measured in the **angular measurement** unit of degrees (°).

No! Scientists have not regressed by using an imaginary dome; instead, it has allowed them to create sky maps showing the apparent location of celestial bodies in relation to each other from day to day throughout the year. The angular distance from one horizon to another, through the **zenith** (highest point) of the sky dome, is 180°. Distance above the horizon is called **altitude**. The angular measurement around the horizon where the imaginary sky dome rests is 360°. A measurement *on* the horizon is called the **azimuth**, which begins at due north, 0°, and ends at due north, completing 360°.

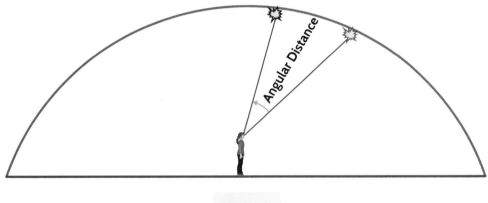

Figure 1

One of the simplest measuring tools to measure angular distance is your hand. While this may not be the most accurate method, hand measurements are good enough to measure approximate angular distances.

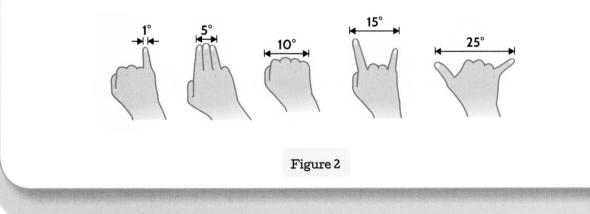

Figure 2

See for Yourself

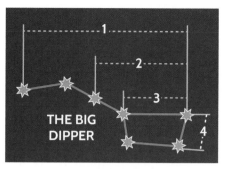

Figure 3

Materials

your hands

What to Do

1. On a clear, dark night, stand outside facing north.

2. Look for a group of stars that look like the Big Dipper in Figure 3.

3. Hold your hand at arm's length, and referring to the hand measurements in Figure 2, measure the five angular distances between the stars in the Big Dipper.

What Happened ?

All hand measurements are to be made at arm's length. The ratio of the size of a person's hand to their arm length is about the same for everyone. Thus, generally, the angular measurements in Figure 2 work for everyone.

The four angular distances between the Big Dipper stars are: (1) 25°; (2) 15°; (3) 10°; and (4) 5°.

Challenge ★

The altitude of celestial bodies is their angular distance above the horizon. **Can you explain how to use your hands to measure the altitude of the Moon or a star?**

Think!

- When the Moon has risen above the horizon, use your hands to determine its altitude.
- The altitude of the Moon in Figure 4 is equal to the angular measurement of two fists, which is equal to 20°. From experience, you know that the Moon's altitude will increase as it apparently moves across the sky.

Figure 4

Sun Shadows

Shadows are the results of light being blocked by an object. Outdoors, objects cast shadows because they block light from the Sun. The length of sun shadows is affected by the Sun's altitude. The direction of sun shadows is affected by the Sun's azimuth, which is its angular direction on the horizon. Azimuth readings give specific angular readings that basically tell **cardinal directions** of north, east, south, and west. Without access to azimuth measurements, sun shadows can be used to discover cardinal directions.

See for Yourself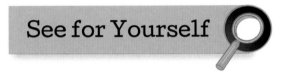

Materials

dowel rod, 24 inches (60 cm) or longer
hammer or large rock

5 or more small stones
outdoor area

What to Do

1. On a sunny day, select an open outdoor area that will not be disturbed during the day.

2. Ask an adult to sharpen one end of the dowel rod.

3. Use a hammer or large rock to beat the pointed end of the rod into the ground. Ask an adult to help you with this. You want the rod to be sturdy and vertical.

4. On the ground, use a stone to mark the tip of the shadow cast by the rod. Record the time.

5. You want to observe and mark the sun shadow cast by the dowel rod at least five times: early morning, mid-morning, solar noon, mid-afternoon, and late afternoon. If you start the experiment after noon, complete the experiment by starting again in the early morning of the next day.

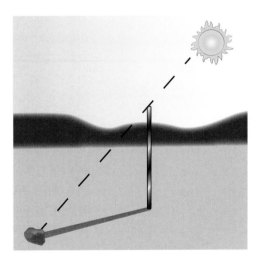

Figure 1

What Happened

The smaller the solar altitude angle, the longer is the sun shadow. At sunrise, the solar altitude angle is equal to zero; when the Sun is rising above the horizon, shadows are very long and pointing in a westerly direction. At sunset the shadows are again long but point in an easterly direction. Thus, the longest sun shadows are always at sunrise and sunset. The shortest shadows are at **solar noon**, when the Sun is at its highest point in the sky. In the Northern Hemisphere, the Sun appears to move across the southern sky; thus, at solar noon the Sun is at its highest altitude and shadows formed point due north.

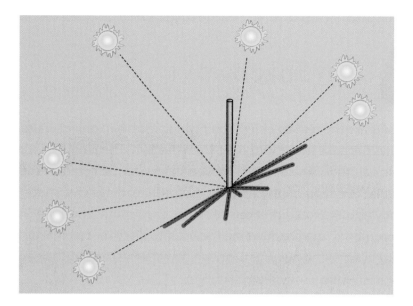

Figure 2

Challenge ⭐

Can you explain how your shadow can be used to determine the directions north, south, east, and west?

Think!

The girl's shadow points opposite the Sun; thus, knowing that the Sun sets in the west, she can identify the other three directions as shown.

FYI: The Sun doesn't rise and set at due east and due west, respectively, all year long, but shadows can give you general directions.

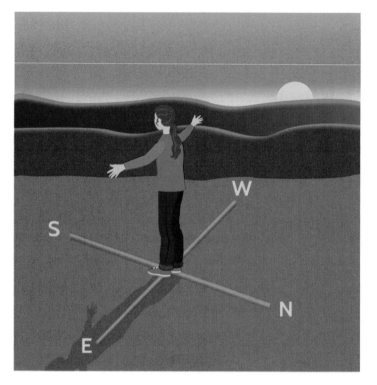

Figure 3

67 Albedo

The reflective power of a celestial body is called its **albedo**, which refers to the ratio of the amount of light received to the amount of light reflected from an object. An albedo of 1 indicates a shiny surface with perfect reflection; an albedo of 0 indicates a totally black surface with no reflection. Earth's albedo is 0.30 and the Moon's albedo is 0.12.

Stars are **luminous** bodies, which means they produce their own light, while planets and their moons are nonluminous. Even though planets and moons do not produce their own light, they shine because they reflect sunlight.

See for Yourself

Materials

black marker
2 sheets of blank paper
transparent tape
medium-size box with one side at least the
   size of the paper

flashlight
3 or 4 books
ruler

What to Do

1. Use the marker to draw a stick figure on one sheet of paper and a circle to represent the Moon on the second sheet.

2. Tape the stick-figure paper to the wall and the paper with the moon to one side of the box.

3. Stand the box about 12 inches (30 cm) from the wall with the paper-covered side of the box facing the stick-figure paper.

4. Use the books to raise the flashlight so that it is at an angle to the moon paper on the box and its light hits the center of the moon (Figure 2).

5. In a darkened room, turn the flashlight on, and then observe the brightness of the stick-figure paper taped to the wall.

Figure 1

Figure 2

What Happened ?

Light from the flashlight illuminated the moon paper. When light hits an opaque surface, like the paper on the box, the surface absorbs some of the light and the rest is reflected. In this activity, the moon paper reflected a lot of the light it received from the flashlight; thus, the stick figure and surrounding paper were illuminated. This models sunlight striking the Moon's surface and being reflected. To an observer on Earth, the Moon appears as a white disk in the sky. You only see the Moon because sunlight reflects off the Moon's surface to your eyes; this reflected light is called moonlight; reflected light from Earth is called earthshine.

Challenge ★

If the bright part of the Moon in Figure 3 is reflected sunlight, **can you explain the source of light being reflected from the dark area?**

Think!

- As the Moon revolves around Earth, sunlight hits different parts of the Moon's surface. Thus, only part of the Moon's surface facing Earth is lit; the parts facing Earth that are not reflecting sunlight are visible because of earthshine.

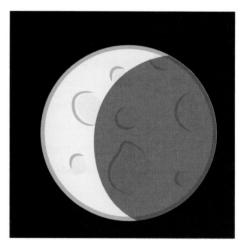

Figure 3

The Moon

The Moon appears as a disk to viewers on Earth. In this unit, you will discover that, although the Moon rotates on its axis as it revolves around Earth, the same part of the Moon always faces Earth. In other words, the "backside" of the Moon has never been viewed from Earth. The Moon rotates, yet only one side faces Earth; this fact will be investigated in this study of the Moon.

Moons are natural satellites, meaning they revolve around another celestial body. As the Moon revolves around Earth, different portions of the Moon disk facing Earth are illuminated by sunlight. The shapes of these lighted areas are called moon phases. When the Moon disk is completely illuminated, the phase is called a full moon. When the Moon disk has no illumination, it is dark and is called a new moon. The time it takes the Moon to go through all of its phases is about 29 days and this is called a lunar month.

During the development of each moon phase, the line of separation between the lit and dark part of the Moon's disk is called the terminator. You will investigate moon phases in this unit and discover how to use the terminator to identify a waxing or a waning phase.

Following the new moon, more and more of the Moon's disk facing Earth is lit by sunlight. The phases are said to be waxing (getting bigger), meaning the lighted part is increasing. The first phase is seen about 24 hours after the new moon phase. This phase is called the waxing crescent phase, and looks like a small, curved section with pointed ends. About 7 days after the new moon, half of the Moon disk facing Earth is lit. This is called the first quarter phase because about one-fourth of the lunar month has passed. The next phase is waxing gibbous, which has a greater lit area than the first quarter phase, but less than the full moon phase. During full moon, the entire Moon disk is lit.

Following the full moon, the Moon goes through the same phases in reverse. These phases are said to be waning (getting smaller), meaning the lighted part is decreasing. The waning phases are waning gibbous; the third quarter, when half of the lit side Moon disk is visible and three-fourths of the lunar month have passed; and waning crescent. Then the cycle begins again with the new moon.

The Moon rotates on its axis while it revolves around Earth. The pull of gravity between Earth and the Moon keeps these celestial bodies together as a unit while they revolve around the Sun.

68 Moon Phases

The Moon is a **natural satellite** that orbits Earth in about 27.5 days. The Moon's orbit is at an angle to Earth; so, when Earth is between the Moon and the Sun, the side of the Moon facing Earth is fully illuminated. This is called the **full moon**. When the Moon is between Earth and the Sun, the lighted side of the Moon faces the Sun and the unlit side faces Earth and is called the **new moon**.

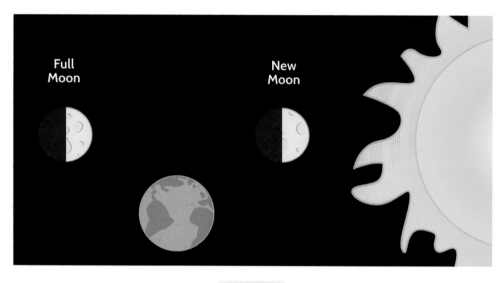

Figure 1

When the Moon is in its orbit around Earth, it appears as a disk in the sky with different portions of the disk lit during a lunar month of about 29 days. The portion of the Moon disk that is lit forms a shape that continuously changes. Each shape has a specific name.

See for Yourself

Materials

2 sheets of black construction paper
piece of white chalk

scissors

What to Do

1. Fold one sheet of black paper in half twice, first from top to bottom, and then from side to side.

2. Use the chalk to draw the largest circle possible on the folded paper, and then cut out the circle, cutting through all four layers. You have four black circles.

3. Repeat steps 1 and 2 using the remaining piece of black paper.

4. Set one of the black paper disks aside. This black disk represents the new moon phase.

5. Use the chalk to color white parts on the remaining seven disks to represent the moon phases shown in Figure 2.

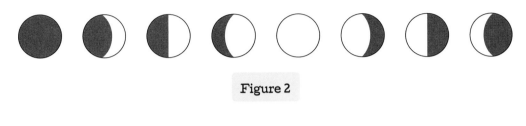

Figure 2

What Happened ?

The lighted and unlighted parts of the moon during a lunar month have been prepared.

Challenge ★

Can you identify the disks that represent each of the eight moon phases?

Think!

- **New:** The entire Moon disk is dark.
- **Waxing crescent:** A largely dark Moon has a crescent white shape on the right. (It looks like a white banana shape to me.)
- **First quarter:** Half of the Moon disk is white on its right side. One-fourth of the lunar month has passed.
- **Waxing gibbous:** The white part has a hump shape or is convex on both sides. The remaining dark area is on the left.
- **Full:** The entire disk is white.

Following a full moon, the moon phases have shapes that are mirror images of those following the new moon.

- **Waning gibbous:** The white part has a hump shape or is convex on both sides. The remaining area on the right is dark.
- **Third quarter:** Half of the Moon disk is white on its left side. Three-fourths of the lunar month has passed.
- **Waning crescent:** A largely dark Moon has a crescent white shape on the left.

The Terminator

Starting with the full moon phase, an observer on Earth sees the Moon as a white, disk-shaped object in the night sky. From one day to the next, the white disk changes shape as the white, lighted part decreases; the moon is waning. One could imagine that a hand is pulling the night sky over the lighted disk until there is only a dark disk. The line separating the lighted and unlighted part of the disk is called the terminator, which in the Northern Hemisphere always moves across the Moon eastward, from right to left.

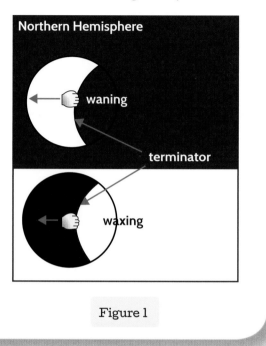

When the moon is waxing, the lighted area is increasing; it changes from a new moon to a full moon. This time, the imaginary hand is pulling a blanket of light across the darkened disk. A dynamic model can demonstrate the movement of the Moon's terminator during a lunar month.

Figure 1

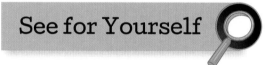

See for Yourself

Materials

2 sheets of blank white paper   drawing compass
pencil   ruler
scissors   black marker

What to Do

1. Fold one of the sheets of paper in half, placing the short sides together. Crease the fold.

2. Mark a line across the bottom edge of the paper and 4 inches (10 cm) from its fold.

3. Using the drawing compass, draw a circle with a 2-inch (5-cm) diameter in the center of the folded paper. Cut out this circle, cutting through only one layer.

4. Fold the open bottom edge of the paper along the line. You want only the two ends of the paper envelope to be open.

5. Cut a long strip from the second sheet of paper with a width of about 3.5 inches (8.75 cm) and a length of 11 inches (28 cm). This is the terminator strip.

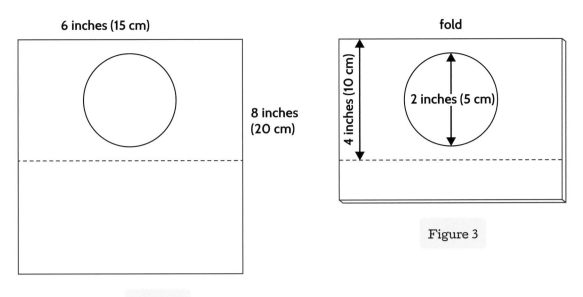

6 inches (15 cm)

8 inches
(20 cm)

Figure 2

fold

4 inches (10 cm)

2 inches (5 cm)

Figure 3

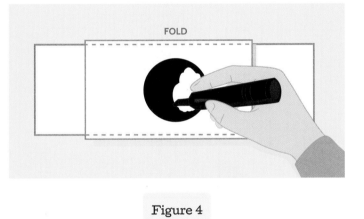

FOLD

Figure 4

6. Insert the strip of paper into the moon phase envelope until the center of the strip is beneath the cutout circle.

7. Use the cutout circle as a guide and the black marker to color a black circle on the terminator strip.

What Happened ?

A dynamic model of the movement of the Moon's terminator line was made.

Challenge ★

Can you use the model to demonstrate how the terminator line moves during a lunar month in the Northern Hemisphere?

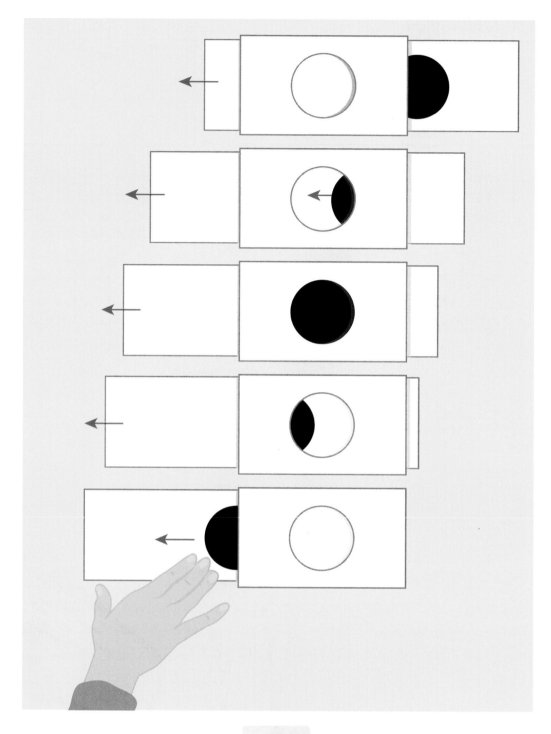

Figure 5

Think!

- Pull the terminator strip through the envelope to the left. The first phase observed in the cutout section is the full moon.
- The terminator line is moving to the left and pulling a black shade over the lit part of the Moon. The phases are waning.
- The Moon has no lit parts. This is the new moon phase. The terminator line always begins on the right side of the Moon. It is now pulling a lit shade to the left over the Moon.
- Back to a full Moon. A complete lunar month has passed.

FYI: Moving the strip to the right demonstrates Moon phases viewed from the Southern Hemisphere.

70 Barycenter

The orbital path of the Moon is not around Earth; instead, the Moon's orbit is around a point inside Earth; this point is called the **barycenter** between the two celestial bodies. Gravity between Earth and the Moon keeps these two celestial bodies together, thus they form a Moon–Earth unit. The center of mass of this unit is their barycenter. The barycenter is within the surface of Earth. Don't be confused about this. The barycenter is not a specific place on Earth, such as in Texas or Germany. Instead, it is a point in space between two objects.

The Earth doesn't stay in position as the Moon circles it. Instead, the Moon and Earth both orbit the barycenter. A model helps to visualize this motion of the Earth–Moon unit.

See for Yourself

Materials

dowel rod, 36 inches (90 cm) long
string, 24 inches (60 cm) long

baseball-size piece of modeling clay

What to Do

1. Place a small ball of clay on the end of the dowel rod.

2. Tie one end of the string near the end of the rod opposite the small clay ball. Secure the free end of the string to the edge of a table where the dowel rod can freely swing around.

3. Use the remaining clay to form a ball around the end of the rod that has the supporting string, so the string is embedded within the surface of clay as shown in Figure 1.

4. Add more clay (and move the string along the rod a little if necessary) until this system balances.

5. Once the system is balanced on the string, push one end so that it spins around the supporting string.

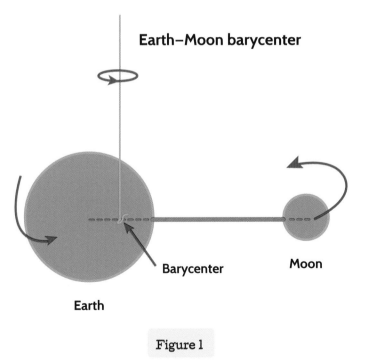

Figure 1

The barycenter is within the larger clay ball; thus, the string sticks out of the large clay ball. The movement of this model represents how the Moon orbits a spot in space that falls within Earth. The model does not properly represent how Earth orbits around this spot.

Challenge

Can you explain Figure 2?

Figure 2

Think!

- A tug-of-war struggle appears to be happening between Earth and the Moon. The gravitational pull of each of these celestial bodies is pulling on the other. There is no winner; instead, they continue to rotate on their own axis but act as a unit that revolves around the Sun.
- There is a big difference between the mass of Earth and the mass of the Moon. When considering the mass of both celestial bodies, the center of gravity of their combined masses lies within Earth's surface. This is the barycenter of these two bodies that are forever bound together.
- If Earth and the Moon were of equal mass, the barycenter would be exactly halfway between them. It's because Earth is so much larger that the barycenter is so much closer to the center of Earth.

71 Moon Motion

The Moon has two motions: **rotation** about its own axis, and **revolution** around Earth. The Moon revolves around Earth and rotates on its axis in about 27.5 days. Since the Moon rotates once during its revolution about Earth, the same side of the Moon always faces Earth.

See for Yourself

Materials

a chair

What to Do

1. Set a chair where you can easily walk around it.

2. Stand facing the chair. Make note of the wall you are facing.

3. Continue to face the chair as you move around it. Make note of how the background changes as you make one complete revolution. Make note of any changes in your body position in order to face the chair.

Figure 1

Figure 2

What Happened ?

You modeled the Moon during one revolution around the Earth when you faced the chair as you moved around it. You modeled the Moon's single rotation on its axis as you made slight adjustments so that you continued to face the chair. This simple activity demonstrates why only one side of the Moon faces Earth.

Challenge ⭐

Can you relate these two Moon movements: revolution about the Earth and rotation?

Think!

- The Moon revolves around Earth once in about 27.5 days.
- The Moon rotates once about its own axis in about 27.5 days.
- The Moon rotates at the same rate that it revolves around Earth.

Constellations

Constellations are groups of stars that appear to form patterns in the sky. What stars you see in the sky depends on your latitude, which is the angle of your location from Earth's equator. When you look at the sky at night, you see only the stars that are above your horizon. Below your horizon is another set of stars that are visible to observers at different latitudes on Earth. The stars an observer would see at Earth's North Pole (latitude 90° N) are totally different from the stars viewed by an observer at Earth's South Pole (latitude 90° S).

At the North Pole, constellations revolve around a center star, Polaris, which is called the North Star: the star the north end of Earth's axis points toward. These constellations are called the northern circumpolar constellations (Figure 1). At the Earth's most northern point, latitude 90°, Polaris is directly overhead with the constellations appearing to move around it. At lower latitudes, Polaris is seen lower in the sky and some of the circumpolar constellations dip down below the horizon. One of the activities in this unit investigates how an observer's latitude affects the position of Polaris in the sky. Note that higher and lower latitudes do not refer to elevation; instead they refer to an angular distance from the equator.

The apparent path of the Sun in the sky is called the ecliptic. Along this path are 12 constellations called the zodiac constellations. These constellations seem to provide a background for the Sun, the Moon, and the planets, which appear to move in front of the zodiac constellations as they move across the sky. Because Earth revolves around the Sun each year, a different zodiac constellation is visible from Earth during different time periods. As you investigate the 12 zodiac constellations in this unit, you will discover what it means for the Sun "to be in" Aquarius or in one of the other zodiac constellations.

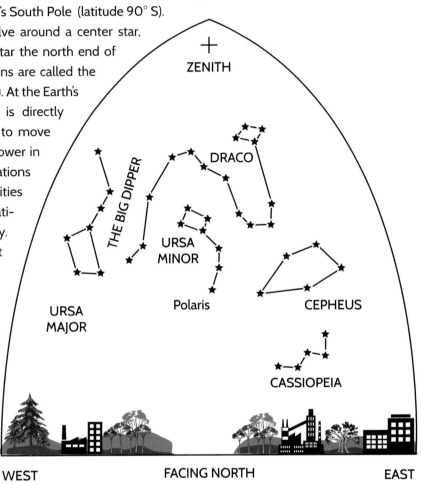

NORTHERN
CIRCUMPOLAR CONSTELLATIONS

Figure 1

Circumpolar Constellations

Polaris is called the Pole Star or North Star because it apparently remains in the same place in the sky: almost exactly above the North Pole, night after night. Face Polaris and you will be facing north. Thus, to your right is east, to your left is west, and directly behind you is south.

Observe the sky for a period of time and you will find that from night to night some stars appear in the sky all year, while others are seasonal. These stars are part of constellations called **circumpolar constellations**, because they move in circular paths around Polaris, the Pole Star. Like horses on a carousel, the stars spin around a center point but still stay in line with one another. Thus, the shapes of constellations do not change even though they appear in different places during the night and on different nights of the year. From latitudes of 40° N or greater, the four most visible northern circumpolar constellations are Ursa Major, Ursa Minor, Cassiopeia, and Cepheus.

See for Yourself

Materials

sheet of black paper
pencil with eraser at end

pushpin
scissors

What to Do

1. Cut a circle as large as possible from the black paper.

2. Fold the circle in half twice, first from top to bottom, and then from side to side.

3. With the pencil and the star pattern in Figure 1 as a guide, mark the position of each star on the paper shown in Figure 1. Mark Ursa Major, Ursa Minor, Cephus, and the other constellations if there is room.

4. Using the pushpin, make a hole in the paper for each star.

5. Turn the circle upside down, and then push the pushpin through the star Polaris and into the end of the pencil's eraser. Turn the paper to hollow out the hole so the paper circle can be easily rotated.

6. During the day, darken the room, and then hold the end of the pushpin against a window.

7. Slowly turn the paper so that it rotates counterclockwise around the pushpin.

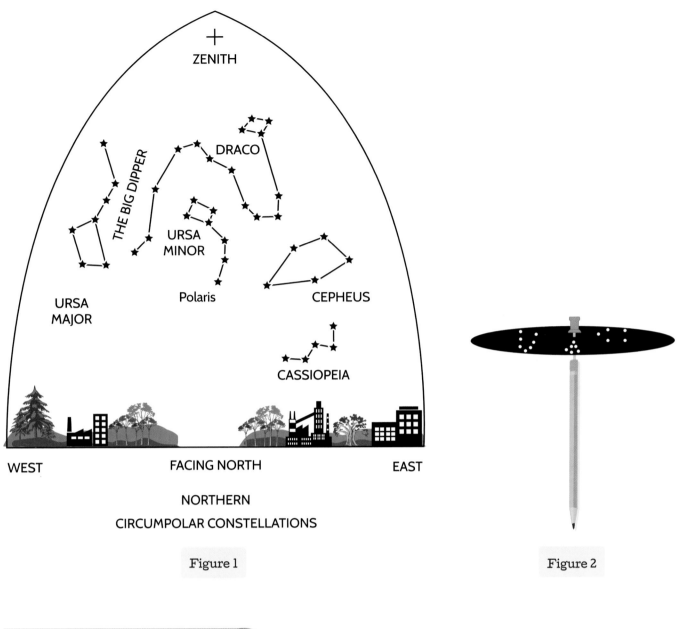

ZENITH

DRACO

THE BIG DIPPER

URSA MINOR

URSA MAJOR

Polaris

CEPHEUS

CASSIOPEIA

WEST

FACING NORTH

EAST

NORTHERN
CIRCUMPOLAR CONSTELLATIONS

Figure 1

Figure 2

What Happened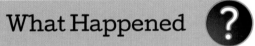

You have made a model of the movement of northern circumpolar constellations. The apparent counterclockwise movement of these stars around Polaris is actually due to the clockwise rotation of Earth about its axis.

Earth not only rotates on its axis, but also changes position in the sky in relation to the stars as it revolves around the Sun. Earth's movement around the Sun causes a slight change in the southern part of the sky seen each day. This results in different stars being visible during each season. But Earth's North Pole continues to point toward Polaris, so the northern circumpolar stars remain the same during the year.

Study Figure 3. Can you choose the star group – A, B, or C – that correctly represents the location of Polaris from the position of the Big Dipper?

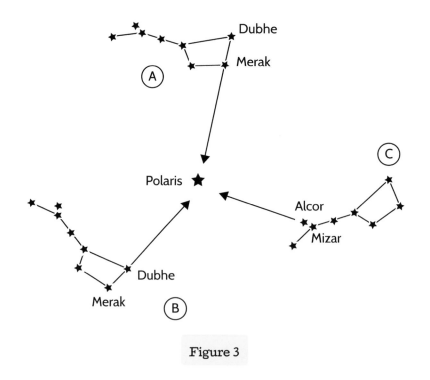

Figure 3

Think!

- The bowl of the Big Dipper always points toward Polaris.
- A line from the star Merak and continuing past Dubhe points to Polaris.
- Position B represents the location of the Big Dipper in relation to Polaris, the North Star.

73 Location of Polaris

Polaris is a star in the constellation Ursa Minor, which translates as "Little Bear." Polaris can only be seen by observers in the Northern Hemisphere. Even there, the position of Polaris above the horizon depends on the latitude of the observer. At the equator (latitude 0°), Polaris is on the horizon; at the North Pole (latitude 90°), Polaris is directly overhead. Thus, as one moves from the equator to the North Pole, Polaris is seen at increasingly greater altitudes above the horizon.

See for Yourself

Materials

masking tape
3 ft (0.9 m) of string
coin
ruler
yardstick (meterstick)
marker
index card
adult helper

What to Do

1. Tape one end of the string to the coin. Ask your helper to tape the free end of the string to the center of the top of a doorframe. Adjust the length of the string so that it is about 6 inches (15 cm) above your head. Note: Choose a doorway that leads into a second room with a far wall.

2. Place a piece of masking tape on the floor beneath the coin. Label the tape "North Pole." Measure 6 ft (1.8 m) from this piece of tape and place a second piece of tape on the floor labeled "equator."

3. Draw a line across the index card and label it "horizon."

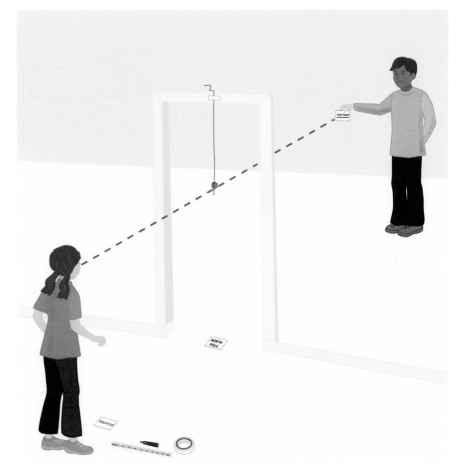

Figure 1

4. Stand behind the "equator" tape. Close one eye and look at the coin.

5. While you are looking at the coin, ask your helper to position the card against the far wall so that the horizon line on the card lines up with the bottom of the coin. The card needs to be taped in this position.

6. As you look at the coin, slowly walk toward it. Make note of how the bottom of the coin lines up with the horizon line on the card.

What Happened ?

At the equator line, the coin appears on the horizon. As you move away from the equator toward the North Pole, Polaris (the coin) rises above the horizon. The same results would happen if you could quickly walk from Earth's equator toward Earth's North Pole. The altitude of Polaris is the same as the latitude of the observer.

Challenge ★

Using the globe in Figure 2, can you determine the altitude that Polaris would be at for each observer, A and B?

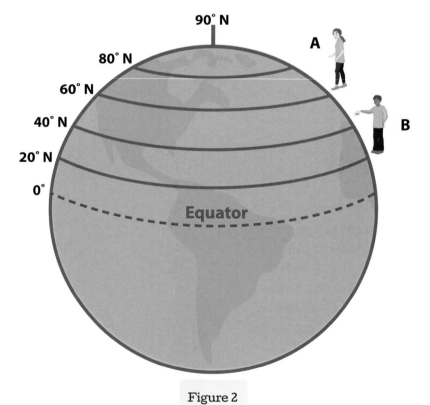

Figure 2

Think!

- The altitude of Polaris above the horizon is equal to the latitude of the observer.
- Observer A is standing at latitude 60° N; thus, Polaris would be visible at an altitude of 60° above the horizon.
- Observer B is standing at latitude 20° N; thus, Polaris would be visible at an altitude of 20° above the horizon.

74 Zodiac Constellations

The apparent yearly path of the Sun around the celestial sphere is called the **ecliptic**. The ecliptic runs through a band on which 12 constellations lie, called the **zodiac constellations**. As seen from Earth, the zodiac constellations provide a background for the other planets. This is because their orbits around the Sun all lie nearly in the same plane as Earth's orbit. The planets appear to move in paths near the ecliptic through the zodiac constellations. The planets that are visible with the naked eye are Mercury, Venus, Mars, Jupiter, and Saturn.

Astronomers sometimes use the zodiac constellations to point to the location of the Sun and the planets at a particular time. At specified times, the Sun and the planets are said to be "in" constellations. Figure 1 represents the position of Earth when the Sun is in Pisces. The brightness of the Sun's light prevents constellations from being seen during the day. If they could be seen, then the end of an imaginary line from Earth through the Sun would point toward the constellation Pisces. The Sun is "in Pisces" from February 19 through March 20.

The approximate dates the Sun is in different zodiac constellations are listed in the following table. The Sun is relatively stationary and does not move in front of the zodiac constellations; instead, it is the Earth's motion around the Sun that apparently changes the position of the Sun during the year.

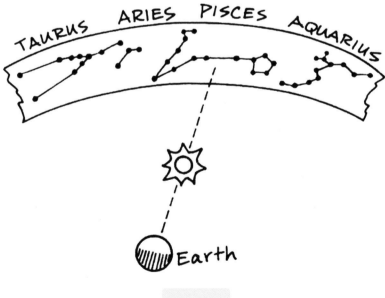

Figure 1

Aries	March 21 – April 19
Taurus	April 20 – May 20
Gemini	May 21 – June 20
Cancer	June 21 – July 22
Leo	July 23 – August 22
Virgo	August 23 – September 22
Libra	September 23 – October 22
Scorpio	October 23 – November 21
Sagittarius	November 22 – December 21
Capricorn	December 22 – January 19
Aquarius	January 20 – February 18
Pisces	February 19 – March 20

See for Yourself

Materials

12 sheets of paper
marker
masking tape

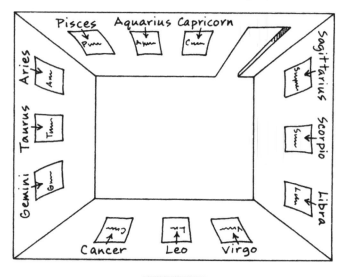

Figure 2

What to Do

1. Print the names of the zodiac constellations on the sheets of paper, one name per sheet.

2. Tape three of the papers to each of the four walls in a room at a height slightly higher than the height of your helper, as shown in Figure 2. Note that the constellations are in a counterclockwise order by dates.

3. Ask your helper to stand in the center of the room.

4. Stand facing your helper so that one of the constellations, such as Aries, is directly behind your helper.

5. Slowly walk around your helper in a counterclockwise direction, but continue to face your helper.

6. As you walk, notice the constellations on the wall directly above your helper's head. Stop when you get back to Aries.

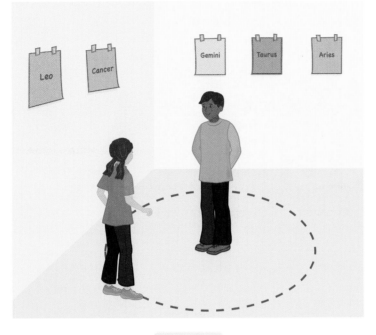

Figure 3

What Happened ❓

Different constellations appear above your helper's head as you move. Your helper's head represents the Sun, and you, Earth. The names on the papers and their positions on the wall represent the zodiac constellations in the sky and their positions in the sky (but not their distances from one another). It takes Earth 1 year to make one complete trip around the Sun. During the year, the Sun *appears* to move into each of the 12 zodiac constellations.

Challenge ⭐

Can you identify the zodiac constellation that will be viewed in the nighttime sky when the Sun is in Aquarius?

Think!

- When the Sun is "in Aquarius," you would be facing your helper with Aquarius above your helper's head.
- Facing your helper represents daytime. Since you represent Earth, all you have to do to view the stars in the nighttime sky is to turn around.
- The zodiac constellation directly across from Aquarius is Leo, with Virgo on one side and Cancer on the other.

CAUTION Never look at the Sun. It can permanently damage your eyes. Always use a star map of the zodiac to know when the Sun is "in" a zodiac constellation.

Part IV

EARTH SCIENCE

Earth science is the study of the planet that we live on. Studying earth science, like any other science, hones our problem-solving skills. The different sections on earth science in this unit, as with other units in this book, are presented as exploratory investigations. This means a step-by-step procedure is given with an explanation of what happened. My objective in selecting this style of experimentation is to provide you with research information. Science is all about asking questions, researching, and discovering answers via experimentation.

The three primary fields of earth science studies are geology, meteorology, and oceanography. **Geology** is the study of the solid part of Earth, **meteorology** is the study of Earth's atmosphere, and **oceanography** is the study of Earth's oceans. Geology and meteorology are primarily represented in this book, with some information being given on oceanic tectonic plates.

Earth's **atmosphere** is the blanket of gases that surround Earth. The movement of these gases affects daily weather as well as weather over a region for a period of time, which is called the region's **climate**. The atmosphere is actually very heavy; the weight of the atmosphere on a given area of land depends on the amount of air above that land. Being a gas, the molecules of gas in air can move apart or be squeezed closer together. Thus, the **atmospheric pressure**, which is the weight of air in any specific region on Earth, can change. One thing about atmospheric pressure is that it is not just directed downward. Remember, air is a gas and can move in any direction. Thus, atmospheric pressure pushes things on Earth from all directions. Without air pressure, you would not be able to drink through a straw. You will investigate this, as well as questions such as "why is the sky blue?" and "what is the Coriolis effect (and does it make toilet water swirl differently north and south of the equator)?" I hope you have fun as you discover the geological and meteorological information in this unit.

Geology

Geology means "study of the Earth." This part of earth science deals with the structure and composition of Earth. Geologists study Earth in search of fuel and mineral resources; they study the composition of rocks and minerals and the processes by which they are formed.

Geology includes the study of natural hazards, such as volcanoes. Models for erupting volcanoes make interesting science projects, so one of the activities in this unit provides a procedure for the construction of such a model. Hopefully, this fun model will be a stepping stone leading to inquiring questions about volcanoes, followed by further studies and investigation.

Geology is a study of the internal parts of Earth. Earth is not a solid rock; instead, it is composed of layers with different chemical compositions, densities, and physical states; some layers are solid, some liquid, and one layer is semi-solid, meaning it is not a liquid nor a solid but has properties between these two states of matter and is called non-Newtonian because it doesn't behave like other fluids described by Newton. The composition of Earth is known through studying seismic waves, which are energy waves created by earthquakes, volcanic eruptions, and other disturbances that cause rocks within Earth to vibrate. Seismic waves push and pull on rocks in the same way as sound waves push and pull on air molecules. In this unit, you will investigate the refraction of seismic waves by observing the path of a material moving from one medium into another. Thus, the densities of Earth's layers can be compared by studying the refraction of seismic waves.

Geology is a study of the forces that result in changes in Earth's structure; forces that cause Earth's surface to be deformed and cause earthquakes, volcanoes, faults, and other disturbances of Earth's surface. In other words, geology is a study of geological stress, which is pressure (force per area) placed on rocky structures. In this unit on geological stresses, the idea that Earth's surface is actually broken into huge blocks called tectonic plates that float on the semi-solid mantle of Earth is introduced. Activities in this unit will lead you to answer questions about geological stress, such as "Why is the Atlantic Ocean getting wider, while the width of the Pacific Ocean is decreasing?" and "Why do some parts of Earth crack open under stress while other parts form hills and valleys?"

75 Density of Earth's Layers

Earth is not one big solid rock; instead, it is made up of different layers. The four main layers from inside out are the inner core, outer core, mantle and the crust, the thinnest layer covering the outside. Each layer from the crust to the inner core increases in density, with the center of Earth being the most dense. Scientists use the energy waves released from earthquakes to compare the densities of Earth's interior materials.

See for Yourself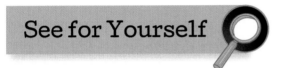

Materials

scissors

ruler

duct tape

large bowl

10 or more coins

helper

pitcher of water

What to Do

1. Cut a 2-inch × 2-inch (5-cm × 5-cm) square piece of tape.

2. Set the bowl on a table, and then stick the piece of tape inside on the center of the bottom of the bowl.

3. Hold one coin between your thumb and index finger. Rest your hand that is holding the coin on the edge of the bowl.

4. Try to drop the coin onto the piece of tape. Adjust the position of your hand until a coin can be dropped onto the tape. Observe the direction of the coin as it falls through the air.

5. Remove the coins from the bowl and ask your helper to fill the bowl with at least 4 inches (10 cm) of water.

6. Repeat steps 3 and 4, dropping coins one at time into the water. Observe the direction of the coins as they pass from air into the water.

Figure 1

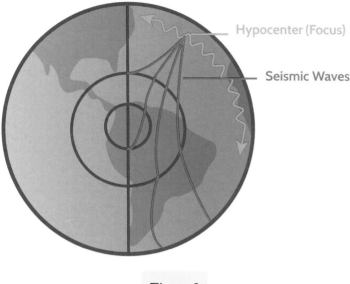

Figure 2

The coins drop straight when falling through the air, but change direction when they move from air to water. This change of direction is much like light changing direction when it passes from air into a glass lens. The change of direction occurs at the boundary between the air and the water, which indicates there is a change in the density of the material. **Seismic waves** are energy waves caused by earthquakes. The underground point where an earthquake starts is called the hypocenter, or focus. These waves would travel in a straight path if the interior materials of Earth were all the same density. **Seismologists** are scientists who study earthquakes. These scientists observe the paths of seismic waves, which, like the falling coins, change direction when passing through the different interior layers of Earth. This gives clues to the position, thickness, and density of materials within Earth.

Challenge ★

Using the basic procedure of the previous activity, can you design a model representing the different density layers of Earth?

Think!

- The coin changed direction because water is denser than air.
- Corn syrup has a density greater than water.
- A simple model could be made using a glass with a layer of corn syrup, water, and air.
- The coin will change direction at the boundary between each layer of material.

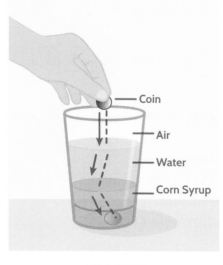

Figure 3

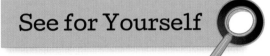
Models can be an important part of a science presentation. A lightweight volcano model that can be easily transported as well as repeatedly used is relatively easy to make with paper and plaster.

See for Yourself

Materials

2 poster boards at least 17 inches (42.5 cm) square

scissors

pencil

empty plastic bottle, 8 oz (240 mL)

masking tape

round tray with a diameter of at least 14 inches (36 cm)

2 cups (500 mL) of plaster of Paris

plastic throwaway container, 3 cups (750 mL)

measuring cup, 1 cup (250 mL)

tap water, 1 cup (250 mL)

plastic spoon

3 liquid tempera paint colors: brown, black, and red

art brush

goggles, face mask and gloves

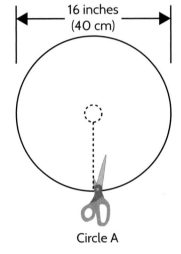

16 inches (40 cm)

Circle A

Figure 1

CAUTION Plaster of Paris is a fine powder. Wear goggles and take care not to get the powder in your nose. Never mix the plaster with your hands because it gets hot and could burn your skin. Never pour plaster down the drain; it could clog the drain. Discard the container and stirring stick used to make the plaster.

What to Do

1. Draw a circle on each poster board, one with an 8-inch (20-cm) radius and the other with a radius of 7 inches (17.5 cm). Let the larger circle be called "A" and the smaller one "B."

2. Cut out the circles.

3. Use circle A to prepare a cone for the volcano using the following:

   - Use the pencil to draw a circle in the center of circle A about the size of a quarter.
   - Cut out this small circle by cutting from one edge of the paper, then around the drawn circle (Figure 1).

4. Stand the plastic bottle in the center of paper circle B. Overlap the cut edges

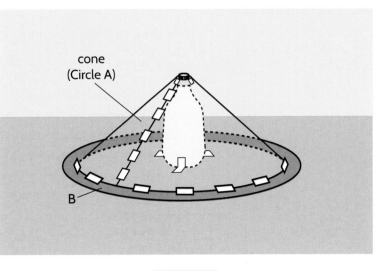

cone (Circle A)

B

Figure 2

Figure 3

of circle A to form a cone with a small open end around the bottle and adjust the amount the edges overlap so that the cone's height is equal to that of the bottle. The mouth of the bottle should be at or near the small open end of the cone. Secure the overlapped edges of the cone with tape.

5. Use tape to secure the mouth of the bottle to the small hole in the cone.

6. With the cone centered on paper circle B, secure the edges of the cone to paper circle B with tape (Figure 2). You have made the foundation for a volcano.

7. Place the volcano foundation in the tray.

8. Prepare the plaster of Paris by pouring the water into the container and then adding the plaster. Stir with the plastic spoon.

9. Spread the wet plaster of Paris over the surface of the paper cone and base. Make the surface as rough as possible. Allow the plaster to dry, which will take 20 to 30 minutes. FYI: As the plaster dries, it gives off heat because an exothermic reaction is taking place.

10. Use the paint to color the volcano. Paint red stripes down the sides to represent lava flow.

What Happened ?

You have made a model of a volcano that has a durable outer structure with a bottle inside that can work as the magma chamber and vent. A magma chamber is a large pool of liquid rock (magma) beneath the surface of the Earth. A vent is an opening to the Earth's surface through which magma can flow. At the surface magma is called lava.

Challenge ★

Can you design a method for modeling a volcanic eruption?

Think!

- You need something that will react and cause fluid and gas to rise out of the volcano model. Effervescent tablets, such as Alka-Seltzer, produce gas bubbles when added to water.
- Liquid dishwashing soap produces large volumes of bubbles when gas is blown into it.
- Lava is so hot that it glows red, so red food dye could be added.
- Pour water, liquid dishwashing soap, and red food dye into the bottle, and then add the effervescent tablet. The amounts needed of each is something that can be discovered experimentally.

See for Yourself

An erupting volcano is always a fun demonstration, especially when it can be repeated. Follow the directions above and see for yourself!

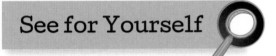

77 Evaporites

Evaporites are a type of rock formed by the evaporation of water from a solution of salt and water. There are different kinds of salt, and table salt, or sodium chloride, is one of them. A solution of sodium chloride and water is called **brine**. Sodium chloride is a mineral in seawater. When seawater **evaporates**, the dissolved minerals can be recovered. **Halite** is an evaporite formed when water from seawater evaporates leaving dry crystals.

See for Yourself

Materials

2 tsp (10 mL) table salt
tap water
measuring cup, 1 cup (250 mL)
stirring spoon
scissors

sheet of black
   construction paper
shallow cooking pan
magnifying lens

What to Do

1. Make a mineral solution by mixing the salt and ½ cup (125 mL) of water in the measuring cup using the stirring spoon.

2. Cut the black paper to fit in the bottom of the pan.

3. Pour the salt–water solution over the black paper in the pan.

4. Set the pan in a warm area where it will not be disturbed. (Outdoors in the Sun if possible.)

5. Periodically observe the contents of the pan until the paper is dry.

6. Observe the halite crystals formed on the paper using the magnifying lens.

Figure 1

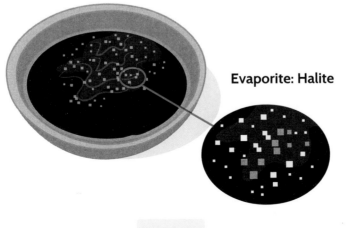

Evaporite: Halite

Figure 2

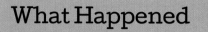
Salt dissolving in water
NaCl + H₂O

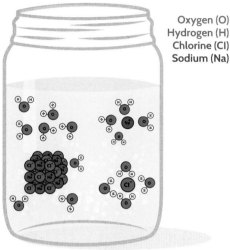

Oxygen (O)
Hydrogen (H)
Chlorine (Cl)
Sodium (Na)

Figure 3

The crystals formed are composed of the ionic compound, sodium chloride. Ionic compounds break up into positive and negative ions when mixed with water. Water molecules are bipolar, meaning they have a a positive and a negative side as shown in Figure 3. The charged sides of water pull on the ions that make up crystals of salt. The water molecules basically pull salt crystals apart. Once separated from the crystal, the salt ions are surrounded by water molecules.

As the water evaporated from the salt–water solution, the distance between the sodium and chloride ions decreased. These positive and negative ions are attracted to each other. With fewer water molecules to separate the charged salt ions they join together forming a cubic-shaped crystal. The size of these crystals depends on the number of layers of sodium and chloride ions. The black paper provided a background making the salt crystals more visible. Sodium chloride crystals formed in nature by the evaporation of water from seawater are considered to be a type of sedimentary rock called halite.

Challenge

Can you explain how sea salt is harvested from shallow outdoor pools of seawater?

Think!

• What has to happen to remove salt from seawater?

The water must be removed, and this can be done by evaporation.

Figure 4

• What effect does the depth of the pools have on recovering the sea salt?

In shallow pools, sunlight can penetrate and heat the water. In deep pools of water, light intensity decreases with depth, thus surface water warms up faster than deeper water. The evaporation rate of water increases as its temperature increases.

• What effect does the surface area of the pools have on the rate of evaporation?

Water molecules evaporate from the surface of a body of water. Thus, the larger the surface area the greater the rate of evaporation.

Fossils

Paleontologists are scientists who study prehistoric life on Earth. They do this by searching for **fossils**, which are traces of the remains of prehistoric organisms buried in the Earth's crust. Preserved remains of prehistoric organisms, such as bones or shells, are known as **body fossils**. Tracks, trails, burrows, and other indirect evidence of prehistoric life are called **trace fossils**.

Figure 1

Fossils are not always the actual remains of organisms; instead, many are just copies. There are three ways that copies of fossils are formed: **imprint fossils** are impressions made in soft materials; **mold fossils** are cavities underground left when the organism decays; and **cast fossils** are formed when minerals fill mold fossils forming the shape of the organism. You can model the process for the formation of a cast fossil.

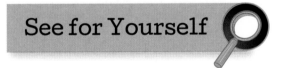

Materials

seashell (found where crafts are sold)
piece of modeling clay twice the size of the
   seashell used
paper plate
jar of petroleum jelly
paper cup, 7 oz (210 mL)

plastic spoon
1 tbsp (15 mL)
plaster of Paris
tap water
goggles, face mask and gloves

CAUTION Plaster of Paris is a fine powder. Wear goggles and take care not to get the powder in your nose. Never mix the plaster with your hands because it gets hot and could burn your skin. Never pour plaster down the drain; it could clog the drain. Discard the paper cup and plastic spoon used to make the plaster.

Figure 2

What to Do

1. Squeeze the clay until it soft and pliable, and then place the clay on the plate.

2. Coat the outside of the seashell with a thin layer of petroleum jelly.

3. Press the lubricated side of the seashell into the clay. You want as much of the shell pressed into the clay as possible.

4. Carefully remove the shell from the clay. If a good imprint of the shell is not made in the clay, repeat the process.

5. Wearing goggles, thoroughly mix together 4 tablespoons of plaster of Paris with 2 tablespoons of water in the paper cup.

6. Pour the plaster mixture into the shell imprint in the clay.

7. Allow the plaster to harden (about 20 minutes).

8. Gently separate the clay from the plaster.

9. Compare the shape and texture of the outside of the shell with that of the plaster cast.

What Happened ?

The imprint of the shell in the clay and the outside of the shell are mirror images. The outside of the plaster cast and the shell are identical.

Challenge ★

Can you explain how the previous activity modeled the formation of fossil imprints, molds, and casts?

Figure 3

Think!

- Pressing the shell into the clay and removing it represents a fossil imprint made in soft mud that was preserved when the mud hardened.

- You removed the shell leaving a **mold** of the seashell. In nature, the shell would have been totally buried in mud that hardened into rock around the shell. Over time, ground water dissolved the seashell, leaving a cavity shaped like the shell.

- You filled the seashell mold with plaster, which hardened into what is called a **cast** (a reproduction that has the same outer shape as the seashell). In nature, the mold of the seashell would be filled with mud or mineral materials that would harden into a cast.

79 Tectonic Plates

Earth's crust and the uppermost layer of the mantle form a layer called the lithosphere. This layer of Earth is believed to be broken into seven large pieces with multiple smaller pieces in between. These pieces are called tectonic plates. The entire lithosphere is like jigsaw puzzle pieces resting on moving magma produced near Earth's core. This hot magma rises and spreads out beneath the tectonic plates where it cools and sinks down again. This rising and falling of magma creates large heat convection cells beneath the plates resulting in their movement. Magma pushes through to the surface in some places, such as the thinner oceanic plates; magma forces plates apart; at Earth's surface, magma is called lava, and it cools filling the void left by the diverging (separating) plates.

Yes, this is happening in the Atlantic Ocean floor; its width increases about ½ inch to 4 inches (1 to 10 cm) each year. No, Earth is not expanding; while the Atlantic Ocean floor is growing at divergent boundaries, between plates the Pacific Ocean floor is shrinking at convergent boundaries where ocean plates are sinking beneath continental plates and continuing down into the mantle. You can model this diverging and shrinking of oceanic plates.

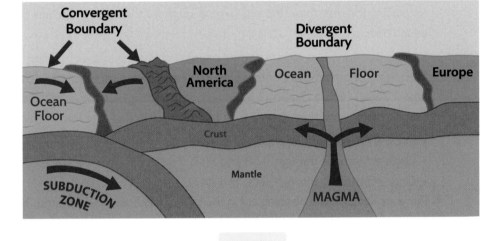

Figure 1

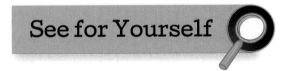

Materials

scissors

roll of adding machine tape

ruler

cardboard shoe box

transparent tape

marker

What to Do

1. Cut a section out of the side of the shoe box so you can easily put your hands inside as shown in Figure 2.

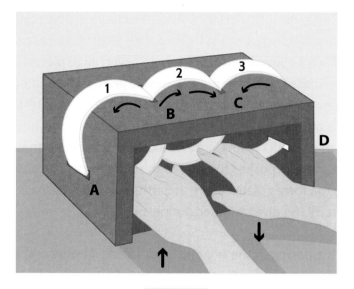

Figure 2

2. Cut four slits in the box, two on the top and one on each side. Use Figure 2 as a guide for placing the slits; make the slits large enough for the adding machine tape to be easily pulled through.

3. You need to construct three separate paper circles using strips of adding machine tape. The length of the tape depends on the size of the box. Once you decide on how long the tape for each circle must be, complete one circle at a time; thread the end through the slits describe below; tape the ends of the paper strip together forming a circle.
   - Circle #1 threads through slit A and slit B.
   - Circle #2 threads through slit B and slit C.
   - Circle #3 threads through slit C and slit D.

4. Put your hands in the opening cut in the side of the box. Hold the strips between your index and second finger of each hand.

5. Slowly and simultaneously pull down on two strips and push up on the other set of strips as shown in Figure 2.

What Happened ❓

The paper circles move in and out of the box. The strips represent the movement of tectonic plates at convergent and divergent boundaries. Divergent boundaries are where tectonic plates are pushed apart and convergent boundaries are where tectonic plates are pushed together.

The place where one tectonic plate is moving beneath another is called a **subduction zone**. Divergent boundaries are called **constructive boundaries** because more land is produced; convergent boundaries are called **destructive boundaries** because one plate sinks under the other or the two plates collide and move upward forming a mountain.

A transform boundary is a third type of tectonic boundary; this boundary is referred to as a conservative boundary because there is just a change in the position of the plates; plates slide sideways.

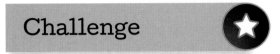

Challenge ⭐

Can you identify the type of tectonic plate boundary that might have caused the movement of Earth's crust shown in Figure 3?

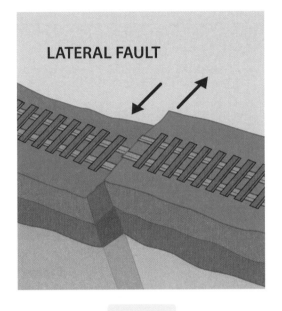

Figure 3

Think!

The crust appears to be split and moving sideways. When tectonic plates converge but the plates are not particularly deformed (instead the two plates are conserved), this is called a transform boundary.

Deformation

The crust of Earth is deformed when put under stress. **Stress** is pressure (force per area) applied to a surface. When stress causes rocks to change shape, the rocks have undergone **deformation**. The degree of deformation of a rock depends on the type of rock, temperature, the type of stress, and where the stress is applied, as well as how long the stress has been applied. Types of deformation can be modeled with a wooden skewer.

See for Yourself

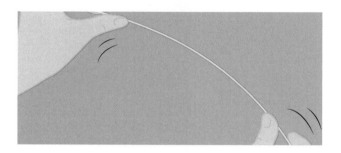

Figure 1

Materials

3 wooden skewers

What to Do

1. Prepare the skewers:

   - Cool one skewer in the freezer.
   - Warm one skewer outdoors in the Sun or another warm place.
   - Leave one skewer at room temperature.

   After 15 minutes or more, continue with the experiment.

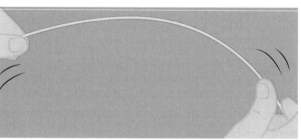

Figure 2

2. Using the skewer at room temperature, hold its ends with your thumbs gently pressing against the skewer. Apply just enough pressure to slightly bend the skewer, and then release it.

3. Using the warm skewer, place your hands as in step 2, but slowly bend the skewer farther without breaking it and hold it in this position for 30 seconds or longer before releasing it.

4. Using the cold skewer, place your hands closer to it center, and then quickly apply enough pressure to break the skewer.

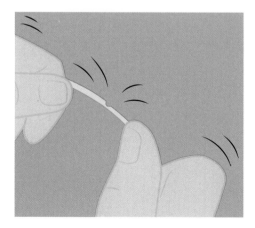

Figure 3

Rocks along tectonic plate boundaries are under stress. When rocks bend but return to their original shape, it is called **elastic deformation**. The bending of the skewer at room temperature modeled this.

When rocks bend under stress but do not return to their original shape, it is called **ductile deformation**. The warmed skewer is an example of ductile deformation. Warming the wooden skewer made the wood more pliable. Keeping the warmed material under stress for a time allowed the wood to cool and remain in the new shape. Hills, mountains, and valleys are formed where the stress of colliding tectonic plates pushes the rock layers upward.

When rocks along plate boundaries break, it is called **brittle deformation**. Any material that breaks demonstrates brittle behavior. Rocks break when they have reached their **elastic limit**. Rocks, or any materials that are cold and receive quick forceful stress, are more likely to break. This was represented by the breaking of the cold wooden skewer.

Challenge ⭐

Can you describe the possible deformation process that occurred in Figure 4?

Think!

- The rock layers are bending upward, thus a compression force has been applied squeezing the rocks together. This resulted in an upward movement of the rock layers.
- The lower layers show plastic or ductile deformation in that they are deformed but not broken.
- Part of the top layer is smooth, but sections have large cracks, representing brittle deformation.

Figure 4

81 Fold Mountains

Fold mountains form as a result of the colliding of two tectonic plates. This usually occurs at a **compression** boundary between two continental tectonic plates. The plates are bent and folded forming a small rocky outcrop, a hill, or a mountain, or, if continued movement occurs, an entire mountain range. This geological process is called **orogeny**, which takes millions of years to occur. You can, however, model orogeny in a few seconds.

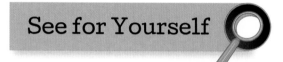

See for Yourself

Materials

4 or more different-colored hand towels

What to Do

1. Stack the outstretched towels one on top of the other on a table.
2. Place your hands on opposite ends of the towels.
3. Slowly push the ends of the towels toward the center.
4. Observe the shape of the towels.

Figure 1

What Happened

Pushing from opposite directions causes the towels to be squeezed into folds. The result is a surface with a wavelike appearance. Forces pushing toward each other from opposite directions are called compression forces. Such forces between two continental tectonic plates can slowly squeeze and push the rocks in these plates upward forming folds like those of the stack of towels. **Folds** are a type of **plastic** or **ductile deformation**.

Challenge

Can you explain why compression stress might cause one material to crumble (Figure 2) while another material forms folds?

Think!

- Materials that are more pliable are more likely to fold under compression stress. This is called plastic or ductile deformation.
- Brittle materials are more likely to break or crumble under compression stress. This is called brittle deformation and is even more likely to occur if the materials are cold and the stress is sudden.

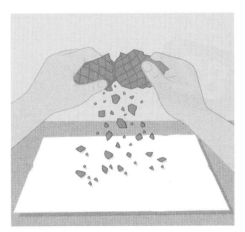

Figure 2

82 Tension

Tension is a type of geological stress that tends to stretch things, much like the rubber hose in Figure 1. If the hose is stretched too far, it will remain deformed. If the tension is released before the elastic deforming limit is reached, the hose will rebound; it will shrink back to its original shape.

Figure 1

When rock layers are stretched, they have a lot of potential energy that converts to rebound energy or kinetic energy when the tension is removed. Rebound energy can be great enough to cause an **earthquake**, which is a violent shaking of Earth's surface. A rubber strip can be used to demonstrate rocks stretching under tension and the affect their rebound energy has on the surface above it when they return to their original shape.

See for Yourself

Materials

scissors
long, thin rubber band
ruler
shallow baking pan

helper
blank sheet of paper
table salt

What to Do

1. Cut the rubber band to make one long strip.

2. Measure the length of the rubber strip. Be sure not to stretch the strip during this measurement.

3. Lay the strip in the center of the pan. Hold the ends of the rubber strip against the bottom of the pan.

4. Ask your helper to lay the paper over the rubber strip and then cover the paper above the rubber strip with salt.

5. Hold tightly to the ends of the rubber strip and stretch the strip as far as possible. Make a note of any movement of the paper and salt.

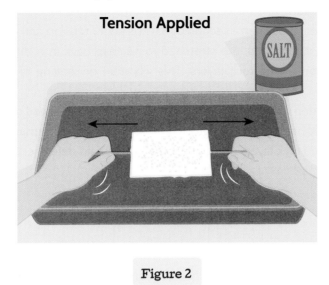

Figure 2

6. Release both ends of the rubber strip at the same time. Observe the movement of the rubber strip, the paper, and the salt.

7. Measure the length of the rubber strip again and compare it with the first measurement.

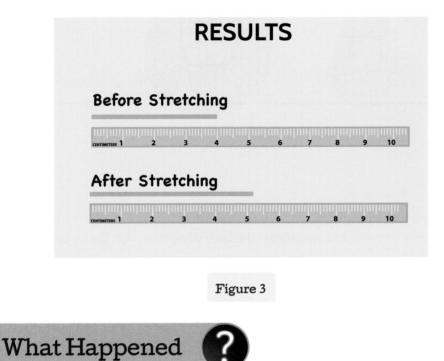

Figure 3

What Happened ?

As the rubber strip was being stretched, there was a slight movement of the paper and salt particles. When the rubber strip was released, the paper moved more and salt was thrown in all directions. If any of the salt was left on the paper, it would have been on either side of an empty space directly above where the rubber strip had been.

The movement of the rubber strip as it stretched tapped against the paper, causing the salt particles to separate. As the molecules in the rubber strip were pulled apart, the **potential energy** (stored energy) inside the strip increased. This potential energy quickly changed to kinetic energy (energy of moving objects) when the rubber strip snapped back to is natural position. This sudden release of energy caused the strip to vibrate, thus causing the paper and salt particles to vibrate.

Like the rubber strip, when a section of Earth is under tension, the rocks are stretched. When the tension is removed, the stretched rocks snap back into their normal position resulting in vibration of the rock layers. This vibration or shaking of Earth is called an earthquake.

If the rubber strip was longer after it was stretched, it represented ductile deformation. If the rubber strip did not change in length, it represented elastic deformation. Like the rubber strip, some stretched rock layers do not rebound and remain deformed while others return to their original shape.

Challenge ⭐

Can you explain the deformation of the black square drawn on the balloon in Figure 4 when the balloon is inflated?

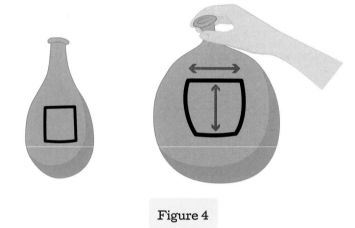

Figure 4

Think!

As the balloon was inflated, the black square was stretched out in all directions. In other words, adding air to the balloon resulted in the latex being stretched; the air applied tension to the latex resulting in the black lines being stretched. The square enlarged.

See for Yourself

When the air is released from the balloon, does the square return to its original shape and size or does it model ductile deformation?

83 Normal and Reverse Faults

Faults are cracks in Earth's crust where parts of the crust move in relation to one another. Typically, faults are formed at or associated with tectonic plates, but they do occur in other places. Normal faults are where the hanging wall moves down; these faults usually occur at divergent boundaries. Normal is not used because they are the most common type of fault, but because one side of the fault moves down in response to gravity. The side that slips down is called the hanging wall and the other block is called the footwall.

A reverse fault (Figure 1) is opposite to a normal fault with the hanging wall moving up due to compressive stress, such as at converging plate boundaries. Figure 1 shows an easy way of identifying the two blocks making up a fault. Note a rock climber is hanging from the hanging wall, while another is sliding down the footwall.

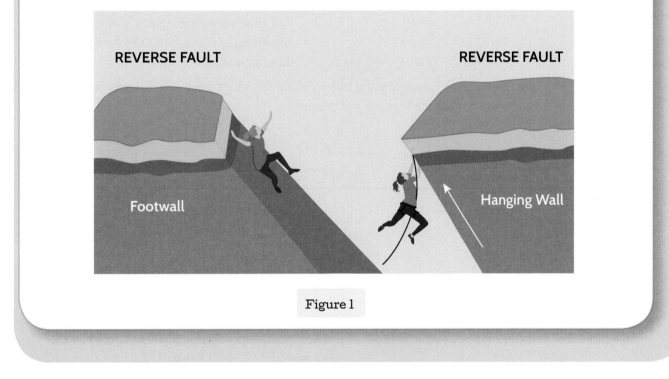

Figure 1

Materials

2 lemon-size pieces of clay of
   different colors
table knife
2 toothpicks

square piece of poster board, 8 × 8 inches
   (20 × 20 cm)
marker

NORMAL FAULT

Footwall

Hanging Wall

Figure 2

What to Do

1. Break each piece of clay in half.

2. Shape each piece of clay into a roll about 4 inches (10 cm) long.

3. Lay the four clay rolls together, one on top of the other, alternating the colors.

4. Press the rolls together into one large clay piece. Flatten the sides of the clay piece by tapping them against a hard surface, such as a table.

5. Use the table knife to cut the clay piece into two parts diagonally.

6. Secure the layers in each section together by inserting a toothpick through the layers, top to bottom.

7. Lay the sections together on the square piece of poster board so that the colored layers match up, then move the hanging wall section of the clay layers down as you hold the footwall section stationary.

8. Repeat step 7, reversing the movement of the hanging wall. Hold the footwall stationary while moving the hanging wall upward.

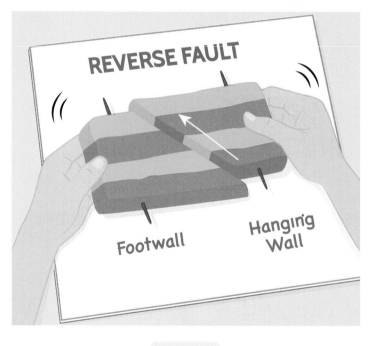

REVERSE FAULT

Footwall

Hanging Wall

Figure 3

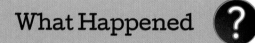

What Happened ?

The clay is cut and shifted so that the layers of colored clay in the two sections no longer form continuous horizontal lines. Each clay color represents a layer of one kind of rock material. Cutting the clay creates two tectonic plates. A crack in Earth's crust doesn't represent a fault; instead, it is the movement of the plates on either side of the crack that designates it as a fault.

The clay pieces were used to first form a normal fault with the hanging wall lower than the footwall. Normal faults generally form when the tectonic plates are diverging; separating from each other. When reversed, a reverse fault was formed. Reverse faults generally form when tectonic plates are converging, slamming into one another.

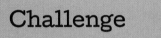
Challenge

Can you identify the normal and reverse faults in Figure 4?

Think!

- Fault A has the hanging wall above the footwall, thus it is a reverse fault.
- Fault B has the hanging wall lower than the footwall, thus it is a normal fault. Remember that this name was arbitrarily given to this structure.
- Fault C was not introduced in the previous activity, but notice the fault blocks are not moving up or down but instead are sliding past each other. The San Andreas fault represents this type of fault, which is a **slip-strike fault**.

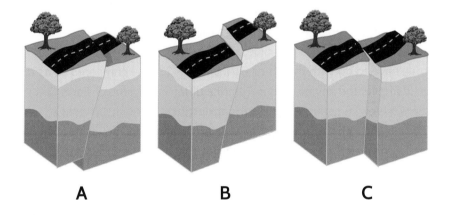

A   B   C

Figure 4

Meteorology

Meteorology is the study of Earth's atmosphere and how it affects Earth. Earth's **atmosphere** is the blanket of gas wrapped around Earth. The atmosphere separates Earth from space; it controls the amount of solar radiation Earth receives by reflecting some of it back into space. It also keeps Earth warm. Earth's atmosphere is what makes Earth's climate moderate compared to the extreme conditions of space.

Weather is the condition of the atmosphere at a specific place and time in regard to air temperature, humidity, wind, rain, cloudiness, and so on. **Climate** is the *average* weather in a specific region over a long period – at least 30 years. The Sun's rays hit different regions of the Earth at different angles, creating distinct climates throughout the world. The effect of the angle of sunrays will be investigated in this unit.

Air, like all matter, has mass, meaning that Earth's gravity will pull the gas particles in air toward the Earth; thus, the atmosphere has weight and applies pressure on Earth's surface. **Atmospheric pressure** is the pressure of the air above an area. You will investigate and see for yourself that air pressure is great enough to push liquids upward against the downward pull of gravity; air pressure can keep a liquid from escaping from a hole in its container.

Sunlight is scattered by molecules of gas in Earth's atmosphere; this action is called **Rayleigh scattering** and can be modeled using a milky colloid solution and a light source. This model explains why the sky is usually blue, as well as why it can be very red at times.

Seasons have to do with the tilt of Earth's axis – 23.5° – compared to its direction of travel. This tilt affects the angle that sunlight hits different regions of Earth during the year. When sunlight travels straight through Earth's atmosphere, the light is not scattered as much as when it travels through the atmosphere at an angle and thus moves through more of the atmosphere. Some areas of Earth receive sunlight that is perpendicular to its surface, while others never do.

Earth's rotation affects the direction of air flow above its surface. The deflection of air masses in the Northern and Southern Hemispheres is opposite; this is due to the **Coriolis effect**, which will be investigated. You will then be able to explain why air masses are deflected differently depending on their geographical location.

84 Climate

Climate is the weather conditions for a region over a long period of time. The **atmosphere**, the blanket of gases surrounding Earth, is responsible for Earth's climate not being as extreme as in space or on other planets. How does the shape of Earth affect its climate? The amount of solar radiation that passes through Earth's atmosphere is the same for all parts of Earth, but because Earth is a sphere, solar rays hit different parts of Earth at different angles. This affects the daily weather as well as the climate of different areas of Earth.

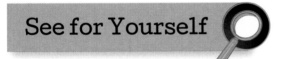 **See for Yourself**

Materials

blank sheet of paper
book about 1 inch (2.5 cm) thick
2 new sharpened pencils with erasers
pen

What to Do

1. Lay the paper on a table.

2. Place the book at one end of the paper.

3. Raise the nonsharpened end of one pencil by resting it on the book so that the pointed end of the pencil touches the paper.

4. Hold the second pencil on top of the first one and slide it downward until its tip just touches the paper.

5. Use the pen to make a mark about 1-inch (2.5-cm) long where each pencil touches the paper. Label the mark "Higher Latitude."

6. Stand the two pencils side by side on the paper.

7. Use the pen to make a mark about 1 inch (2.5 cm) long where the point of each pencil touches the paper. Label the marks "Lower Latitude."

8. Compare the distance between the Higher Latitude marks to the distance between the Lower Latitude marks.

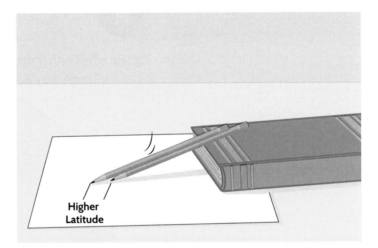

Figure 1

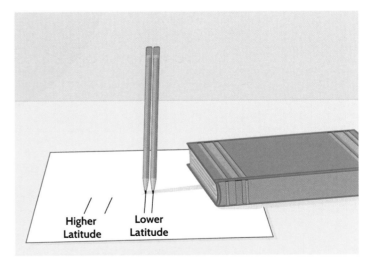

Figure 2

The marks represent parallel rays from the Sun hitting the Earth at different latitudes. Because Earth is a sphere, the rays at higher latitudes are more slanted and are farther apart than those at lower latitudes. Generally, the hottest climates on Earth are at or near the **equator** at latitude 0°, which receives the most direct rays from the Sun. This is represented by the marks for a "Lower Latitude."

As one moves north or south of the equator, the rays of the Sun are more slanted. The slanted marks for "Higher Latitude" are farther apart, thus slanted light rays are more spread out. Generally, the coldest climates are at or near the North Pole and South Pole at latitudes, respectively, of 90° N and 90° S. Climates between latitudes 0° and 90° N or S progressively get cooler as you move to higher latitudes.

Challenge ★

Can you explain why Earth is divided into three climate zones: cold, temperate, and hot?

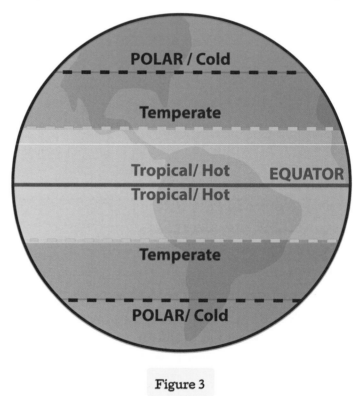

Figure 3

Think!

- The two cold climate zones are near the Earth's North and South Poles.
- At the ends of the Earth, sunrays strike the surface at the greatest angle, thus these zones are heated the least.
- The **tropics** are the two hottest climate zones bordering both sides of the equator. This band receives the most direct sunrays, and thus these zones are heated the most.
- The two temperate zones are between the poles and the tropics. Thus, they are generally hotter than the poles and cooler than the tropics.

85 Atmospheric Pressure

An **atmosphere** is a layer of gas wrapped around a planet or moon. Although Earth's atmosphere extends into space to about 6,200 miles (10,000 km), most of the air is within the first 10 miles (16 km) from the surface.

Atmospheric pressure is the weight of air pressing on a surface. Pressure is a force pressing on a specific area. At sea level, the pressure of air is about 14.7 pounds per square inch (1 atm). This is about a ton of air pushing down on your body. You are not crushed by air because the gases inside your body push back. Since air molecules are moving in all directions, air is pushing on you and every other material on Earth from every direction.

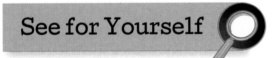
See for Yourself

Materials

pushpin
1 qt (1 L) empty soda bottle with lid
masking tape (or duct tape)

tap water
shallow baking pan
helper

What to Do

Prepare the bottle using the following instructions:

1. Use the pushpin to make two holes in the bottle, one hole at the bottom of the bottle and one at the top.

2. Cover the holes with small strips of tape.

3. Fill the bottle about three-fourths full with water. The water's surface should be below the hole at the top of the bottle. Close the bottle with its lid.

4. Hold the bottle above the pan and ask a helper to remove the tape covering the hole at the bottom.

5. Ask your helper to remove the remaining piece of tape covering the hole at the top of the bottle.

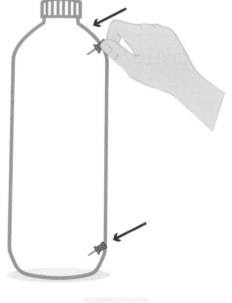

Figure 1

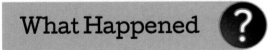
What Happened ?

The air pressure in the closed bottle equals the air pressure outside the bottle. Water did not exit the hole in the bottom of the closed bottle because it had a "skin-like" covering of

Figure 2

Figure 3

Figure 4

water across it. This covering is surface tension due to the attractive forces between surface water molecules and with the molecules surrounding those on the surface. The pressure of the air inside the bottle was not enough to push the water out the hole. Plus, water cannot leave unless air can enter. Any leaking of water would allow the air to spread out, creating a lower pressure.

Removing the tape from the top hole allowed the air outside the bottle to move in so that the air pressure inside and outside the bottle was the same. Now, simultaneously water exits and air enters.

Challenge ⭐

Can you explain how drinking through a straw depends on air pressure?

Think!

- When a straw is placed in a liquid, does the liquid automatically flow up and out of the straw? No.
- It is incorrect to say we suck a liquid through a straw. Technically, air pressure pushing down on the surface of the liquid is forcing the liquid into our mouths.
- First, you have to make a space for the liquid; this means the air inside the straw and your mouth must be removed. Yes, you suck this air out.
- Then, the difference in pressure inside the straw and your mouth and the air pressure pushing on the liquid forces the liquid up the straw and into your mouth.

86 Sea and Land Breezes

Sea and land breezes occur because of thermal convection currents of air above the land and the sea. As shown in Figure 1, during the day the Sun provides the energy that heats both the land and the sea. Note that during the daytime the air above the land rises while the air above the water sinks. The rising air above the land produces a low-pressure area; the sinking air above the water produces a high-pressure area. Air masses move from a high-pressure area to a low-pressure area. Thus, the cooler air above the water moves toward the land. Horizontal movement of air masses is called wind, or in this case, since it originates from the sea, sea breeze.

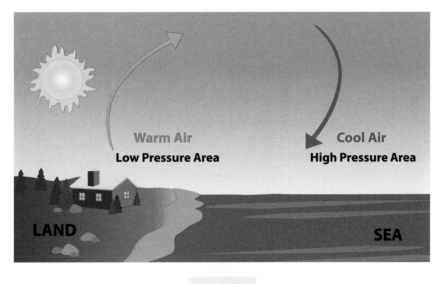

Figure 1

At night the cycle is reversed, with the air above the land being cooler than the air above the water. The direction of the breeze is reversed; it moves from the land toward the water and is called a land breeze. The reason for the differences between the temperature of the land and the water is due to heat capacity, which is the amount of energy needed to change the temperature of one gram of a substance by one degree. Water has a higher heat capacity than the land. This means it takes more energy to raise the temperature of water than the land; in reverse, to cool water it must lose more energy than the land.

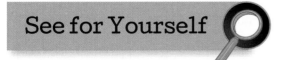

See for Yourself

Materials

2 plastic cups
2 thermometers
¼ cup (63 mL) soil

¼ cup (63 mL) water
a freezer

What to Do

CAUTION Take care when using the thermometers: they can break.

1. Stand a thermometer in each of the cups.

2. Pour enough water in one cup to cover the bulb of the thermometer.

3. Add the soil to the second cup so that it is at the same height as the water.

30 Minutes in the Freezer

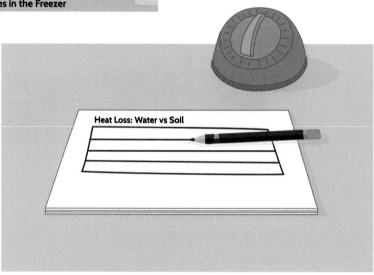

Figure 2

4. Read and record the initial temperature of both the soil and the water in a data chart such as the one shown. Note that the temperatures do not have to be the same.

Heat Loss: Water vs. Soil

Medium	Temperature, Initial (T_i)	Temperature, Final (T_f)	Temperature Change (T_Δ)
Water			
Soil			

5. Place the two cups in a freezer for about 30 minutes.

6. Remove the cups and immediately read and record this final temperature of the soil and the water in the data chart.

7. Calculate the temperature change for each cup by finding the difference between the two temperatures. The equation for this calculation is:

$$T_\Delta = T_f - T_i$$

8. Using the results from step 7, determine which has the highest heat capacity.

What Happened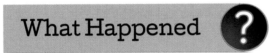

Generally, soil cools faster than water. This is because water has to lose more heat than soil to lower its temperature. Water has the highest heat capacity compared to other common substances.

The breezes created on an ocean shore result from differences in air pressure. When air above a warm surface rises there is less air pressing on the surface, thus a low air pressure area is formed. The reverse is true when the air sinks toward a cool surface, producing a high air pressure area. Air from a high-pressure area will move toward a low-pressure area, producing wind.

Challenge

In Figure 3, imagine there is smoke coming out of the chimney. Can you predict the direction of this smoke?

Think!

- The Moon is a clue that it is nighttime.
- Without solar heating, the land and seawater start to cool.
- Water cools slower than most substances, thus the land cools faster.
- The air over the water is warm and rises, creating a low-pressure area.
- The cooler air over the land sinks, creating a high-pressure area.
- High-pressure air from the land moves toward the low air pressure area over the sea. The smoke from the chimney will move toward the water.

Figure 3

87 Rayleigh Scattering

Scattering means to spread out in all directions. In 1871, a British physicist, Lord Rayleigh, described the redirection of short wavelengths of sunlight as light scattering. The blues in visible light have shorter wavelengths than red or green light. Lord Rayleigh explained that the gas molecules in air, such as oxygen and nitrogen, were responsible for the blue light waves from sunlight being scattered; thus, the sky above Earth appears blue.

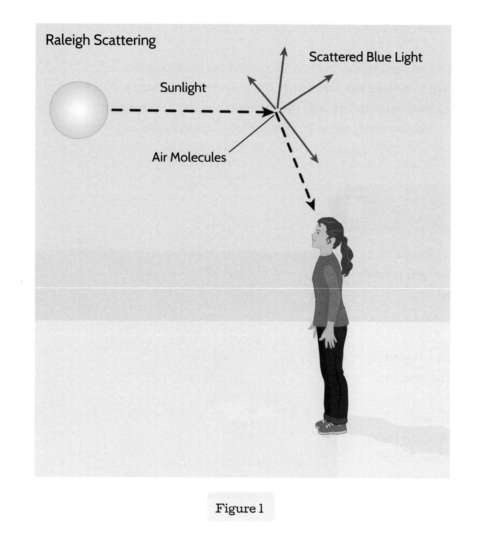

Figure 1

Light shining through a colloid solution, such as milk, can demonstrate the scattering of blue light.

Materials

transparent glass

small box

flashlight

tap water

¼ tsp (1.25 mL) of milk

eyedropper

spoon

What to Do

1. Fill the glass with water and stand the glass on a table.

2. Use the box or other flat objects to support the flashlight so its light shines through the water in the glass.

3. Turn on the light and make your observations by looking at the side of the glass as shown in Figure 2. You want to view at a 90° angle to the path of the beam of light from the flashlight. Make note whether the light is visible as it passes through the water in the glass.

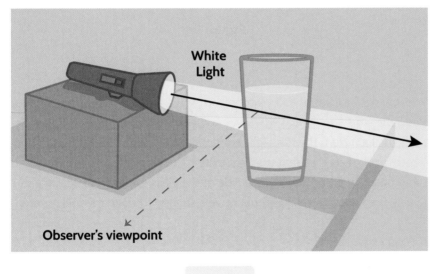

White Light

Observer's viewpoint

Figure 2

4. Use the eyedropper to add 10 to 12 drops of milk to the water. Stir and repeat step 3.

5. Repeat step 4 until there is a definite color change in the milky water.

What Happened

Light is only visible when it reflects from a surface to your eyes. Although shown in the figure, light is not visible as it passed through air and water, but the milky solution took on a bluish color. This is because part of the light entering the milky water was scattered by the molecules of fat and protein in milk, in the same manner gases in air scatter blue light from sunlight.

If white light is produced by the Sun, can you describe how the previous investigation could be used to explain why the Sun appears to be yellow instead of white?

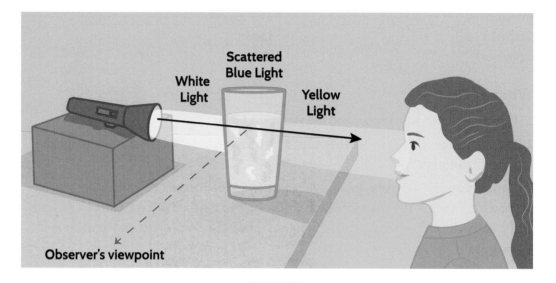

Figure 3

Think!

- When observing the glass of milky water from a 90° angle, you observe the blue scattered light.
- The remaining light from the flashlight continues in a straight line.
- A screen could be placed so that the light exiting the glass shines on it. Or, you could move your observation position to the side of the glass opposite the flashlight. You will see the yellowish unscattered light that travels straight through the milky water.

See for Yourself

Set up a screen or move your observation position so that you view the side of the glass where the unscattered light is exiting.

FYI: Increase the amount of milk by small amounts and more of the light will be scattered. Eventually the exiting light will be red, just like red skies at sunset and sunrise.

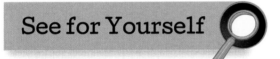

88 Seasons

Seasons are the four divisions of the year marking a specific type of weather and the number of daylight hours. These seasons are spring, summer, autumn, and winter. A model representing the change in daylight around the Earth can be used to identify the seasons in the Northern and Southern Hemispheres.

See for Yourself

Materials

drawing compass

piece of white poster board, 8-inch (20-cm) square

piece of black poster board, 8-inch (20-cm) square

ruler

pen

protractor

scissors

paper brad

What to Do

1. Use the compass to draw a large circle on the piece of white poster board.

2. With the ruler and pen draw a line across the center of the circle. Label the line "Equator" as shown. Make two marks at the top and bottom of the circle to represent the North and South Poles.

3. Use the protractor to make a mark for the west and east ends of the 63.5° N latitude line.

4. Flip the protractor over and then repeat step #3 to mark the ends of the 63.5° S latitude line.

5. Draw lines for the 63.5° N and S latitude lines. Label the Arctic Circle, equator, and Antarctic Circle as shown in Figure 2. Add labels for the Northern Hemisphere and the Southern Hemisphere.

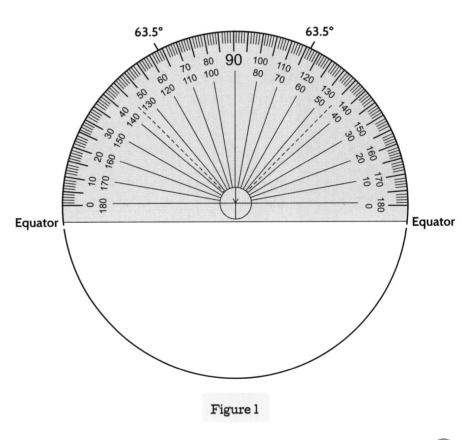

Figure 1

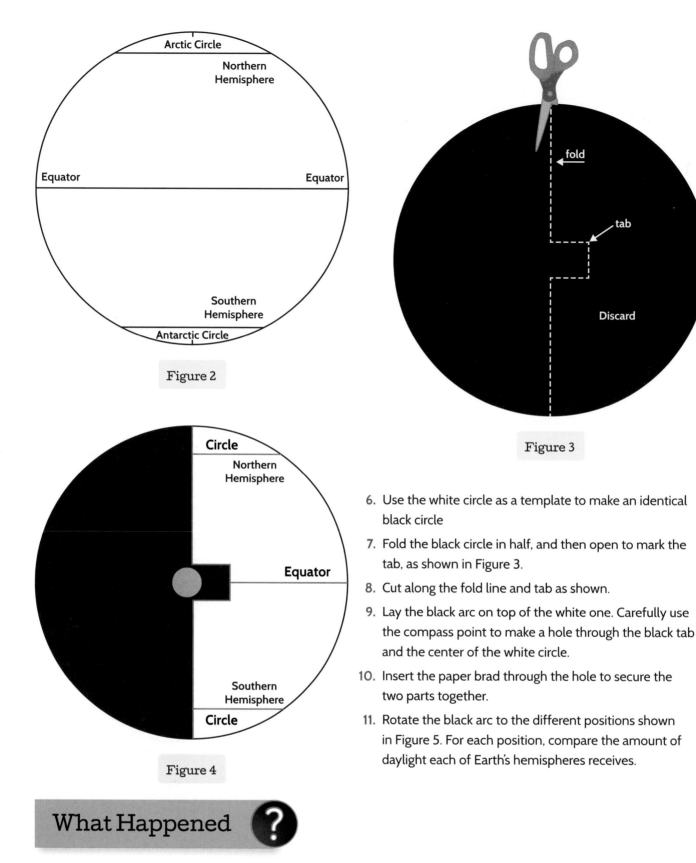

Figure 2

Figure 3

Figure 4

6. Use the white circle as a template to make an identical black circle

7. Fold the black circle in half, and then open to mark the tab, as shown in Figure 3.

8. Cut along the fold line and tab as shown.

9. Lay the black arc on top of the white one. Carefully use the compass point to make a hole through the black tab and the center of the white circle.

10. Insert the paper brad through the hole to secure the two parts together.

11. Rotate the black arc to the different positions shown in Figure 5. For each position, compare the amount of daylight each of Earth's hemispheres receives.

What Happened ?

At any moment in time, half of the Earth is covered in sunlight. In Figure 5, the Northern Hemisphere has more daytime than the Southern Hemisphere in diagram A, equal daytime in B, and less daytime in diagram C.

One factor responsible for seasonal changes is the number of hours of sunlight each day. Another factor, and one that is very important, is the angle that sunlight hits Earth's surface. Thus, even though either of Earth's poles might be experiencing summer, the climate in these regions is very cold, but not as cold as during the winter months. Winter receives the fewest daily hours of sunlight and summer the greatest. Autumn and spring start off with equal amounts of daily sunlight.

Note that, at the poles, there is no sunlight during the winter and the Sun never sets during the summer.

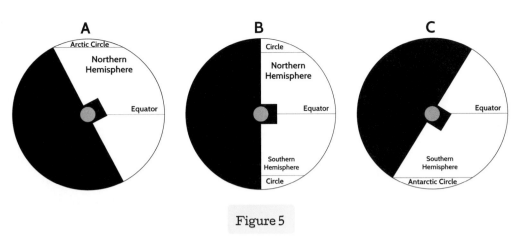

Figure 5

For the Northern Hemisphere, can you identify the order of the seasons in Figure 6?

Think!

- Illustrations 1 and 3 are identical; to identify them you have to identify the season that follows or precedes it.
- Illustration 2 shows more than half the Northern Hemisphere bathed in sunlight, thus the season for this part of Earth is summer.
- Starting with illustration 1, the order of the seasons is: spring, summer, autumn, winter.

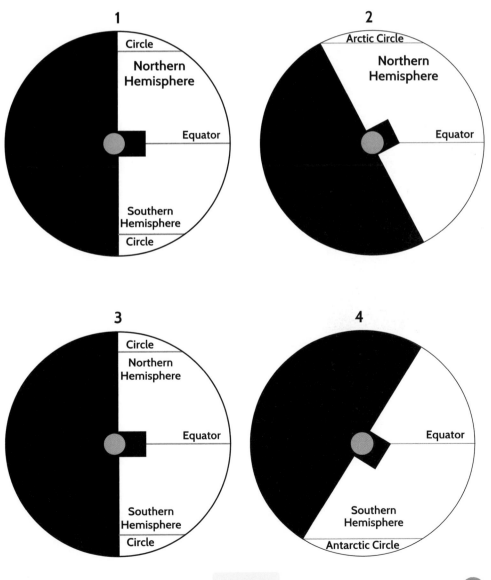

Figure 6

89 Coriolis Effect

The movement of the air in the lower layer of Earth's atmosphere produces major wind systems across Earth. Air moves from areas of higher atmospheric pressure to areas of lower atmospheric pressure. **Wind** is described as the horizontal movement of air while vertical movements due to unequal heating of Earth's surface are called convection currents. One type of major wind system occurs between latitudes 30° S and 30° N; these are called trade winds or easterlies. As shown in Figure 1, trade winds are deflected toward the west. The name "easterlies" tells the basic origin of the wind.

The major wind systems are all deflected by the **Coriolis effect**, which is a force due to Earth's rotation. Earth's rotation is in one direction, counterclockwise. Even so, fluids in the Northern Hemisphere are deflected to the right, and fluids in the Southern Hemisphere are deflected to the left.

North Easterlies Trades

South Easterlies Trades

30° N

30° S

Figure 1

See for Yourself

Materials

sheet of blank paper
pencil

helper

What to Do

1. Write "North Pole" at the top of the long side of the paper. Draw a small circle to the left of the North Pole, and label it #1. Repeat, drawing a circle to the right and labeling it #2.

2. Turn the paper around and write South Pole at the top of the paper, and then repeat step 1 drawing labeled circles at the top, but reversing their order.

3. Fold the paper in half placing the long sides together and with the circles on the outside. Lay the folded paper on a table with the North Pole side up and the folded edge toward you.

Figure 2   Figure 3

4. Hold the pencil with its point in circle #1. Close your eyes and as best as you can draw a straight line down the paper toward the folded edge. Place an arrow head on the end of the line to denote direction (Figure 2).

5. Place the pencil's point in circle #2, which is on the right side. As you draw the line with your eyes closed, ask a helper to hold the right edge of the paper and slowly pull it to the right.

6. Turn the folded paper over with the South Pole at the top and the folded edge toward you. Repeat steps 4 and 5.

7. Unfold the paper and draw a line across the fold. Label this line "equator." Compare the direction of the lines drawn from the North Pole toward the equator with those drawn from the South Pole toward the equator (Figure 3).

What Happened ?

The straight lines drawn represent the direction of air masses without the Coriolis effect. The movement of the paper toward the right represented the rotation of Earth toward the east. Notice that air is deflected toward the right in the Northern Hemisphere and toward the left in the Southern Hemisphere.

When determining right and left, there has to be a reference point. With wind movement, imagine yourself standing at its origin facing in the direction of motion. Now, no matter where the start of an air mass is in the Northern Hemisphere, it is going to be deflected toward the right. The reverse is true for the Southern Hemisphere: standing at the start, wind will be deflected toward the left.

Know that there are more factors involved, but for now just being able to determine the direction of deflection is a very good start.

Can you determine the direction of deflection for the two labeled wind systems, A and B, in Figure 4?

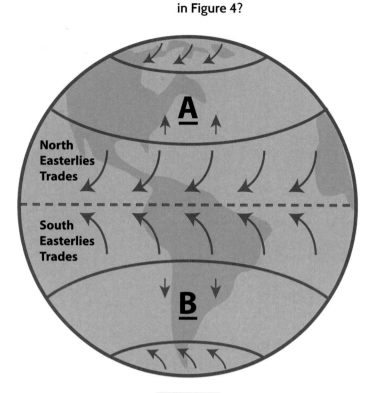

Figure 4

Think!

- Note that the winds are moving away from the equator toward the two poles.
- Winds in section A are in the Northern Hemisphere, thus the winds will be deflected toward the right, toward the east.
- Winds in section B are in the Southern Hemisphere, thus winds will be deflected toward the left, toward the east.
- These winds are called westerlies because they originate from the west.
- Figure 5 shows all the major wind systems across Earth. Those at the poles are called polar winds.

FYI: The Coriolis effect doesn't affect the rotation of water going down drains or toilets; instead, the shapes of the drains cause this. Thus, water in drains doesn't swirl in a different direction above or below Earth's equator.

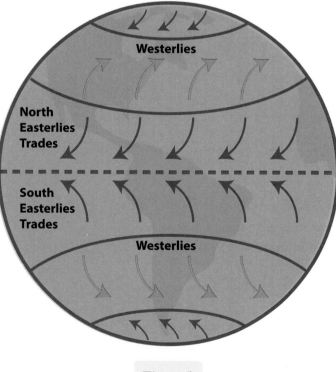

Figure 5

Part V

BIOLOGY

Biology is concerned with the study of living organisms: plants, fungi, algae, animals, and humans. **Biologists** are scientists who specialize in the study of all different aspects related to living organisms, such as how organisms interact with each other and their environment. For humans, this interaction is due to sensory receptors. **Sensory receptors** are specialized nerve cells that respond to stimuli, such as light, sound, odors, tastes, heat, and so on. Sensory receptors send a message via nerves to the brain for interpretation and perception. Basically, you see, hear, smell, taste, and feel because of the many different sensory receptors in your body.

Sensory receptors, and all other parts of your body, are made up of building blocks called cells. While the cells in all organisms have similar characteristics, they differ depending on the function they perform.

The human body is a walking chemical laboratory with all the different chemical changes going on night and day. When a chemical reaction occurs in an organism it is referred to as a **biochemical change**. "Bio" is a prefix meaning "life"; thus, biochemical reactions are chemical reactions that occur in living organisms. Some biochemical processes are investigated in this unit, such as denaturing different types of **protein**. The prefix "de" means reversal, removal, and negation; so, when something has been *denatured*, it is no longer in its natural form. If you observe an egg being fried, you are observing the denaturing of the egg's protein.

There are so many physical and biochemical changes going on around you every day! I hope the activities in this unit will tweak your interest, and you will not only be more aware of but have a desire to learn and investigate more about biology and life science.

The Nervous System

The **nervous system** of your body has two parts: the **central nervous system** composed of the brain and spinal cord, and the **peripheral nervous system** composed of nerves from the spinal cord that reach every part of your body.

All body systems have cells as the starting blocks. This section will first present **eukaryotic cells**, which are in all living organisms except bacteria and archaea, the latter two having **prokaryotic cells**. The difference between these two types of cells is in cell organization. I visualize eukaryotic cells as being very organized, with each type of organelle, such as the nucleus, having a membrane keeping all the genetic material safe. Prokaryotic cells have no bound organelles; nuclear materials are not enclosed by a membrane.

The cell itself is at the first level of organization and there are many different types of eukaryotic cell, including blood cells, skeletal cells, skin cells, muscle cells, and photoreceptor cells, as well as the different kinds of nerve cells responsible for you interacting with the world around you.

Groups of similar cells with similar functions form the second level of organization called **tissue**. Muscle cells form muscle tissue, which is responsible for movement. You will investigate why it takes a pair of muscles just to raise your forearm.

The different colors of the world you see around you are down to photoreceptors in your eyes. But it takes more than just receiving information to perceive colors; the information has to be sent via nerve cells to your brain, where the message is interpreted, and *voila*, you perceive that leaves are green and the sky is blue.

The brain can only process the information it receives, and sometimes what you perceive as color isn't really there. Also, the timing of messages received can affect your reaction time. This phenomenon is called the **Stroop effect**, which will be investigated.

90 Eukaryotic Cells

The human body contains trillions of eukaryotic cells. Each cell has a job to perform, and all cells must work together for the body to maintain good health. Groups of similar cells form tissues; tissues working together form organs; organs working together form systems; all systems working together form an organism, such as you. But the bottom line is that cells are the building blocks of organisms. Figure 1 shows three types of cell: muscle cells, red blood cells, and nerve cells. Note the different shapes; each kind of cell has the shape needed for the special job it performs. For example, nerve cells have long fibers that carry messages around your body. Plant cells, like animal cells, have basic parts: a **cell membrane** (a barrier around a cell that controls what enters and leaves the cell), **cytoplasm** (a gel-like material that fills the cell, includes all cell parts except the nucleus), and a bound **nucleus** (contains genetic materials and controls all cell activities). But animal cells are more pliable than are plant cells. Making a three-dimensional animal cell model can help to better understand how eukaryotic cells in animals can be gently pushed and pulled without breaking.

Red Blood Cells

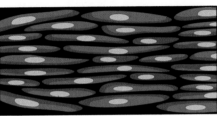
Muscle Cells

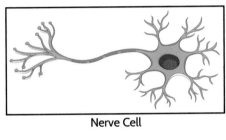
Nerve Cell

Figure 1

Figure 1 is a bowl of lime gelatin that can be used to represent the cytoplasm in a cell model.

See for Yourself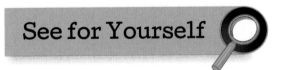

Materials

box of lemon gelatin mix
resealable plastic bag, 1 pint (568 mL)
bowl, 1 qt (1L)
green and purple grapes

adult helper
labels and a pen
show box

What to Do

1. With adult assistance, prepare the gelatin using the instructions on the box.

2. When the gelatin has cooled, but is still a liquid, pour it into the plastic bag, seal the bag, and set it in the bowl.

3. Place the bowl with the bag of gelatin in a refrigerator until the gelatin has set, meaning it is a jiggly solid (3 to 4 hours).

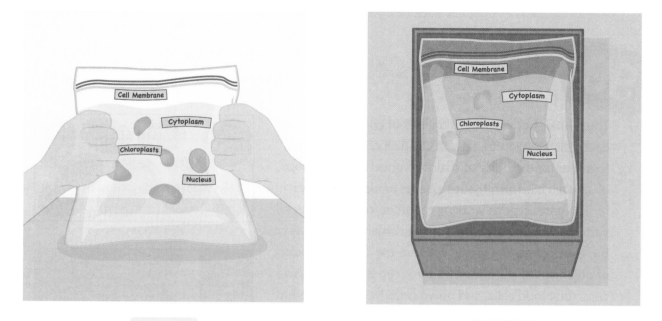

Figure 2

Figure 3

4. When set, remove the bowl with the bag of gelatin from the refrigerator and insert the purple grape into the gelatin. Reseal the bag and place it on a flat surface. Observe the shape of the bag.

5. Gently squeeze the bag with your hands and observe any changes in the shape of the bag.

6. Insert the green grapes into the gelatin and then label the bag as shown in Figure 2.

7. Place the bag in the shoe box.

What Happened ❓

A model of a eukaryotic cell with its basic three parts has been made. Squeezing the model or placing it on a hard surface causes its shape to change. All the cells in your body, like the model, have three parts: a cell membrane, cytoplasm, and a nucleus. As shown in Figure 2, the cell membrane is represented by the plastic bag. The pale-yellow gelatin is the cell's cytoplasm, and the purple represents the nucleus. The peel of the grape represents the nuclear membrane binding the contents of the nucleus.

Plants, unlike people and animals, do not have bones for support; instead, their cells have a firm structure surrounding them called a **cell wall**. Plant cells also have green chloroplasts represented by the green grapes. **Photosynthesis** is the process of of using sunlight to make foods from carbon dioxide and water; this occurs in chloroplasts.

Challenge ⭐

Can you identify the structure representing the cell wall in the plant cell model in Figure 3?

Think!

A very basic plant cell model is like an animal cell, with one big structural difference, which is that plant cells have a cell wall on the outside of their cell membrane. The model that has been constructed has a box representing the cell wall. Another difference is the presence of chloroplasts.

91 Muscles

Your body is like a **marionette**, which is a puppet with strings attached to different parts of its body. As the strings are pulled, the puppet's parts move. Instead of having strings attached to your body, you have **muscle tissue**, which is the tissue found in animals that causes the animal to move. When muscles contract (shorten) and relax (lengthen), motion occurs. Muscles attached to bones pull on the bones making them move, much like the strings move the parts of the marionette. Without muscles you could not move. A working model of how muscles move your arm can be made.

See for Yourself

Materials

2 pieces of poster board, 3 × 8 inches (7.5 cm × 20 cm)

2 pieces of thick string, one 14 inches (35 cm) long and one 18 inches (45 cm) long

2 tags

paper hole punch

paper brad

labels

marker

What to Do

1. Use the following instructions to prepare an arm:

   - Place the poster board strips together. With the hole punch, cut a hole through both strips about ½ inch (1.25 cm) in from the center point on one end.
   - Bind the two pieces together by inserting a brad through the holes, and then bend back the metal tabs.
   - Swivel one of the strips around the brad so that the strips are in a straight line, and then label the upper arm and forearm as shown in Figure 2.
   - Use the paper hole punch to cut two holes at the end of the upper arm and two holes on the forearm at least ½ inch (1.25 cm) from where the brad attaches the two paper pieces.

2. Use the following to attach muscles to the arm:

   - Tie the ends of the shorter string to the holes on the top edge of the arm model as shown in Figure 3. Use a tag to label this string "A."
   - Tie the longer string to the holes on the bottom edge of the arm model. Tag this string "B".

3. Instructions for bending and straightening the arm:

   - Hold the upper arm against a table's surface, and then pull string A away from the arm as shown in Figure 4. Note the motion of the forearm.
   - Release string A and pull string B away from the arm. Note the motion of the forearm.

Figure 1

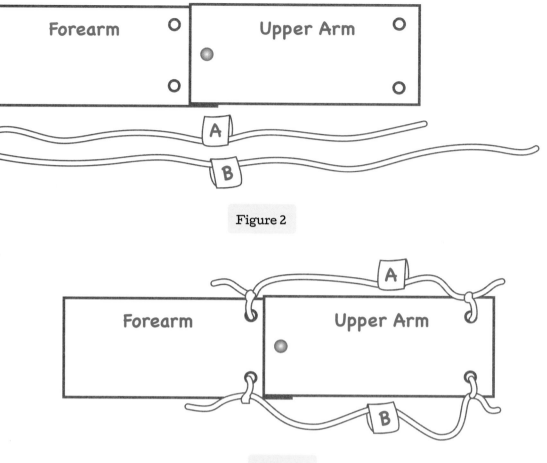

Figure 2

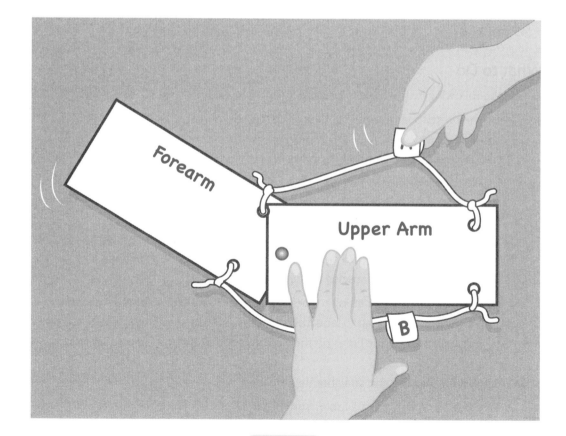

Figure 3

Figure 4

You have made a model of an arm. Pulling on string A lifts the forearm and pulling on string B lowers the forearm. Muscle can only pull, they cannot push. Thus, muscles at joints (places where two bones meet) such as the elbow come in pairs; flexors bend the arm and extensors straighten it. In the arm model, string A represents the biceps muscle, which is the large flexor muscle on the front side of your upper arm. String B represents the extensor muscle on the back of the upper arm called the triceps muscle. These two muscles control the bending and straightening of your arm at the elbow.

Some skeletal muscles are attached directly to bones, while others, such as the biceps and triceps muscles, are attached to bones by tendons (tough, nonelastic tissues that attach muscles to bones).

Challenge ⭐

Can you design a way to identify the muscles and tendons in the arm model?

Think!

- One way is to color-code the string. Use a red marker to color the string about 1 inch (2.5 cm) at each end. The red section represents the tendons and the white string the muscle.
- You could cut out a hand shape from poster board and tape it to the end of the forearm. Add a legend as shown in Figure 5.

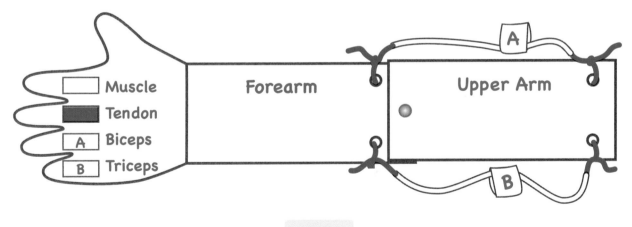

Figure 5

Afterimage

Light enters your eye and is focused on the **retina**, which is a light-sensitive membrane that lines the inner surface on the back of your eye. The retina has specialized cells called **photoreceptors**. Your eyes have two types of photoreceptor: **rods** that function in low light but produce no color vision and **cones** that do produce color vision. These cells send electrical impulses carried by the optic nerve to your brain. The brain interprets the message and *voila*! You see the world around you.

An **afterimage** is a visual image that continues to appear after exposure to the original image has ceased. For example, after a bright flash of light, you see dark spots, which are afterimages. If you stare at one color for a time and then look at a white surface, you will see a colored afterimage. But the afterimage is a different color.

See for Yourself

Materials

Figure 1 and Figure 2

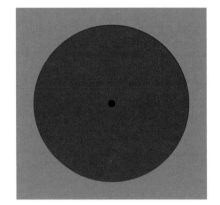 

Figure 1   Figure 2

What to Do

1. Stare at the center of the blue circle in Figure 1 for 20 seconds. Measure this time by counting very slowly to 20.
2. At the end of 20 seconds blink a few times, then stare at the white square in Figure 2.
3. Make note of the color, size, and shape of the afterimage you see on the white area.

What Happened

The rods in your eyes are responsible for vision at low light levels; cones give you color vision. Your eyes have three basic color-sensitive cones that respond to red, green, and blue light. White light stimulates all three color cones. Light from the blue-colored circle in Figure 1 stimulated the blue cone cells in your eyes. After a time, these blue cone cells became fatigued. The white light reflected from the white square simulated all of the cones: red, blue, and green. But, being over stimulated, the blue cones did not respond as before. Thus, the green and red cones responded and the brain interprets the combination of red and green as yellow, Thus, the afterimage appeared as a yellow circle.

The color wheel in Figure 3 shows the resulting color for different combinations of red, blue, and green light.

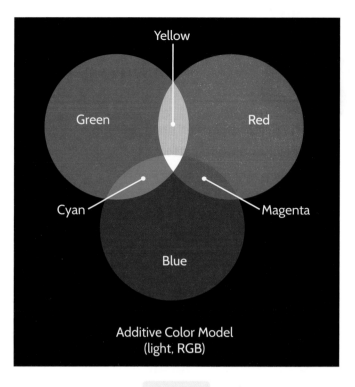

Additive Color Model
(light, RGB)

Figure 3

Challenge

Can you explain why the green background around the blue circle in Figure 1 appears to be pale magenta in the afterimage?

Think!

- Staring at the green background caused the green cone cells be fatigued and not respond as usual to white light.
- The two remaining color-sensitive cells, red and blue, did respond to the white light.
- The color wheel in Figure 3 shows magenta as the color the brain interprets for the combination of red and blue light.

93 Perception of Color

An English toymaker, Charles Benham, created and sold a top with a black and white pattern like the one shown in Figure 1. When the top was spun, colors were seen.

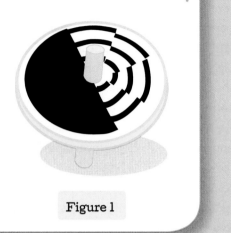

Figure 1

See for Yourself

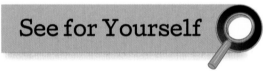

Materials

drawing compass
blank index card, 3 inches × 5 inches
   (7.5 cm × 12.5 cm)
scissors

ruler
black marker
pushpin
pencil with eraser

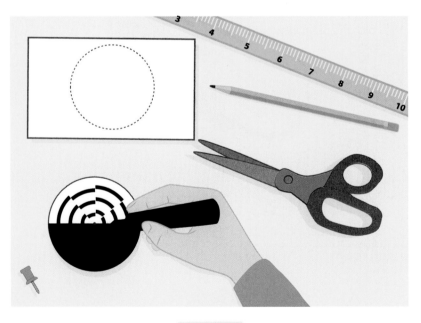

Figure 2

What to Do

1. Draw a circle with about a 2-inch (5-cm) diameter in the center of the index card. Cut out the circle.

2. Use the ruler to draw a straight line across the center of the circle, and then use the marker to color half of the circle black.

3. Use the black marker to draw the curved lines as shown in Figure 2.

4. Push the pushpin through the center of the circle, and then into the eraser of the pencil.

5. In a lighted area, roll the pencil between the palms of your hands so that the card spins clockwise. As the card spins, look at the patterns and make note of any change in the pattern as well as color on the spinning disk.

What Happened ❓

Most but not all people see four concentric colored circles. How vivid the colors appear depends on several variables, one being how fast the disk rotates. More colors are generally seen when the disk rotates slowly, but then not too slowly. The order of the rings of colors is shown in Figure 4. The diagram shows vivid colors, but I do not see the colors with such intensity.

There are different explanations for this perception of colors. One is that the photoreceptor cones in your eyes have different activation and deactivation times. This means that one color cone might switch on faster and turn off faster than the others. When the disk is spun, the white light from the white section activates all three color receptor cones: red, green, and blue. The black parts of the disk interrupt or, we might say, shut off the cones. It is thought that the cones are switched on and off at different time intervals, thus the brain is interpreting messages from the optical nerve as flashes of color that overlap forming colored circles. The bottom line is that you see color where there is no color.

Figure 3

Challenge ⭐

Can you give a hypothesis of the results if the disk is spun in a counterclockwise direction?

Think!

Reversing the direction of the spin reverses the time sequence, thus one might assume that the colors would be reversed as in Figure 5.

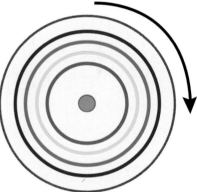

Figure 4

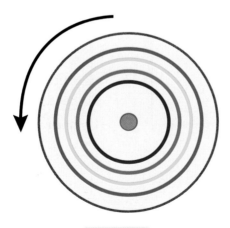

Figure 5

See for Yourself

Spin the spinner counterclockwise to test this hypothesis.

94 Reaction Time

Reaction time is how fast you can complete a task. It is also how fast you respond to a stimulus, which is anything your body reacts to. In the 1930s, an American psychologist, John Ridley Stroop, designed a test that demonstrates a slower reaction time when two tasks are being completed at the same time. The test is simple: You only have to identify the ink color used to print different words. Most people find this to be surprisingly difficult.

See for Yourself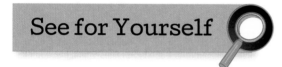

Materials

helper
timer

Stroop tests in Figure 1 and Figure 2

STROOP TEST Number 1

1. RED
2. PURPLE
3. BLUE
4. GREEN
5. YELLOW
6. PINK
7. GREY
8. BROWN
9. BLACK
10. ORANGE

Figure 1

STROOP TEST Number 2

1. RED
2. PURPLE
3. BLUE
4. GREEN
5. YELLOW
6. PINK
7. GREY
8. BROWN
9. BLACK
10. ORANGE

Figure 2

What to Do

1. The task for each test is to identify the ink color for each word. For example, in test #1, the *ink color* for 1 is red, 2 is purple. For test #2, the *ink color* for 1 is green, 2 is orange.

2. Cover test #2 while you take test #1. Ask a helper to time your results. Repeat test #2.

3. Compare your results for the two tests. Which test, 1 or 2, was more difficult?

What Happened ❓

Each test involves one task being performed, which is to identify the ink color of each word. The photoreceptor cells in your eyes that respond to color are called cones, which send a message to your brain. At the same time, your eyes are relaying to your brain the sequence of letters making up the names of each color.

Test #1 is easy because the words spell out the ink color the words are printed with. The same words are used in test #2, but they are printed in a different color. When looking at the word **RED**, your brain receives two messages: (1) the color the word spells out; (2) the color of the letters. Even though you really try, you cannot stop yourself from reading the words, and it is difficult not to blurt out what you read. This slows your reaction time when completing the task of identifying ink color. When interference affects your reaction time in completing a task, this is called the **Stroop effect**.

Challenge ⭐

With your understanding of the Stroop effect, which driver in Figure 3, A or B, is more likely to have a faster response time?

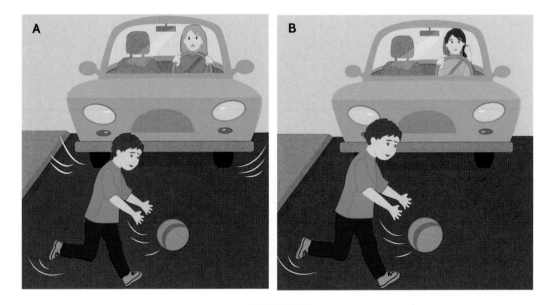

Figure 3

Think!

1. Which driver is most focused on the road?
   This is a no brainer: driver A.
2. Which driver is most likely to have a slower response time in the emergency situation shown?
   Driver B because he is trying to drive and text on his phone. He is less likely to have the needed response time to stop in time.

95

Sensory Receptors

When the body is stimulated (excited), different sensations can be felt, such as touch, pressure, heat, cold, and pain. Except for pain receptors, all the skin sensory receptors in Figure 1 are specialized sense organs at the end of nerve fibers. Pain sensors are naked nerve endings. Note that each receptor is a bundle of nerves, except pain receptors, which consist of separate nerve fibers.

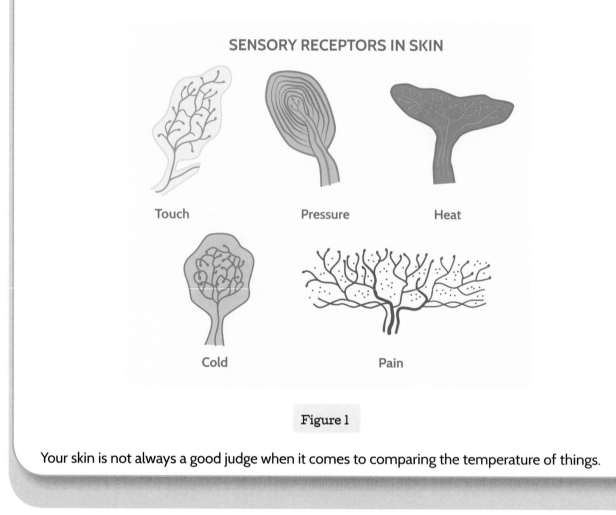

SENSORY RECEPTORS IN SKIN

Touch   Pressure   Heat

Cold   Pain

Figure 1

Your skin is not always a good judge when it comes to comparing the temperature of things.

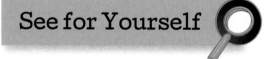

See for Yourself

Materials

3 bowls, 2 qt (2 L)   spoon
cold and warm tap water   thermometer
6 to 8 ice cubes

What to Do

CAUTION Take care when using the thermometer: they can break.

1. Fill two of the bowls three-fourths full with cold tap water.

2. Add all of the ice cubes to one of the bowls of water. Stir the water until the ice cubes are about half melted. This bowl will be the cold water.

3. Fill the third bowl about three-fourths full with warm tap water. It should be about 113°F (45°C).

CAUTION If any hotter, add cold tap water, and check the temperature before proceedings. You do not want the water to burn your skin.

4. Place the three bowls on a table with the icy water on your right side and the warm water on your left side. Place the remaining bowl of water between them; this will be the medium temperature water.

5. Put your right hand in the icy water and your left hand in the warm water. After 20 seconds, remove your hands from the outer bowls of water and put both hands in the center, medium temperature water.

Cold   Medium   Warm

Figure 2

CAUTION Remove your hand from the icy water if you feel pain. Some people's skin is more sensitive to cold than others.

What Happened ❓

The medium temperature water feels warm to your right hand and cool to your left hand. This is because the heat sensory cells respond to a loss or gain of heat in your skin. Placed in the icy water, heat was transferred from your warm skin to the cold water. Thus, the temperature of the skin on this hand was colder than normal. When placed in the medium temperature water, heat from this water moved to your right hand. Heat sensory cells recognized this heat being taken in and it was interpreted by the brain that the water was warmer than it really was. The opposite occurred with your left hand that was first warmed and then put in the cooler medium-temperature water. Since the water was cooler than your skin temperature, heat was transferred from your hand to the water. This time, the heat sensory cells in your hand reported that heat was being lost, and your brain interpreted this as the water being cool.

Study Figure 3. Can you explain from the action in Figure 3 why the brain interprets the lower side of the finger touching the pencil to be numb?

Think!

- The top part of the finger is actually being touched, thus a message from both index fingers is sent to the brain and interprets that this section of the finger has good sensory reception.
- When the thumb rubs the pencil instead of the underside of the finger, only the thumb is sending a message. There is a message missing, thus the brain interprets this as the sensory receptors in the underside of the finger on the pencil are not functioning properly, and so this area is numb.

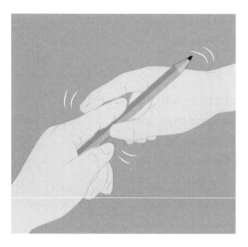

Figure 3

Physical and Biochemical Changes

Physical changes in life science can be the falling of leaves from trees, the growth of plants, or even the changes in the size of animals and people. The most obvious physical changes are those that can be seen, such as the changing of leaf colors in autumn or lumps in milk, which gives you a big clue that something has happened to cause this.

Generally, the cause of physical change is chemical change, which in living organisms is called biochemical change. You will investigate and discover how color pigments can be separated by a process called chromatography; this is the process that can be used to separate and identify different color pigments in a material.

The lumps in milk are called curds and the liquid they are floating in is called whey. If you cause milk to curdle by adding an edible acid, such as vinegar or lemon juice, the curds and whey formed are edible. These are the curds and whey that Little Miss Muffet was eating before the spider dropped down beside her and frightened Miss Muffet away. Curds and whey formed when milk spoils are not edible.

Milk curdling as well as the changes in the color of the whites of eggs when heated or beaten is all about the denaturing of protein in these foods. Denaturing means to change from a natural state. When egg whites are cooked, they turn from a liquid to a solid. The protein in the egg whites has been uncoiled and cannot return to its former state. The same is true when egg whites are beaten until stiff; they have lost their elastic nature and the change is not reversible.

Many physical and biochemical changes happen in foods, such as the ripening of fruit. In this unit, you will investigate and discover how to speed up the ripening process. Changing the speed of a biological process often requires the aid of a helper, called an enzyme. Enzymes are chemicals that change the speed of a chemical reaction but are not changed in the process. This means that the enzyme can be used again and again. You will use a working model to demonstrate how an enzyme brings two chemicals together but remains unchanged. This will be related to the enzyme necessary for bioluminescence, which is light produced by living organisms.

96

Chromatography

Chromatography is a technique for separating mixtures. This requires a stationary phase and a mobile phase. Components in a mixture have varying attraction to the two phases. The same basic technique used by scientists to separate and study chemicals in living organisms can be used to separate the different components in black ink.

See for Yourself

Materials

coffee filter

ruler

water soluble black marker

small glass

tap water

sheet of paper

What to Do

1. Fold the filter paper in half twice.

2. Make a mark on the front and back side of the folded paper 1 inch (2.5 cm) from the pointed end.

3. Unfold the paper, and using the two marks as a guide, draw a thick circle on the paper. Allow the black ink to dry.

4. Refold the paper. Open the filter into a funnel shape by placing your finger between the third and fourth layers.

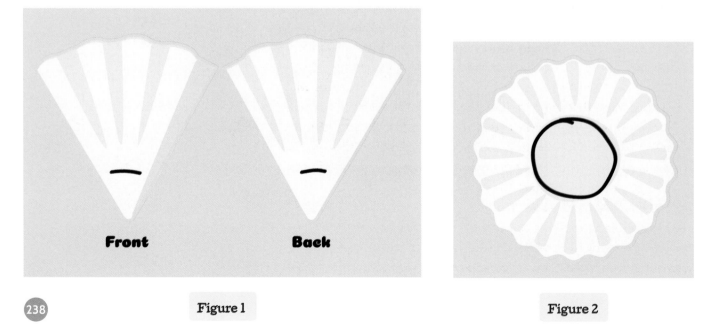

Front   Back

Figure 1   **Figure 2**

Figure 3

Figure 4

5. Stand the paper funnel in the empty glass. At eye level, mark a line on the glass midway between the tip of the funnel and the black mark on the paper. Remove the funnel.

6. Fill the glass with water up to the mark.

7. Replace the paper funnel in the glass. It is important that the ink mark is above the water level in the glass.

8. Observe the paper funnel for 1 minute or longer, then make observations periodically for about 1 hour.

9. When there are no further changes, remove the funnel from the glass. Open the paper funnel, then lay it flat on a sheet of paper and allow it to dry.

Figure 5

What Happened ?

The filter is the stationary phase and the water is the mobile phase. The black ink is the mixture of components that will be separated.

A water-soluble ink mark is necessary so that the ink will dissolve in the water as it climbs up the filter paper. The water moves by **capillary action**, which is the movement of a liquid through narrow spaces with no outside force assisting it. As the water passes through the ink mixture, the ink dissolves in the water and moves with it. There is an adhesive attraction between the pigments and the paper, as well as between the pigments and the water. Figure 6 shows the separation of the different colors in the black ink mixture. The order of the colors from the outside edge is blue, red, and yellow. The blue pigment's attraction is greatest to water and least to the paper. The reverse is true for yellow, with the red having a medium attraction for the paper and water. Thus, the blue pigment moves farther than the other pigments, with yellow moving the shortest distance.

Figure 6

Using Figure 7, can you suggest why spinach has green leaves when there are yellow and orange pigments besides green chlorophyll?

Plant Chromatography

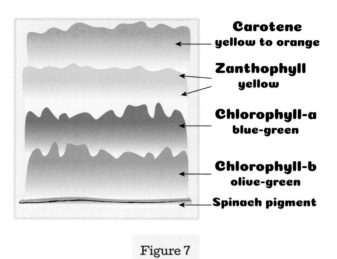

Figure 7

Think!

With previous knowledge plus Figure 7, we might hypothesize that leaves are green because chlorophyll masks the other pigments. Without chlorophyll, other colored pigments are visible in leaves. In autumn, when plants receive less intense sunlight needed for chlorophyll production, chlorophyll disappears, and other pigments are visible. Leaves turn red when the sugars and other chemicals in the leaves produce a red pigment called anthocyanin.

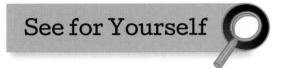

Denaturing Egg Protein

Denaturing refers to not being natural. Thus, denaturing a protein means changing it from its natural structure. Proteins can be denatured by heating or changing their pH, as well as by mechanical means, such as beating them with a whisk.

See for Yourself

Materials

3 or more egg whites at room temperature   whisk
mixing bowl (use only glass, stainless steel,
   or copper)

NOTE   It is very important that the bowl and whisk are very clean. Be sure to wash and rinse these items.

CAUTION   Raw eggs can contain Salmonella bacteria. Wash hands, utensils, equipment, and work surfaces with hot, soapy water before and after they come in contact with raw eggs.

What to Do

1. Pour the egg whites into the bowl.
2. Observe and make note of these physical properties of the egg whites: color, state of matter, viscosity, and volume.
3. Beat the egg whites with the whisk until you can lift the whisk and a white foamy peak forms on the surface.

What Happened

Proteins are polymers, which are macromolecules made up of repeated units. The units in protein are amino acids. Egg white protein is a type of globular protein, which means the protein molecules fold over and curl into a spherical shape, much like a ball of yarn. Weak chemical bonds between different parts of this tangled molecule help to keep the protein in its ball shape.

Figure 1

About 87 percent of egg white is water, 4 percent minerals, and the remaining 9 percent balls of globular protein molecules dispersed throughout the water. Light is able to travel through this liquid mixture; thus, it is clear. Globular protein has both **hydrophobic** (water-hating) and **hydrophilic** (water-loving) properties. When curled, the hydrophilic parts are on the outside and the hydrophobic parts are tucked away inside the ball away from the surrounding water.

Beating the egg whites causes the protein to stretch out, thus exposing the hydrophobic areas. The stretched molecules bond with each other forming a network with captured air bubbles. The air bubbles keep water away from the hydrophobic parts of the protein molecules. The color of the egg white changes because the reconfigured protein structure is no longer transparent; instead, the new foamy structure reflects light in a similar manner to a white fluffy cloud in the sky. When a liquid, such as natural egg whites, changes to a solid or semi-solid, the process is called **coagulation**.

Challenge

Can you describe the process of egg white coagulation in Figure 2?

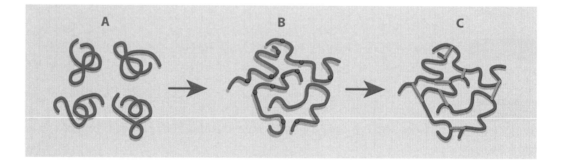

Figure 2

Think!

- Egg protein in its natural form is coiled, thus diagram A represents natural protein.
- Diagram B shows the strands of protein stretched out; thus, the natural structure has been changed. The protein has been denatured.
- The strands of protein are bonded to each other in diagram C, which represents the coagulation of egg whites.

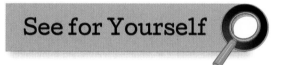

98 Denaturing Milk Protein

Denaturing means changing from a natural structure. Casein and whey are the two main proteins in cow, sheep, and goat milk. The casein proteins group together forming sphere-like structures called micelles. These micelles are small enough to stay suspended in the liquid whey. Acids denature individual microscopic casein micelles in milk; the unraveled protein strands bond together resulting in their clumping together forming a gelatinous mass called curd. This change from a liquid to a solid is called coagulation.

See for Yourself

Materials

½ cup (125 mL) of milk
shallow bowl

1 tbsp (15 mL) of vinegar
stirring spoon

What to Do

1. Pour the milk into the bowl.

2. Stir the milk with the spoon. Lift some of the milk in the spoon and observe its physical properties (Figure 1).

3. Add the vinegar to the bowl.

4. Stir the mixture in the bowl. Lift the spoon and observe the physical properties of its content, as in Figure 2.

Figure 1   Figure 2

What Happened

Milk is a white liquid. When vinegar is added, milk separates into curds and whey. Curds are the solid parts and whey is the liquid. Curd results when casein protein in the milk is denatured. Casein forms microscopic spheres called micelles. The proteins on the outside of the micelle spheres have a negative charge. Because of this charge, the individual micelles repel each other resulting in them being well dispersed throughout the liquid. Acids denature the casein micelles by neutralizing their negative charges. Without the negative charges, the casein micelles can combine, forming curd.

Challenge

Bacteria causes the lactose sugar in milk to form lactic acid. Can you explain how this acid affects the milk?

Think!

- The addition of vinegar (acetic acid) to milk causes milk curds to form. The formation of lactic acid will have the same results as other acids, thus causing milk curds to form. The milk is said to spoil.
- Bacteria are found everywhere. Milk sold in stores has been pasteurized, meaning it is heated to kill bacteria, but some always remain. In time, the bacteria multiply and cause milk to spoil. This is why manufacturers date milk. It doesn't mean that the milk spoils on that date, but that the milk may be old enough to spoil.

99 Ripening Hormone

Hormones are chemicals that stimulate specific biochemical changes in living organisms. **Ethylene gas** serves as a hormone in plants. It affects a plant at different stages of development by stimulating or regulating different biochemical processes, such as the **abscission** (shedding) of leaves, the opening of flowers, and the ripening of fruit. But there can be too much of a good thing.

Figure 1

See for Yourself

Materials

5 green bananas
1 overripe banana

3 zipper-locking freezer bags

What to Do

1. Place two green bananas in one of the bags.

2. In a second bag, place one green banana and the overripe banana.

3. In the last bag place one banana, and then close the bags and place them where they will not be disturbed.

4. Place the remaining green banana on the surface next to the bags.

5. Observe the bags daily for signs of ripening, which will be any change from green to yellow. Make note of the banana that shows the first signs of ripening.

Figure 2

What Happened ?

The plastic freezer bags help to contain the natural production of the ethylene gas hormone as the bananas ripen. The overripe banana produced more ethylene than did the green bananas. Thus, the unripe banana in the bag with the overripe banana should be the first to show signs of ripening. Second should be the two green bananas in a bag because more ethylene would be produced than with one banana, and next the banana that is alone in the closed bag because the ethylene was trapped inside the bag. Last to ripen should be the banana that was not enclosed. The ethylene this banana produced would have mixed with the air surrounding it and, like all gases, being in constant motion it would move away from the banana.

If you want fruit to ripen faster, put the fruit in a closed plastic bag or even a paper sack. Keep the fruit separated and where there is good air circulation if you want your fruit to ripen slower. Temperature changes affect most chemical reactions; you might want to investigate how it affects the rate of fruit ripening.

Challenge ⭐

Can you explain how a crate of good apples could be spoiled by one bad apple?

Think!

- First, a "bad apple" is overripe or rotten.
- Overripe fruit produces more of the ethylene hormone.
- Apples in a crate are close together, and the ethylene gas released by the rotten apple gets trapped. Ethylene gas speeds up the ripening of the other apples. Given enough time, all the apples will overripen more quickly than if the bad apple had not been present.

Figure 3

Bioluminescence

Chemiluminescence is a chemical reaction that produces light. This occurs when electrons in the atoms of the products absorb energy and move away from the nucleus. These excited electrons release this extra energy in the form of light. The color of the light depends on the chemical reaction. When chemiluminescence occurs in plants or animals, it is called **bioluminescence**.

Many creatures, including bacteria, insects, jellyfish, and fish, are bioluminescent. Their bodies manufacture substances called luciferase and luciferin. **Luciferase** is an enzyme, which is a type of catalyst in organisms that causes or changes the speed of a chemical reaction. Remember that catalysts are necessary for some reactions to occur, but are not part of the reaction. This allows the catalyst to be used over and over until it wears out. Luciferase aids in the chemical reaction between **luciferin** and oxygen producing a product that emits visible light. A magic trick can model the function of an enzyme in the combination of two substances.

Figure 1

See for Yourself

Materials

ruler
pencil

9-inch × 3-inch (22.5-cm × 7.5-cm) strip of paper
2 different-colored paper clips

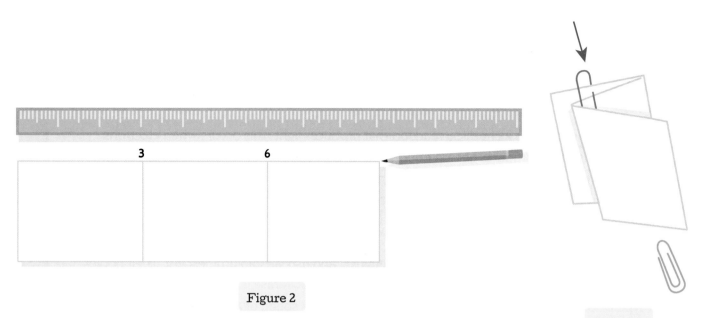

Figure 2

Figure 3

What to Do

1. Use the ruler and pencil to draw two lines across the paper strip: one line at 3 inches (7.5 cm) and the second line at 6 inches (15 cm) from one end of the strip.

2. Fold the paper strip along one of the lines. Connect the top and second layer with one paper clip as shown in Figure 3.

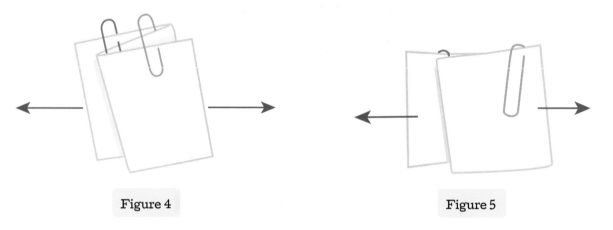

Figure 4

Figure 5

3. Fold the paper backward along the second line. As in step 2, connect the top and second layer with one paper clip as shown in Figure 4.

4. Holding the ends of the paper strip in each hand, quickly pull the ends in opposite directions, as in Figure 5.

The paper straightened and resulted in the two paper clips attaching to each other. Note that the paper can be used again to attach other paper clips, as can enzymes. While this is much like a magic trick, there is nothing magic about the way enzymes change the rate of chemical reaction and in some cases are necessary for the reaction to occur.

Challenge

Using Figure 6, can you explain how fireflies produce light?

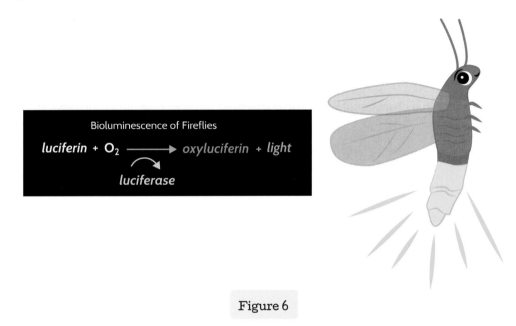

Figure 6

Think!

- Fireflies produce light by combining luciferin and oxygen in their bodies.
- The oxidation of luciferin requires the enzyme called luciferase. The luciferin and oxygen are used up in the reaction, but the enzyme luciferase is used again and again as noted by the curved arrow.

Glossary

abscission

In reference to plants, it is the natural detachment of plant parts, such as dead leaves and ripe fruit.

acceleration

The change in velocity per unit of time. *See also* linear acceleration; angular acceleration.

acid

A chemical that donates protons in a chemical reaction; a chemical that turns blue litmus red; has a pH of less than 7.

acid indicator

A substance that changes color when in contact with an acid; blue litmus indicates an acid by turning red.

aerosol

A type of emulsion in which water droplets are dispersed in air; fog.

afterimage

A virtual image due to the tiring of light sensory receptors, called cones, in the eye.

air resistance

Friction on objects moving through air.

albedo

The measure of the amount of sunlight that nonluminous celestial bodies reflect.

altitude

The angular height above the ground.

angular acceleration

The rate of change in angular velocity per unit time or in the direction of revolving or rotating objects.

angular measurement

Distance around a curved path in degrees; a circle has 360°; one angular degree is 1/360 of a circle.

angular velocity

How far an object moves on a curved path per unit time.

anion

An atom that has gained electrons, forming a negatively charged ion.

apparent measurement

This type of measurement is only how large or distant celestial bodies appear to an observer on Earth.

apparent size

In reference to an observer on Earth, apparent size is how large a celestial body appears to be.

apparent weight

The weight of an object when gravity is not the only force acting on it; weight of objects in fluids.

apparent weightlessness

A feeling of being weightless when there is no external contact force pushing or pulling on you; freefalling; astronauts in spacecraft, who are actually falling around the Earth.

astronomical unit (AU)

A unit of measurement for the distance between celestial bodies; 1 AU is the mean distance between Earth and the Sun, which is 93 million miles (150 million km).

astronomy

The study of the physical Universe as a whole; the study of celestial bodies.

atmosphere

The blanket of gases surrounding Earth or any celestial body.

atmospheric pressure

The pressure on a surface created by the weight of the gases in the atmosphere; on Earth, air pressing down on Earth's surface.

atom

An atom is the smallest building block of an element that retains the properties of the element; the atoms of an element all have the same number of protons.

atomic mass

The mass of one atom of an element.

atomic number

The number of protons in the atoms of an element; every element has a specific number of protons, thus every element has a specific atomic number.

azimuth

The angular measurement around the horizon of an observer with north being zero degrees; used to identify the location of celestial bodies.

balance

In reference to stability, it is a state of being stable, meaning that there is no net rotating force acting on an object; when the torque on either side of the center of gravity is equal but in opposite directions. In reference to a measuring instrument, it is an equal-arm-type device in which the mass on one side is compared to the mass of materials on the opposite side.

balanced forces

Two equal forces acting in opposite direction on an object.

barycenter

The center of gravity (center of mass) of the Earth–Moon system; found inside the Earth near its crust.

base

In a chemical reaction, a base accepts protons; turns red litmus blue; common bases release a hydroxide ion $(OH)^{1-}$ in solution.

battery

A device that changes chemical energy into electric energy.

biceps

Muscle in the upper part of the human arm that raises the lower arm.

binary compound

A compound with two kinds of element.

biochemical change

A chemical change within a living organism.

biologist

A scientist who specializes in the study of all aspects of living organisms.

biology

The study of living organisms.

bioluminescence

Luminescence in living organisms; light produced in living organisms by chemical reactions.

bipolar

In reference to chemicals, it is a molecule with a negative side and a positive side, such as a water molecule.

body fossil

The most common fossils found; formed from hard parts of organisms, such as teeth, bones, shells, or woody parts of plants.

bond

An attraction between the particles in a chemical compound; electrostatic attraction between anions and cations.

bonded

In reference to chemical compounds, an attraction between atoms making up the compound; linked together.

breath

Exhaled waste gases from animals.

brine

A solution of sodium chloride in water.

brittle deformation

In reference to rock and rock structure, brittle deformation is the shattering of rock.

buoyancy

The ability to float in a fluid.

buoyant force

The upward force of a fluid on an object submerged in it; a buoyant force is equal to the weight of the fluid that is displaced by the submerged object.

capillary action

The ability of a liquid to move in narrow spaces without any outside forces; movement can even occur against gravity.

carbonated

Contains dissolved carbon dioxide; dissolved carbon dioxide in water produces carbonic acid.

cardinal direction

The four cardinal directions are north (N), east (E), south (S), and west (W); due north is toward the Earth's North Pole; due south is toward Earth's South Pole; do not lineup with compass directions, which instead are directed towards Earth's north and south magnetic poles.

casein

The solid parts of milk separated by a decrease in the pH of the liquid.

cast

The hardened material that is shaped by a mold.

cast fossil

A fossil formed when minerals fill a mold fossil, forming the shape of the organism.

cation

An atom that has lost valence electrons, forming a positively charged ion.

caustic

Able to burn skin.

celestial bodies

Natural bodies in space.

cell membrane

A combination of proteins, fats and other chemicals that form a barrier around a cell; controls what enters and leaves a cell.

cell wall

The rigid structure around the cell membrane of a plant cell.

center of gravity

A location on an object where the weight of an object or system is considered to be concentrated; if supported at this point, the object can be balanced.

central nervous system

The part of the nervous system composed of the brain and spinal cord.

chemical change

When a substance combines with another or breaks apart to form a new substance.

chemical equation

Elemental symbols and chemical formulas used to represent a chemical reaction; starts with reactant(s) and yields product(s).

chemical formula

A combination of elemental symbols showing the kinds of elements as well as the number of atoms of each element.

chemical property

A characteristic of a substance observed when it participates in a chemical reaction.

chemical symbol

A code of one or two letters that represents the name of an element.

chemiluminescence

A chemical reaction that produces light.

chemist

A chemist is a scientist who specializes in studying chemistry.

chemistry

Chemistry is the study of matter, its physical and chemical properties, and how it interacts, combines, and changes to form new substances.

chloroplast

Part of a plant cell that converts light energy into sugars in the process of photosynthesis. The sugars can be used by the cell.

chromatography

A technique for separating mixtures.

chromophore

A part of a dye molecule that absorbs light.

churning

A process of agitating cream to form butter.

circuit

In reference to electricity, a circuit is the path that an electric current flows through.

circumpolar constellations

Constellations that never set below the horizon as seen from a specific location on Earth.

climate

The average weather in a region for about 30 years.

closed circuit

In reference to electricity, a closed circuit is one with no breaks in its path.

coagulation

When a liquid, such as natural egg white, changes to a solid or semi-solid.

colloid

A mixture with suspended microscopic, undissolved particles dispersed throughout it.

combustion

The process of burning; combination with oxygen.

compound

A substance composed of two or more different elements bonded together.

compression

A type of stress that squeezes material together; at convergent boundaries mountains and valleys are produced when rocks are squeezed upward.

concave lens

A diverging lens; thicker at its edges; parallel light rays are refracted away from the principal axis.

concentration

In reference to a solution, it is the ratio of the amount of solute to the amount of solvent.

conduction

The process of energy being transferred between two objects in contact with each other; heat conduction moves from hot regions to cooler regions; electric conduction moves from high potential energy to lower potential energy.

conductivity

The rate at which heat or electricity passes through a specific material.

conductor

A material through which energy (heat or electricity) passes easily; metals are good conductors of both heat and electric current.

cone

A photoreceptor cell in the retina of the eye; responsible for color vision. The other type of photoreceptor cell in the retina is the rod cell.

constellation

A group of stars that appears to form a pattern in the sky.

contact force

Force applied directly to an object. *See also* air resistance; buoyant force; drag; friction; torque.

convection

A heat transfer process in fluids; heat energy is transferred from an area of higher heat energy to an area of lower heat energy.

converge

When things meet; parallel light rays entering a convex lens converge when exiting the lens.

convergent boundary

Where two tectonic plates come together.

convex lens

A lens that is thicker in the center than at its edges; curved outward; a converging lens.

coolant

A substance used to remove the heat from another material.

Coriolis effect

On Earth, the effect of Earth's rotation results in air masses as well as ocean water being deflected to the right in the Northern Hemisphere and to the left in the Southern Hemisphere.

covalent bond

An attraction between atoms that share valence electrons; links atoms together.

covalent compound

A compound in which covalent bonds hold the atoms of the compound together.

crescent

In reference to the Moon, it is a thin, curve shape that is thicker in the center and tapered on the two ends; a moon phase.

cross-linked polymer

A polymer with bonds between its separate molecules.

curd

The solid parts of milk that coagulate when the pH of the milk is lowered.

current

In reference to electricity, current is the rate of electrons moving past a point; measured in amperes (A).

current electricity

The movement of electrons.

cytoplasm

Gel-like material inside a cell that includes all cell parts except the nucleus.

decant

To pour off the liquid from a mixture.

deceleration

Negative acceleration; a decrease in velocity in a specific amount of time.

decomposition

When a single substance breaks apart, forming new substances.

deformation

A change in the physical shape of a material.

degree

Temperature is a measure of the average kinetic energy of the particles in a substance; temperature is measured in degrees Fahrenheit ($^\circ$F), degrees Celsius ($^\circ$C), or kelvin (K); altitude is measured in angular degrees.

denaturing

To change from a natural form.

density

The measure of mass per volume; the quantity of matter in a specific volume.

destructive boundary

Another name for a convergent boundary where one plate moves under another.

diatomic molecule

A diatomic molecule is a molecule with two atoms of the same element covalently bonded together. Seven common diatomic molecules are hydrogen, nitrogen, oxygen, fluorine, chlorine bromine, and iodine.

diffusion

The spontaneous movement of particles in a fluid from an area of high particle concentration to an area of lower particle concentration; to spread out in all directions.

dilute

In reference to a solution, it refers to reducing the concentration by increasing the amount of solvent.

dispersion

In reference to solution, dispersion refers to solutes being spread throughout a solvent; in reference to light, dispersion is the splitting of white light into its separate colors.

displace

To take the place of; submerged objects displace the fluid they are in.

diverge

When things separate; parallel light rays entering a concave lens diverge when exiting the lens.

divergent boundary

In reference to tectonic plates, a divergent boundary is where two plates move away from each other.

down

A vertical direction; on Earth, down is toward the center of Earth.

drag

The retarding force of fluids on objects moving through them.

ductile deformation

In reference to the deformation of rock structures, ductile deformation is when rocks stretch under pressure and do not return to their original form; also called plastic deformation; the stretching of materials into a thin wire.

earthquake

A sudden and violent vibration or shaking of Earth's upper crust; results from movement of tectonic plates as well as volcanic actions.

Earth science

The study of Earth.

Earth's gravity

The force of attraction of things toward Earth's center; accelerates things at a rate of 32 feet/s² (9.8 m/s²) toward Earth's center.

earthshine

Sunlight reflected from Earth.

easterlies

The prevailing east-to-west winds in regions near Earth's equator; also called trade winds.

eclipse

To block the light of a luminous body; a solar eclipse occurs when the Moon blocks sunlight from reaching Earth; a lunar eclipse is when Earth blocks sunlight from reaching the Moon; when one object moves in front of and blocks the view of another object.

ecliptic

The apparent path of the Sun around Earth.

effort arm

The side of a lever where the effort force is applied; the side of an equal arm balance to which a known force is applied.

effort force

The known force you apply to one end of a lever; known force on one side of an equal arm balance.

elastic deformation

Deformation as a result of a tension force in which the material is stretched; the material springs back to its natural form when the force is removed if it has not exceeded its elastic limit.

elastic limit

The limit to which a material can be stretched and still return to its natural form when the stretching tension force is removed.

electric circuit

The path that an electric current flows through; a loop of conductors forms the path.

electric current

A flow of electric charges; the strength of the current is equal to the amount of electric charges passing a given point per second; measured in amperes.

electrical energy

Electricity.

electricity

A form of energy associated with the presence and movement of electrical charges. *See also* current electricity; static electricity.

electromagnetic radiation (EMR or ER)

Energy in the form of waves that can move through space or material mediums; light radiation.

electromagnetic spectrum

All the different types of electromagnetic radiation in order of wavelength; the spectrum from longest wavelength (least energy) to shortest wavelength (greatest energy): radio waves, microwaves, infrared light, visible light, ultraviolet light, x-rays, and gamma rays.

electron cloud

The cloud of negative charges around the nucleus of an atom.

electronegativity

The measure of how strongly electrons are attracted to the nucleus of an atom; least electronegativity in a period is to the left; least electronegativity in a group is at the bottom.

electrostatic attraction

The attraction between two unlike charges; attraction between cations and anions forming ionic bonds in ionic compounds.

element

An element is a substance that cannot be broken down into simpler substances by ordinary means; each type of element is made of only one kind of atom.

emulsification

When an emulsifier is added to a mixture of two immiscible liquids in order to bind them.

emulsifier

A substance that binds two immiscible liquids so they do not separate, such as the oil and water in milk, cream, and butter.

emulsion

A mixture of two immiscible liquids that separate unless they have an emulsifier to bind them together; a fine dispersion of minute liquid droplets in another liquid in which it is not soluble.

energy

The ability to do work; work = force × distance moved; examples of energy include heat, light, and electricity; types of energy: kinetic and potential.

energy ball

A device designed with an open circuit. When the circuit is closed the ball lights up and buzzes.

energy level

Energy levels or orbitals are at fixed distances from the nucleus of an atom, with the electrons (e^{1-}) in each level having different amounts of energy.

enzyme

A chemical that changes the rate of chemical reaction in living organisms; a catalyst.

equator

The imaginary line around the center of Earth that separates the Northern and Southern Hemispheres.

esophagus

The tube leading from the mouth to the stomach.

ethylene gas

A gas given off by ripening fruit that speeds up the ripening process.

eukaryotic cell

A cell containing bound organelles, including a nucleus.

evaporate

The physical change of a liquid to a gas at a temperature below the boiling point of the liquid.

evaporite

Crystal formation as a result of the evaporation of water from a mineral solution; halite is an evaporite formed by the evaporation of water from a brine solution.

excited state

A state in which electrons with extra energy exist farther from the nucleus of an atom for a short time before losing the excess energy and returning to ground state.

exothermic reaction

A chemical reaction in which energy in the form of light and/or heat is a product.

explosion

A rapid increase in volume resulting in a container breaking with a release of energy; usually caused by the production of gas in a closed container.

extensive property

A property that depends on the quantity of material.

extensor

Muscle that pulls on a bone resulting in the body part being straightened.

fading

In reference to colors, fading is the reduction of color intensity.

family

In reference to the periodic table, a family is a vertical column of elements; also called a group.

fault

A fracture in Earth's crust in which the blocks on either side of the break move in relation to each other.

filtrate

The liquid separated from a solution by filtration.

filtration

The process of separating solids from liquids in a mixture using a filter.

first quarter

In reference to the Moon, the first quarter is when the Moon's disk is half lit on the side facing the Sun; in the Northern Hemisphere the lighted side would be on the right.

flexor

Muscle that pulls on a bone so that the bone is raised; for example, raising of the lower arm.

fluid

A substance that has no particular shape and can flow; a liquid or gas.

fluorescence

The property of certain substances that can absorb high-energy light and emit lower-energy light.

fluorescent

The property of a substance that can fluoresce; producing light when activated by high-energy light, such as ultraviolet light.

foam

A type of emulsion in which air is mixed into a liquid or a solid; for example, when air is whipped into liquid cream.

focal length

The distance from the center of a lens to its focal point.

focal point

The point where converging light rays meet; the point where diverging rays of light appear to lead back to.

fold mountain

Mountain formed when two converging tectonic plates meet and rise upward, one plate folding over the other.

folds

In reference to land structure, folds are wavelike formations.

force

A push or pulling action on an object. *See also* contact forces; noncontact forces; turning force.

fossil

A preserved remains of any once-living thing from a past geological age. *See also* body fossil; trace fossil.

freefall

To fall with Earth's gravity being the only downward force acting on the body.

frequency

In reference to light, frequency is the number of waves that pass a point in a specific time.

friction

A contact force that retards the motion of two surfaces moving against each other. *See also* static friction; kinetic friction.

fulcrum

The point where a lever rotates; pivot point.

full moon

The moon phase in which the entire Moon disk is lit.

galaxy

Part of the Universe; a system composed of stars, gas, dust, asteroids, and planets that are all bound together by gravity and move as a unit; our Solar System is part of the Milky Way galaxy.

gel

A type of emulsion in which water is trapped within a network formed by gelatin; it jiggles; jelly.

geocentric

An ancient model of the Universe in which all celestial bodies revolved around Earth.

geological stress

Stress in geology is the force per unit area on rocks in Earth's crust; tension is a stress that stretches at divergent boundaries; compression is a stress that squeezes at convergent boundaries; shearing is a stress that causes lateral shifting or sliding at transform boundaries.

geology

A study of the Earth, its physical structure and composition, its history, and the processes that result in changes.

globular protein

A protein whose physical shape is spherical; somewhat soluble in water.

gravity

The force that attracts objects toward the center of Earth or towards any other body with mass. *See also* Earth's gravity.

ground state

The natural location of an atom's electrons.

group

In reference to the periodic table, a group is a vertical column of elements; also called a family; elements in a group have similar chemical and physical structures and properties.

halite

An evaporite formed from the evaporation of water from a brine solution; a type of sedimentary rock.

heat

The transfer of thermal energy; heat flows due to a difference in temperature from hot to cold.

heat capacity

The amount of heat needed to raise the temperature of a substance.

heat conduction

The transfer of heat between materials that are in contact with each other.

heliocentric

An ancient model of the Universe proposed by the Polish astronomer Nicolaus Copernicus (1473–1543) in a book published after his death; a model of the Universe in which all celestial bodies rotate around the Sun.

heterogeneous mixture

A mixture that is not the same throughout.

homogeneous mixture

A mixture that is the same throughout; a solution; a colloid.

hormone

A substance in organisms that regulates specific processes, such as the ripening of fruit.

hydrophilic

Water loving; an emulsifier molecule has a hydrophilic end that attaches to water.

hydrophobic

Water hating; an emulsifier molecule has a hydrophobic end that will attach to oil.

hypothesis

A testable prediction of an answer to a science question that is based on knowledge of experience and/or research.

ignition temperature

The temperature at which a substance will burn.

immiscible

In reference to liquids, immiscible liquids will not mix to form a homogeneous mixture.

imprint fossil

An impression made by pressing something onto a softer substance so that its outline is reproduced; tracks made in soft clay of sediments.

incandescence

The emission of light due to being heated; examples include bonfires, some light bulbs, and the Sun as well as all other stars.

incident light

Light striking a surface is referred to as incident light.

indicator

A chemical indicator makes a distinct observable change to indicate the presence of a specific substance; litmus is an indicator that changes color to indicate the presence of an acid or base.

inertia

The property of matter that resists any change in its state of motion unless acted on by a net force; if an object is moving it continues to move at a constant velocity unless acted on by a net force; stationary objects remain stationary unless acted on by a net force.

insulator

A substance that retards the movement of electric current as well as heat; nonmetals are insulators, as are plastics and air.

intensive property

A physical property of matter that doesn't depend on size or amount of material; density and temperature are examples of intensive properties.

ion

An ion is an atom or group of atoms with a positive or negative charge; particle produced when an atom gains or loses electrons; cations are positive and anions are negative.

ionic bond

A bond between cations and anions that is formed by the transfer of valence electrons from one atom to another; an electrostatic attraction between positive and negative ions.

ionic compound

Ionic compounds are made of cations and anions; ionic bonds hold the ions of this type of compound together; $NaCl$ is an ionic compound.

isotope

Atoms with the same number of protons but a different number of neutrons in their nucleus are isotopes; symbols of the isotopes of an element show the atomic weight, such as H-1, H-2, and H-3 for the three isotopes of hydrogen.

joint

In reference to the skeletal system, it is where two bones are attached.

kinetic energy

The energy that an object has because it is in motion.

kinetic friction

The retarding force between an object and the surface it is moving across; also called sliding friction or simply moving friction.

land breeze

Wind from the land blowing toward the sea; occurs at night because the land cools faster than the water, thus air above the water is warmer and it rises, producing a low-pressure area. Air moves from a higher-pressure area to a lower-pressure area.

latitude

The angular distance north or south from the equator.

Law of Conservation of Mass

Matter is neither created nor destroyed during chemical reactions.

leavening agent

A substance that causes dough and batter to rise; baking powder and yeast.

LED

Light-emitting diode; this device does two things: gives off light and allows the current to flow in only one direction, which is from the positive terminal to the negative terminal.

lens

A transparent material, such as glass, with curved surfaces; a convex lens is thicker in the center than at the edges; a concave lens is thicker at the edges than in the center.

lever

A rigid bar with three parts: pivot, effort arm, and load arm; the bar rotates about the pivot point; force is applied to the effort arm; the substance to be moved is on the load arm.

Lewis dot diagram

An element's symbol with dots spaced around it representing the valence electrons of the element's atoms.

light

Wave energy; electromagnetic radiation (EMR or ER).

light-year

An astronomical measurement for distance; 1 light-year is the distance that light energy travels at a speed of 1.86×10^5 miles/s (3×10^5 km/s) during one Earth year (365 days).

linear acceleration

The velocity of an object moving in a straight line.

linear measurement

Straight line measurements; Imperial linear measurements include inches, feet, yards, and miles; SI linear measurements include centimeters, meters, and kilometers.

linear motion

Motion in a straight line.

lithosphere

Earth's crust and the upper part of Earth's mantle; part of Earth that is broken into sections called the tectonic plates.

load

In reference to levers, which are simple machines, the load is the substance being moved.

load arm

The end of a lever supporting the load.

luciferase

An enzyme necessary for luciferin to generate bioluminescence.

luciferin

A light-emitting chemical found in organisms that generate bioluminescence.

luminescence

Emitting light not caused by heat; also called cold light.

luminescent

When a substance emits light without having been heated.

luminous

Bright or shining; relates to light as perceived by the eye.

lunar month

The amount of time it takes for the Moon to pass through all of its phases.

machine

A device used to perform a specific task.

marionette

A puppet with strings attached to different parts. As the strings are pulled the parts move.

mass

The amount of matter in a material; common Imperial units for mass are ounces (oz) and pounds (lb); common SI units for mass are grams (g) and kilograms (kg).

mass number

The sum of the protons and neutrons inside the nucleus of an atom for a specific element.

matter

Matter is anything that takes up space and has mass; the stuff the Universe is made of.

meniscus

The curved surface of a liquid inside a container.

metal

An element that is typically hard, solid, and easy to bend or stretch into a wire.

metalloid

An element that has both metallic and nonmetallic properties; a semiconductor.

meteorology

A study of Earth's atmospheric changes and how they can be used to forecast the weather.

micelle

A cluster of atoms, ions, or molecules forming one particle; generally has a hydrophilic and a hydrophobic side.

mixture

A mixture is the combination of two or more materials with no change in the chemical identity of the materials.

mold

A hollow container that gives shape to materials that harden in it; a cast is the hardened material that is shaped by a mold.

mold fossil

A fossil formed when an organism dies and is covered by sediment; its flesh and bones decay leaving a cavity below the surface.

molecule

A molecule is composed of two or more atoms covalently bonded together; the smallest part of a molecular compound that can exist independently.

momentum

Mass in motion; momentum = mass × velocity; a vector quantity.

moonlight

Moonlight is sunlight reflected from the Moon's surface.

moon phase

The sunlit portion of the Moon's disk as viewed by an observer on Earth.

muscle tissue

Muscle tissue is composed of muscle cells; animals are able to move because of muscle tissue contraction.

natural element

An element that occurs naturally in nature; there are 94 known natural elements.

natural satellite

A celestial body that orbits a planet or a star.

nervous system

A system in animals composed of a brain, spinal cord, nerves, and specialized receptors that respond to the world around them.

net force

The resulting force after all other forces acting on an object have been considered; a net force has direction; resultant force.

neutral

In reference to the pH of a substance, neutral is not being acidic or basic in nature; pH 7 is neutral.

new moon

New moon is the moon phase in which no part of the Moon's disk is lit; occurs when the Moon moves between the Sun and the Earth.

Newton

A Newton (N) is the SI unit for force.

Newton's First Law of Motion

The law of inertia; objects tend to not change their state of motion unless acted on by a net force; objects at rest do not move unless acted on by a net force; objects in motion continue to move at a constant velocity unless acted on by a net force.

Newton's Second Law of Motion

A net force acting on an object causes it to accelerate; the net force on an object is equal to the product of the object's mass times its acceleration; $F = ma$.

Newton's Third Law of Motion

For every action there is an equal and opposite reaction; when one object pushes on another, the second object pushes back with an equal force but in the opposite direction.

noncontact forces

Forces, such as gravity, that act on an object without ever coming in physical contact with it; Earth's gravity causes objects to accelerate toward the ground.

nonmetal

An element that is typically a dull solid with characteristics opposite to those of a metal.

non-Newtonian fluid

A fluid whose viscosity increases when under sudden stress.

northern circumpolar constellation

A constellation that appears to revolve about Polaris, the North Star.

nucleus

In reference to atoms, the nucleus is the atom's center with protons and neutrons in it. In reference to cells, the nucleus directs cell functions and is where genetic material is stored.

oceanography

A study of the ocean and the organisms in it.

oil-in-water emulsion

An emulsion in which oil drops are dispersed throughout water; milk is an oil-in-water emulsion.

opaque

Characteristic of a substance which blocks visible light; cannot be seen through.

open circuit

In reference to electricity, an open circuit is one with a break in its path.

optical center

In reference to a lens, the optical center is the center point of the lens; light rays passing through the optical center of a lens do not change direction.

orogeny

A process in which a part of Earth's crust is folded and deformed when tectonic plates are pushed together; folded mountains are created through this process.

paleontologist

A scientist who studies prehistoric life on Earth via fossils.

parallel circuit

In reference to electricity, a parallel circuit has more than one conducting path for an electric current to flow through.

Particle Theory

All matter is made up of small particles that are in constant motion.

period

A row on the periodic table of elements; elements in a row have the same number of atomic energy levels.

periodic table

A table of all known chemical elements in order of atomic number in periods (rows). Elements with similar atomic structure and chemical properties are in vertical columns called groups or families.

peripheral nervous system

The part of the nervous system outside the brain and spinal cord.

phosphor

A substance that emits visible light when its electrons are activated by a high-energy source such as ultraviolet light.

phosphorescence

Light emitted by phosphors; cold light because it is produced without a heat source; continues to glow for a time after the activating energy source is removed.

phosphorescent

Something that exhibits phosphorescence.

photodegradation

The fading of dye due to the exposure to light, generally sunlight.

photon

A bundle of light energy; released when an atom's excited electrons return to the ground state.

photoreceptor

In reference to vision, photoreceptors are nerves that respond to light; cones are photoreceptors in the retina that are responsible for color vision; rods are more receptive to light, thus responsible for night vision, but produce no color vision.

photosynthesis

The process in plant chloroplasts that uses sunlight to synthesize sugars from carbon dioxide and water.

pH scale

A scale for measuring the concentration of acids and bases; scale is from 1 to 14, with a pH of 7 being neutral; the lower the pH value the more acidic the substance is; the higher the pH value the more basic.

physical change

A change in the physical properties of a substance but which does not change its chemical identity.

physical property

A physical property is a characteristic of a substance that can be measured and/or observed using the five senses of sight, hearing, touch, taste, and smell.

physicist

A physicist is a scientist who specializes in the field of physics.

physics

The study of matter and energy and how they interact; the study of how forces affect the motion of objects.

pivot

The point about which an object rotates; balancing point of a seesaw; center of a merry-go-round; fulcrum of levers.

plastic deformation

A change in the shape of a solid object without breaking it; the change is not reversible; also called ductile deformation.

plumb bob

An instrument used to determine a vertical line; a weight hanging on a string.

Polaris

A star in the constellation Ursa Minor; the star that the north end of Earth's axis points to.

pollution

Material whose presence negatively affects living organisms.

polyvinyl adhesives (PVA)

Glue containing polyvinyl acetate.

potential energy

The energy of an object due to its position; stored energy, such as energy in chemical bonds; energy in a compressed spring; energy of something at the top of a ramp.

precipitate

In reference to a solution it is undissolved solute that settles out of the solution; a solid that falls out of solution.

pressure

Force applied to a specific area.

principal axis

In reference to lenses, the principal axis is a straight line going through the center of a lens.

product

In a chemical reaction, a product is the end result.

prokaryotic cell

A cell that does not have a bound nucleus or any other bound organelles; cells of the archaea and bacteria.

protein

A large molecule made up of one or more amino acids; present in all living organisms.

pure substance

Used to refer to an element or a compound.

quinine

Chemical from the bark of the cinchona tree; contains a phosphor that emits blue photons when activated by ultraviolet light.

rate of diffusion

How quickly a substance evenly spreads throughout another substance.

Rayleigh scattering

The scattering of light waves from the Sun by the gases in Earth's atmosphere; nitrogen and oxygen molecules scatter light waves in the blue section of the visible light spectrum.

reactants

The starting materials in a chemical reaction.

reaction time

The time it takes to respond to a stimulus.

real image

An image produced by a lens that can be projected onto a screen.

refract

The bending or the changing in direction of light rays due to a change in speed as they pass from a medium with a different density from the medium they are entering.

relative density

A comparison of the density of different materials.

residue

Undissolved material collected on filter paper by filtration.

resultant force

The net force and its direction when all forces acting on an object are considered; an unbalanced force.

retina

The area on the back inside layer of the eye that contains photoreceptors.

revolution

In reference to revolving object, it is the movement of one object around another, such as the Earth around the Sun.

rod

A photoreceptor cell in the retina of the eye that is very receptive to light. It is responsible for night vision, but produces no color vision. The other type of photoreceptor cell in the retina is the cone cell.

rotation

The turning of an object about its own axis; turning around a fixed point called a pivot.

saturated solution

A solution in which no more solute can be dissolved in a solvent at a specific temperature and pressure.

scattering

In reference to light, it is the absorption of light by particles and emitting the light in different directions.

sea breeze

Wind that blows toward the land from the sea due to a difference in air pressure.

season

A division of the year with a specific type of weather: summer, autumn, winter, spring.

seismic wave

An energy wave created by an earthquake.

seismologist

A scientist who studies earthquakes and the effects of earthquakes.

sensory receptor

A nerve ending that responds to specific types of senses such as touch, pain, hot or cold, and pressure.

series circuit

In reference to electricity, a series circuit is a conducting path that makes a single loop through which an electric current flows.

shadow

A dark shape produced when a body blocks a light source.

simple machine

The simplest device used to change the direction or magnitude of a force, including levers, pulleys, and wedges; used to do work.

slime

A material with non-Newtonian fluid characteristics; under stress it acts like a solid, otherwise it flows like a liquid.

slip-strike fault

A fault in the Earth's crust in which the walls move sideways, not up and down.

sol

A type of emulsion in which solid pigment particles are dispersed throughout water; paint.

solar eclipse

Occurs when the Moon blocks sunlight from reaching the surface of Earth.

solar noon

Position of the Sun when it is at its highest altitude during the day.

Solar System

In relation to our Solar System, a tiny part of the Milky Way galaxy which is composed of the Sun with celestial bodies moving around it at different distances, including the Earth.

solid aerosol

A type of emulsion in which solid particles mix with air; smoke is carbon from a fire mixed with air.

solid foam

A type of emulsion in which a framework of solid material surrounds gas-filled spaces; gases mixed with hot lava from a volcano become trapped when the lava cools, forming a solid framework around the gas bubbles. This makes pumice rock after cooling.

solid sol

A type of emulsion in which solid colored particles are mixed with hot liquid glass; when cooled, the solid particles remain dispersed throughout the glass.

solubility

A measure of how much solute will dissolve in a solvent at a specific temperature and pressure.

solute

The material that dissolves in the solvent of a solution.

solution

Formed when a solute dissolves in a solvent.

solvent

The material that a solute dissolves in when a solution is formed.

sound waves

A type of energy produced by vibrations that travel through a fluid; received by hearing organs, such as your ears, and perceived as sound.

stability

A measure of the ability of a body to remain upright; resistance to falling over.

stable

In reference to balance, a stable object is not easy to tip over; in reference to chemicals it means the chemical does not spontaneously change.

states of matter

States of matter are the physical forms in which matter exists that depend on the kinetic energy of the atoms making up the substance; four of the states of matter are solid, liquid, gas, and plasma.

static electricity

A collection of electric charges in one place.

static friction

A "gripping" type of friction between stationary objects and the surface they are sitting on.

stimulus

Something that causes a specific reaction in a living organism.

stress

The stress on a material is the force applied per unit area on the material.

Stroop effect

Demonstrates how cognitive interference can delay reaction time of a task; shows that the brain processes words and colors differently, with reading having a stronger influence than the ability to say a color.

subduction zone

In reference to tectonic plates, a subduction zone is where two tectonic plates meet and one plate moves below the other plate.

substance

Common term used for any material, mixture, and so on; pure substances are elements and compounds.

surface tension

A skin-like surface across liquids due to the electrostatic attraction between the molecules of the liquid; water has a strong surface tension.

suspension

In reference to mixtures, a suspension is a heterogeneous mixture with particles that do not dissolve and which will settle on standing.

synthetic

Any material that has been made by people; not found naturally in nature.

synthetic element

An element that has been made by people; there are 24 synthetic elements.

tectonic plate

One of the sections that Earth's lithosphere is divided into; there are seven large plates and many small plates.

tendon

A strong fibrous tissue that connects muscle to bone; flexible but not elastic.

tension

A type of stress that pulls materials apart; a stress that stretches rocks at divergent boundaries.

terminal

In reference to a battery, it is one of the ends where an electric circuit is attached.

terminator

The line between the lighted and unlighted parts of the Moon disk.

thermal convection current

Movement of fluid due to the differences in temperature of two areas.

third quarter

The moon phase in which the lighted part of the Moon's disk is opposite that of the first quarter; in the Northern Hemisphere the left side of the Moon disk is lit.

tissue

A group of cells working together to perform a function.

torque

A turning force that causes an object to rotate; torque = force × distance to the pivot.

trace fossil

Fossil remains of footprints, or other traces of the presence of an animal, but not any part of the animal itself.

trade winds

The east-to-west prevailing winds in regions near Earth's equator; also called easterlies.

transform boundary

Places where two tectonic plates slide past each other.

translucent

The property of a material that allows some light to pass through but changes the direction of the light.

transparent

The property of a material that allows light to pass through with no change in its direction.

transverse wave

A wave that vibrates at right angles to the direction the wave is moving; ocean waves vibrate up and down as the wave energy moves toward shore; light waves are also examples of transverse waves.

triceps

Muscle in the upper part of the human arm that straightens the arm.

tropics

The two hottest climate zones bordering both sides of the equator. This band receives the most direct sunrays, and thus is heated the most.

true solution

A homogeneous mixture in which the dissolved solute particles are too small to be filtered out; transparent to light, meaning it allows light to pass through unaffected.

turning force

Torque, which is the force applied times the distance to the center of the object being rotated.

Tyndall effect

Process where light is used to test for the presence of a true solution; the Tyndall effect is the scattering of light by particles in a colloid or suspension; some suspensions have so many particles light cannot pass through the mixture.

types of elements

The periodic table is divided into three basic types of element: metals, semi-metals, and nonmetals.

unbalanced force

A net force; no forces are acting against it.

Universe

The name for all things in space, including Earth.

unstable

In reference to balance, unstable means the object easily tilts over; in reference to chemicals it means the chemical spontaneously decomposes.

valence charge

The charge on an atom determined by the number of valence electrons it donates or gains during a chemical reaction.

valence electrons

The number of electrons in the outside energy level of an atom.

vector

A measurement with magnitude and direction; examples include velocity, gravity, and acceleration.

velocity

The speed of a moving object in a specific direction.

virtual image

An image produced by a lens that can be seen but not projected onto a screen.

viscosity

A measure of how fast a fluid flows; the thicker the fluid the greater is its viscosity and the slower it flows.

volume

The amount of space an object takes up; common SI measurements are milliliter (mL) and liter (L).

waning

In reference to moon phases, when the lit part of the Moon disk in the sky is getting smaller.

water-in-oil emulsion

An emulsion in which water drops are dispersed throughout oil; butter is a water-in-oil emulsion.

wave

A wave is a transfer of energy without transporting material; a disturbance that moves through a medium without transporting the medium.

wave frequency

The number of waves that pass a point in a given time period.

wavelength

The distance between one wave and the next; for water waves it is the distance from crest to crest or from trough to trough.

waxing

In reference to moon phases, when the lit part of the Moon disk in the sky is getting larger.

weather

The condition of the atmosphere at a specific place and time as regards the temperature, humidity, wind, rain, and so on.

weight

Weight is the measure of the gravitational force acting on an object.

weightlessness

Without weight; nothing can actually be weightless because no matter where the object is in the Universe, gravity is acting on it.

whey

The liquid part of milk when the solid particles, called curd, are removed.

white light

White light is produced by the combination of all the visible light energy in the electro-magnetic spectrum.

wind

Wind is the horizontal movement of air masses from an area of high atmospheric pressure to an area of low atmospheric pressure.

work

Work is the product of the force applied to an object and the distance the object moves; work = force × distance.

zenith

In reference to an observer, the zenith is a point straight overhead; in reference to the Sun, it is the highest altitude of the Sun during the day.

zodiac constellation

A constellation along the solar eliptic path of the Sun; there are 12 zodiac constellations.

Index